We Came to Play!

We Came to Play!

Writings on Basketball

Edited by

John Ross and Q.R. Hand, Jr.

North Atlantic Books
Berkeley, California

We Came to Play!
Writings on Basketball

Published by
North Atlantic Books
P.O. Box 12327
Berkeley, California 94712

This is issue #54 in the *Io* series.

Cover art by Spain Rodriguez
Cover and book design by Paula Morrison
Typeset by Catherine E. Campaigne

Printed in the United States of America

We Came to Play! Writings on Basketball is sponsored by the Society for the Study of Native Arts and Sciences, a nonprofit educational corporation whose goals are to develop an educational and crosscultural perspective linking various scientific, social, and artistic fields; to nurture a holistic view of arts, sciences, humanities, and healing; and to publish and distribute literature on the relationship of mind, body, and nature.

Library of Congress Cataloging-in-Publication Data

We came to play! : writings on basketball / edited by John Ross and
   Q.R. Hand, Jr.
       p.   cm.
   ISBN 1-55643-162-7 (pbk.)
       1. Basketball—Miscellanea.   2. Basketball—United States—
Miscellanea.   3. Basketball stories.   I. Ross, John, 1938 Mar. 11–
II. Hand, Q.R. (Quentin R.), Jr. 1937 Jan. 18–
GV885.W387   1995
796.323—dc20   95-45632
                                                                    CIP

1   2   3   4   5   6   7   8   9 / 99   98   97   96

Table of Contents

Part One: Youngblood

Part Two: School Daze

Part Three: Chasin' the Game

about the editors and the back ground of the book

I

in harlem on my mind   there's a picture
of my daddy van der zee's magic camera made
seated on the steps of the alpha phi alpha house
with his team mates gathered about the game of basket ball

in the negro in sports there's a picture
of my grand father   my momma's daddy   standing
amongst his team mates
                           washington ymca national champs '09–'10

in the room of disappointments where my heart is
constant replaying of me failing at basket ball
on every court   in doors and out   i ran on
                                       and that's a whole lot
stirs me to filch out stills of
how the failure began in bed stuy
continued through new england harlem and north philly
then returned to the magic island of manhattan
where the eighty seventh street old man's basket ball association
held court for almost a year
                           we gloriously shoveled snow to
                                              in '68

II

stills flicking and flickering in
to one
            an other
                           cavalcading images
be hind the back
                  be tween the legs
                                       then flight

lost ins i'm fixed at viewing
                    collagings
                              all labors of all loves
                              of this more than game
                              o' i swear
                                        more than

there's lennie wilkens getting his chops together
in the low ceilinged court of holy rosary with alton walden
and tommy watkins jr   lennie was an altar boy there too

there's lennie at the garden
in the finals of the nit my father took me to
leading providence to a championship
                              determined left handed
                              dribble then the little pop shot
                              again and again

there's lennie in the midst of the boys' high ethos
from which young men brought skills and pride
to many peoples all over this land
                              finally   the world
si hugo green
solly walker
al barden
billy burwell
eddie simmons
john lagoff
jackie jackson
tommie davis
connie hawkins
vaughn harper

there there were the guys from lane
                              art howard
                              the daniels brothers
                              jake jordan
                              richie chink gaines

at madison park in bed stuy
a play ground legend like shu miles
taught the young by example for many years

III

you can sight these things in the '50s
where tenn st sends a 5 to the pros but don't get invited no wheres
    barnett   barnhill   finley   warley   et al
where sherman white and leroy smith don't get a chance to transform
    the game with our new thing and we must wait for elgin and oscar
where the sense of eliteness and egalitarianism entwined often elicited
   an ambiance of the polis as popular and positive
                      more seemed possible
where but on these basketball courts

in this space I virtually reek of
films   stories   poems   novels
                calling for vernacular artists
                to even take this now to cyberspace
                so that the fall out of history
                descends in the true full colors
                it arose from
                    pre green powers
when i'd return from boarding school
where i'd shoot baskets on saturday nights
                often alone
rather than attend the movies all students saw
billy pickens made sure i got to see the hot teams

when my family moved to harlem
john and ed norton
            the whole eddie's cabal
turned me on to the battle ground
              the rucker's tournament

i can remember a little court in the school yard of ps 43
where al lynch and eugene pilgrim and eddie simmons would
to no avail try to help me improve my game
                                        my spirit was all
                                        ways better than my skills

one year i saw clinton upset boys' at the city champs
in the same tournament the next year i saw head to head
connie hawkins and roger brown
                                roger was seventeen for 34   total of 39
                                no tellin how many would be 3s now
                                but boys' wouldn't blow the finals again
                                and the hawk really did fly then

IV

there's a slow mo of me scoring
fewer and fewer in california
where i sight the knicks finally   winning
                                after all the times
                                me and pop had been to the garden
                                and they'd lost
                                                since '49
on a tv in a motel room in redding
with a lovely woman who'd more than befriended me
                                                in spite of my selves
and the director of the local poverty program
i'd gone up there to do a job for
                                clyde   skull   dollar bill
                                topping the wilt and jerry show

she and i were still companions where
i literally bumped into john ross who
picked up the ball i'd fumbled away
in the editing of this book
                                he scored any way

as i scrambled to group therapy
one saturday morning in seventy one
from her apartment on romolo place in north beach

john and i hadn't seen each other since '58
when he left greenwich village for chiapas

   his book documenting the organized struggle of
   native american peoples against entrenched forces of greed there
   won an american book award last year from
   the before columbus foundation

                     rebellion from the roots
                     common courage press

and he and i had met in sag harbor long island
due to friends family and the fortuity of bad weather
which drove his camping family to seek shelter
at least on the porch of a running buddy's folks' summer home

 this was the summer of '50   or was it '51 john

                          now in mexico
the start of a long friend ship

it turns out that his mother and my aunt had collaborated
occasionally doing theatrical publicity in the big apple
that was during the 2nd world war   his step father
who left the war from the merchant marines and
did stints with the sf art institute and a globe trotter b team
before his career on canvass as an abstract expressionist
had placed a basket with a net in the grand loft
they lived in on west broad way

                   no stock brokers there then

it was a place visions grew from
a palace and play ground all in one
to us raised in the brown stone traditon
we sub wayed there   and in a few years

the loft became salon and party pad

the cops came more than once
up six flights

no elevator

where hungry and high spirits found
miles and camus and ellison and yoga
and chicago green and oscar and elgin
mixed with monk and la playa's coco secos
talking and dancing till the night time
slipped into the right time before the coming of light

some of these brothers and sisters
we did significant growing up with
john and i are still in touch with
as well as a whiff of turpentine and oil paint
and sun beams within the net
under the sky light

V

John couldn't play basket ball any better than me
but that didn't stop him either and he says a certain group
of non spanish speaking hoopsters on the dusty court in chiapas
have nick named him el swish

now there's a story

since the seventies though
each of us has done more watching
and talking about basket ball than playing

david henderson's one of the persons i talked to
he'd been one of us psychedelic swashbucklers
running full court ball on eighty seventh street
much nearer to columbus ave than central park west

we ran on a shortened court but we ran and ran

and there too was salon and party   the women
indulging our sweat and funk to sly and 'trane
as we comingled round ball with liberation talk
and poetry and painting in a neighborhood where
one side of the court was gentrified brown stones
and the other rail road tenements which
a neighborhood group led by an ex national guardian writer turned
     organizer
would ultimately liberate from a housing authority
with little concern for poor people with large families
i brought the drama of this court
to the work i did with john o'neal
and a team of writers and performers
who made "ain't no use in goin' home"
and it crucially informed one of the scenes
when it was produced at alice arts in oakland
in the late '80s
                    john o in the role of junebug jabbo jones

is it coincidence or synchronicity
john ross and david henderson are
friends of mine   each of whose poetry
has influenced me and my writing over the years
about a basketball book or project or
                              who knows
                                   what about johnnie ace
so that when richard grossinger
got in touch with me   it was about
this book through david who'd remembered
and passed it on

VI

at the time of this writing i work
as a community mental health counselor
in the mission district of san francisco

where i've lived for many years now though
all of my family's in the north east and
my father who also played for the harlem ymca
died on cape cod where he'd retired with his beloved blossom

john ross is living and writing in mexico city
and his family is in the north east too
his son dante is a knick fanatic
and a producer of rap

the confluence of spirit and matter
involving persons touched by round ball
surprise me still
       in a sports column here several years ago
       kc jones cited mr sadalla a math and gym teacher
       at a jhs here who'd encouraged him   and gail sadalla
       and his daughter helped keep the spirits of john and i
       together
       so each of us were trying to write and be active
       in spite of our selves
                and because
                       just because
     at a cal poets in the schools' benefit
the grand son of one of my father's team mates is a performer too
and his partner in performance was the son of a painter
a running buddy of john wideman at u of p

out of this stuff comes my participation
in this book my father and his friends
hipped me to years before my eyes began to recognize possibilities

this book that wouldn't exist without the work of jr
   or the conversations with david
              or the phone calls
              and persistence of richard

enjoy
     qr hand jr

History of We Came to Play

We Came to Play is an anthology of some of the best basketball writings from the last four decades. This book had its origins in an earlier basketball collection published by North Atlantic Books. *Take it to the Hoop* (edited by Daniel Rudman) appeared in 1980 and was initially quite popular, selling almost one entire edition to public libraries and being adopted for classroom use in the New York City Public School System. However, by 1990, the book had become dated and, after the last copies were destroyed in a warehouse accident, it was not reprinted.

We Came to Play was born in 1992 when the director of the Boston Celtics' Stay in School Program contacted us about getting additional copies of *Take it to the Hoop* or, hopefully, a more current anthology. Initially North Atlantic and the Celtics' Stay in School Program sought to develop a wholly new volume customized for the Celtics' use. Our concept was to include a discrete section in the center of the anthology with Boston poets, writers, and school kids interviewing Celtic players. This, however, required NBA approval. By the time North Atlantic completed the process of requesting and receiving such approval, a new person was in charge of the Celtics' Stay in School Program, and she felt that the book—as proposed—was too sophisticated for school children to use. She elected not to pursue the project with us.

Having taken matters that far, North Atlantic decided to look for another team. The most convenient choice was the local Golden State Warriors. Their publications office quickly accepted the idea but wanted reaffirmation of League approval. This time NBA approval was granted for a basic anthology that could be adapted to any team's use.

At the same time, North Atlantic offered the Warriors project to local poet (and longtime pickup hoop star) Q.R. Hand, Jr. who in turn enlisted his colleague John Ross. These two writers assembled the basic collection that appears in this book.

Ross undertook setting up player-writer interviews. He invited Kathy McAnally of Youth Radio (a journalism training program for teenagers in Berkeley) to train and shepherd students to interview Warrior players. Unfortunately, we could not have picked a worse time to work with the Warriors. During the period in which we attempted to carry out this project not only did the coach and many of the players change but the ownership and virtually all of the staff who were helping us changed too. The intent of cooperation was there, but interviews were invariably cancelled or postponed indefinitely, and finally the writers and students got discouraged. Ultimately the Warriors and North Atlantic agreed mutually to void the contract and discontinue the project.

Because the anthology was nearly assembled and permissions were in hand, North Atlantic then decided to proceed without a particular team Stay in School affiliation. John Ross and Q.R. Hand, Jr. decided not to commit any more time to the anthology, given that the book was so significantly delayed and publication itself was in jeopardy. The project was turned over to North Atlantic intern Herschel Farbman who fine-tuned the editing. He made somewhat different selections of sections to excerpt, picked some pieces of his own, and, while attempting to finalize the permissions, ended up cutting those pieces on which there was either no response or an unfavorable one. After his internship ended, his work was continued by editorial assistant Jana Israel and North Atlantic publisher Richard Grossinger. These two also collaborated on the history of basketball.

Thus, *We Came to Play* represents only in part the collection put together by Ross and Hand. It includes many of their selections, a few additional pieces chosen by Farbman, and a somewhat different editing and organization of the whole. Two pieces came out of the Warrior experience, an interview with Al Attles by John Ross and a Youth Radio interview with Tim Hardaway. Despite the fact that this is no longer a Stay in School anthology customized for the Warriors, we have left this section in the book out of respect to the work of those who compiled it.

Much of the material in *We Came to Play* is certainly above the reading level of most Stay in School programs. However, when *Take it to the Hoop* was used both by the Celtics and the New York Public Schools, it was extremely popular, and students tended to reach up to the level of the book because they liked it. Though this new anthology is just as mature and sophisticated, all the editors have made an effort to reach out to young readers as well as to adult basketball fans.

The original Stay in School concept remains available to any team that chooses to have a local, customized anthology. Although North Atlantic Books cannot provide the personnel to set up writer and student interviews with players in other NBA cities, it can certainly provide editorial assistance in the process, and, using its own financial resources, it can publish a new book (keeping the core) with a different team section replacing and expanding the brief Warrior section that appears in *We Came to Play*. Additionally, a more appropriate team-oriented title than *We Came to Play* (a Warriors slogan) could be used on each anthology. A Raptors, Jazz, or Nets Stay in School anthology would need its own distinctive name.

North Atlantic's plan with the Warriors was to provide 500 copies for free in exchange for the interviews and the rights to distribute the book nationally. All profits from the project were to go back into paying for additional books for the Warriors' Stay in School Program. In the absence of profits, additional books were to be made available to the Stay in School Program at cost. In the unlikely event of greater earnings than could be used in one Stay in School program, funds were to be used to develop anthologies for other Stay in School programs. The entire undertaking was conceived as a nonprofit educational project, drawing on The Society for the Study of Native Arts and Sciences [the 501(c)3 organization within which North Atlantic Books is a program].

Because times have changed since the lapsed agreement with the Warriors (for one, paper prices have more than doubled), the same precise arrangement is no longer possible. However, equivalent arrangements are available, and The Society for the Study of Native Arts and Sciences remains willing to prepare and fund versions of this anthology for individual team Stay in School programs on a nonprofit basis. Interested programs should contact Lindy Hough, Richard Grossinger, or Anastasia McGhee at North Atlantic Books (510-559-8277 by phone; 510-559-8279 by fax).

Other sports anthologies available from North Atlantic Books:

Baseball I Gave You All the Best Years of My Life edited by Lisa Conrad and Richard Grossinger

The Temple of Baseball edited by Richard Grossinger

The Dreamlife of Johnny Baseball edited by Richard Grossinger

Into the Temple of Baseball edited by Kevin Kerrane and Richard Grossinger

North Shore Chronicles by Bruce Jenkins (surfing oral histories)

Risk! by Steve Boga (rock climbing, hang-gliding, cycling, etc.)

Take it to the Hoop edited by Daniel Rudman, hardcover only, limited copies

Publisher's Preface

Basketball did not emerge fullblown with Michael Jordan twisting under the basket and tossing spiral ricochets through the twine or Shaquille O'Neal slam-dunking and shaking the backboard. The earliest forms of the game we call basketball shared as much with tiddlywinks, horseshoes, and knocking down kewpie dolls as they did with today's athletic, break-dancing sport.

The story of basketball's beginnings are no less charming for having been told hundreds of times. The name of the inventor and the site of the first experimental attempt at play are recorded historically as they are for no other major sport, but subtleties distinguish each retelling of James Naismith's derivation of basketball with a combination of genius and luck. Some accounts emphasize how the boys did not want to play girls' indoor gym games; thus, a new sport had to be invented to keep them from misbehaving. Other stories focus on the opposite extreme—the intent to keep the boys from massacring one another on hard floors in scrimmages like rugby. Basketball's distinctive large rubber ball was initially meant to serve as a buffer, an intentional encumbrance, cutting down on physical contact between participants. This is but one of the ironies in the evolution of basketball from a variant of golf played at a minute scale and on a vertical axis with a large hole to a virtual martial art or swordplay complete with one-on-one aikido-like challenges and in-your-face punctuations of scores.

In November of 1891, Naismith was a gym instructor at the YMCA International Training School in Springfield, Massachusetts. His students had become so bored with calisthenics that they routinely rebelled, so Naismith got permission from his superiors to launch a more amusing game. In his own words:

"We decided that there should be a game that could be played in the evenings and during the winter seasons. I began to think of the fundamental principles of all games. I discovered that in all team games some kind of ball was used. . . .

"I tried soccer and we smashed all the windows. I tried lacrosse and smashed most of the fellows' arms. Rugby football finished the students up until they were ready to quit on recreative games. In a day or two I would have to report to the faculty on the success or failure of my attempts. So far they had been all failures. How I hated the thought of admitting that, after all my theories, I too had failed to hold the interest of the class."

This soon-to-be-inventor of Air Jordan and the Shaq Attack had an unusual personal history. He grew up in Bennie's Corners in northern Ontario. Orphaned at eight, he quit school to work as a logger and farmhand. Later, however, he managed to study theology at McGill University in Montreal, and he earned an M.D. from Gross Medical School in Denver.

Naismith's basic intent with his rowdy group was to imitate rugby in some fashion. However, his modified version couldn't involve tackling because of the hard floor. Why, he wondered, did rugby require tackling? It was obviously because players could run with the ball, and tackling was the only way to stop them. Thus, if running with the ball were prohibited, tackling could also be outlawed. "No running with the ball" is not only Naismith's fundamental principle of basketball; it also distinguishes basketball from football. Running with the ball allows ownership of the means of scoring points. Extended domination of the ball itself defines success in football (i.e., time of possession, during which the opponent cannot score). In basketball, contrarily, possession of the ball is ephemeral and requires instant resolution in a play. In baseball, defense and offense are separated from each other by the most fundamental boundary in the game—that between fielders and batters. In basketball, defense and offense turn seamlessly into each other even as attackers become defenders and then attack again. In such an environment, a steal is hardly as fatal as an interception or fumble in football. The rhythm of possession goes back and forth because the ball can never be owned in any lasting way.

Dribbling was later added to basketball as another method of slowing things down and restricting physical interaction. This supposed impediment ironically became a catalyst for all sorts of fancy, daring action.

As long as a player could not run with the ball, he had to throw it immediately from the spot at which he caught it, the rules making allowances only for catching the ball on the run and coming to a prompt stop. From the spot of catching, a player could throw or bat the ball in any direction with one or both hands (though not with a fist).

But what was to be the object of all this activity? How were points to be scored?

"The next step," recalled Naismith, "was to secure some kind of goal through which the ball could be passed. In thinking of upright goals, [I realized] that the more force that was put on the ball, the more likelihood there was of having it pass through the goal. It then occurred that if the ball were thrown in a curve, it would not be necessary or advisable to put too much force on the ball."

There was a game played in rural Ontario that Naismith recalled from his childhood. It was called "Duck on a Rock." The object was to smack an opponent's rock off a boulder with another rock, both the ammunition and target about baseball or golfball size. From years of play, participants came to understand that the best kind of shot for accomplishing the dislodgement had to be one with a good deal of arc. The rock could not be fired at the target like a baseball; it had to be looped.

"I decided that [if I made] the goal horizontal the ball would have to be thrown in a curve, minimizing the severe driving of a ball. In order to avoid having the defense congregate around the goal, it was placed above their heads, so that once the ball left the individual's hands, it was not likely to be interfered with."

On this basis Naismith raised his targets up above the gym, ten feet in the air because that was the height of the Springfield Y balcony. His "ducks" were peach baskets. Actually Naismith had wanted square boxes, but the janitor, failing to find these, offered the round baskets in their stead. These were nailed to the balcony.

Now, in the emerging newborn game, the rules stated that goals were to be scored only when the ball was thrown or batted from the ground into the basket and remained there. Additionally, if, while the ball rested on the edge of the basket, the opponent jiggled the basket in any way, a point was scored whether the ball subsequently fell into the basket or not.

By raising the game ten feet off the ground, the inventor of basketball prevented simple baseball-type strikes or soccer kicks through an open target and also ostensibly reduced the opportunity for opponent interference with shots. However, quite unintentionally, he created a game for tall people and turned shot-blocking (since it could not be accomplished simply) into a high art of natural height and learned timing.

Much as nature fashioned the giraffe by growing taller and taller trees, Naismith set conditions that not only led to taller and taller basketball players but ultimately drew the tallest people from all continents of the planet to play his game. Less than a hundred years after he hung his peach baskets, it was impossible for a seven-foot-tall man anywhere on the Earth, be it Nigeria, Romania, or Mongolia, not to be spotted by an ambitious scout or encouraged by a desperate coach and virtually compelled at least to make an attempt to play basketball. These consequences of Naismith's vision were unlikely and dramatic, both in their interpretation and their scope. After all, he was merely trying to avoid archery and kewpie dolls, not trying to invent dunking and rejections.

"The manner of putting the ball into play was then considered. Two individuals were selected and took their stations in the middle of the floor. The ball was thrown up so as to land between them, giving as nearly equal chance as possible."

As noted, this ball at the heart of the game had to be large. "The nearest approach to the [size] needed was a soccer ball, which we selected."

There was no initial rule governing the number of players on a team. Because Naismith's gym class had eighteen students, the earliest basketball lineups replicated baseball nines. Only after 1900 was the number of players allowed on the court at one time restricted to no more than five.

Most remarkably, Naismith's ten-foot-high basket and thirteen basic rules, devised in two weeks, for all intent and purposes continue to govern basketball today. The commandments of basketball's creator forbade running with the ball, pronounced that the ball could only be held in the hands and that the arms and body (including the feet) could in no way be used for holding it, set the terms for how the ball might be advanced, determined scoring, and defined fouls as shouldering, holding, pushing, tripping, striking, and hitting the ball with the fist.

Basketball was meant to be fun, even creative chaos. But the players on the floor were not allowed to come into direct personal contact. Violation of any of the foul rules resulted in a penalty. No free shot was granted initially, but a player's second foul disqualified him from the court until the next goal was made. If a foul was judged flagrant, with intent to injure, the player committing the foul was disqualified for the whole game (without substitution). The way fouls entered into the scoring was that three consecutive fouls by one team (without an intervening foul by the opponent) were scored as one goal. These original rules also set two fifteen-minute halves with a five-minute break between them, plus a sudden-death overtime (though only after the agreement of both captains). The overtime was ended by the first goal scored.

Other rules defined the duties of the umpire and referee and gave them authority of scores, fouls, and reentering the ball in play after it found its way out of bounds. The player throwing the ball back from out of bounds came from the team that was not immediately responsible for its departure and was allowed five seconds unmolested to make a play. If there was a dispute about who sent it out of bounds, the umpire threw it directly back onto the court with the recipient, the person first touching it, allowed the same five seconds to make his move.

Naismith's rules, when set in motion in a real game, produced a democratic scrimmage in which the players from two opposing squads mingled completely (but without blocking and tackling), each of them allowed to receive, dribble, pass, and shoot a large ball. The sport was most similar to hockey and soccer (European football), though basketball defined possession and scoring in more radically choreographed acts. It was hockey without ice and without weapons, meant for city pavement, imitative of the dances—both bellicose and joyful—that already took place the urban streets. It was soccer with sleight-of-hand magic and a small elevated goal. The difference between basketball and soccer can be measured by imagining the difference of agility between the Harlem Globetrotters and *any* soccer squad.

As with soccer and ice hockey, however, the early basketball matches were extremely low-scoring. When two squads met for the first time in February, 1892 (the rivals representing the Central and Armory Hill YMCAs, respectively), the final was 2–2. Armory Hill won a rematch in March 1–0. The difficulty of scoring was partly the result of Naismith's requirement that a center jump follow every score. It was also the result of a new game that no one yet knew how to play. The game was a tournament of innovation and surprise before players developed skills within the rules. Then the rules followed the skills instead of being stymied by them. If Julius Erving had arrived magically out of context in 1892, he would not have been seen as playing basketball at all. His moves would have been irrelevant to the game as it was understood then. It took basketball evolving into some other thing to accomodate and welcome Doctor J, Magic, and Clyde the Glide.

Backboards were added in 1893 because spectators tried to help their own team by swatting away the attempts of the opponents.

The removal of the bottom of the peach basket also came later when it took too much time to climb a ladder and retrieve the ball after every score.

Early basketball was played, like pickup, on courts of many different sizes. The game was adapted to armories, auditoriums, dance halls, theatrical stages, skating rinks, warehouses, urban sidewalks, and barns. Many of the original indoor courts were supported by central pillars. Thus, the "post play" originated quite literally when offensive players intentionally ran opponents into a formidible and immovable obstacle.

The foul penalties were the most flawed of the original rules and required quick adjustment. Free throws were soon substituted for automatic scores and, in order to distinguish between these uncontested shots from baskets made from the field, the latter were awarded two points instead of one. That technical change doubled the score of the average game. The center jump after each score remained until 1937; its elimination allowed the refinement of the fast break and further increased the scoring.

Modern basketball's formal origin can be directly traced to Naismith's invention, but its subsequent popularity and spread probably represent the archetypal nature of the game. There is something natural about a looping shot at an open target. A kid crumples up an old exam, drifts and shoots for the waste-paper basket in his room. A school-girl tosses the remains of her apple in the air toward a garbage can on the street. Beer cans are flipped competively by group members toward a trash pile. The basketball arc is perhaps not as primal as the attack of *Homo erectus* firing a rock at the forerunner of a zebra or caribou, but it has the formative intelligence of the early primates looking for new ways to accomplish strategic goals or merely to play. Even ancient Europeans tossed balls into boxes and baskets for sport. Kids juxtaposing balls and containers of all sorts continue to reinvent basketball regularly. In Terre Haute, Indiana, Larry Bird started his basketball journey with a coffee can and a little round sponge.

At the time of European contact the Aztecs played a game they called *ollamalitzli*. Contestants tried to heave a small rubber ball through a stone ring raised on a post above the ground on a large outdoor stone ballcourt. It must have been difficult because anyone who scored thusly could claim the clothing of *all* the spectators. The leader of the losing team was sometimes sacrificed. Versions of this game were played by the Mayans and sixteenth-century Indians of present-day Arizona. American Indians in Florida played a similar game.

In an entirely different part of the hemisphere the Abenaki of Eastern Canada competed in a match which involved keeping an air-filled bladder aloft (somewhat like volleyball). An early eighteenth-century episode in Quebec account was observed by ethnographer Stewart Cullin:

"Their ball is nothing but an inflated bladder, which must always be kept up in the air and which in reality is upheld a long time by the multitude of hands tossing it back and forth without ceasing. . . ."

North American Indian tribes also played a version of "hoops," but spears "replaced" balls, and the hoop was not only detached from any support but rolled along the ground. Additionally, the players got to "shoot" at more than one opening in the hoop, with scores depending not on the spot from which the shot was made but the region of the hoop through which it passed. Basketball today would certainly be a wild game with rolling hoops and multiple openings of different sizes.

Cullin describes the target hoops among the Cheyenne as bent saplings intricately laced and cross-hatched with nets of rawhide so as to give a spider's web appearance, "the leather passing forty-eight times around the edge. Half the net on one side of the principal division is painted blue and the other half red; the colors are reversed on the opposite side." The Cheyenne gave this popular game the imposing title of *tititipanatuwanagi*.

Among the Grosventres of Montana an equivalent pastime was called *hatchieb:*

"In playing, the wheel is rolled forward on the ground, when the players hurl toward it slender spears, or darts, the object being to pierce one of the holes formed by the buckskin lacing of the wheel. These holes vary in size, and each has its own proper name and value.... The holes are named as follows: Large hole in center, *ita,* or heart; holes enclosed within the parallel lines crossing at right angles, *anatayan,* or buffalo bulls; small triangles formed at points of cross lacing, *wuuha,* or buffalo calves; large holes next to the wooden ring, *chadjitha,* or wolves; small holes formed by the crossing of the thongs next to the wooden ring, *caawu,* or coyotes."

For a similar game among the Apache, it was reported that "misses were more frequent than scores." Among the Navaho, the spear was more of a pole and decorated with the "claws of wildcats or of the mountain lion, bear, eagle, etc., which [were] attached to the strings, and as the claws [caught] the hoop a point [was] scored."

Such embellishments might truly enliven an NBA game. Players could hang their totems on the ball rather than on themselves. One is reminded of an interaction between African center Manute Bol (who was reported routinely to have speared wild animals in his youth) and American-born forward J. R. Reid. After a block by Bol not to his liking, Reid followed his tall opponent off the court, taunting, "This ain't Africa here. I ain't no lion. I ain't no tiger. I'm a man."

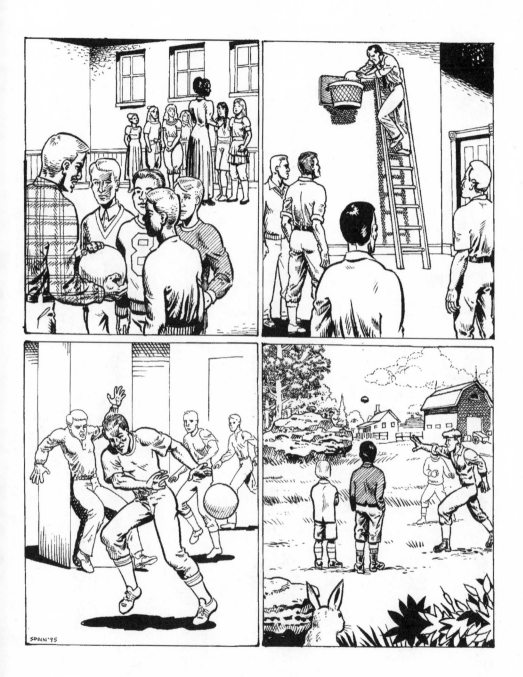

Part One

Youngblood

Darcy Frey

The Last Shot

Russell Thomas places his right sneaker one inch behind the three-point line, considers the basket with a level gaze, cocks his wrist to shoot, then suddenly looks around. Has he spotted me, watching from the corner of the playground? No, something else is up: he is lifting his nose to the wind like a spaniel, he is gauging the currents. He waits until the wind settles, bits of trash feathering lightly to the ground. Then he sends a twenty-five-foot jump shot arcing through the soft summer twilight. It drops without a sound through the dead center of the bare iron rim. So does the next one. So does the one after that. Alone in the gathering dusk, Russell works the perimeter against imaginary defenders, unspooling jump shots from all points. Few sights on Brooklyn playgrounds stir the hearts and minds of the coaches and scouts who recruit young men for college basketball teams quite like Russell's jumper; they have followed its graceful trajectory every since he made varsity at Abraham Lincoln High School, in Coney Island, two years ago. But the shot is merely the final gesture, the public flourish of a private regimen that brings Russell to this court day and night. Avoiding pickup games, he gets down to work: an hour of three-point shooting, then wind sprints up the fourteen flights in his project stairwell, then back to the court, where (much to his friends' amusement) he shoots one-handers ten feet from the basket while sitting in a chair.

At this hour Russell usually has the court to himself; most of the other players won't come out until after dark, when the thick humid air begins to stir with the night breezes and the court lights come on.

But this evening is turning out to be a fine one—cool and foggy. The low, slanting sun sheds a feeble pink light over the silvery Atlantic a block away, and milky sheets of fog roll off the ocean and drift in tatters along the project walkways. The air smells of sewage and saltwater. At the far end of the court, where someone has torn a hole in the chicken-wire fence, other players climb through and begin warming up.

Like most of New York's impoverished and predominantly black neighborhoods, Coney Island does not exactly shower its youth with opportunity. In the early 1960s, urban renewal came to Coney Island in the form of a vast tract of housing projects, packed so densely along a twenty-block stretch that a new skyline rose suddenly behind the boardwalk and the amusement park. The experiment of public housing, which has isolated the nation's urban poor from the hearts of their cities, may have failed here in even more spectacular fashion because of Coney Island's utter remoteness. In this neighborhood, on a peninsula at the southern tip of Brooklyn, there are almost no stores, no trees, no police; just block after block of gray cement projects—hulking, prison-like, and jutting straight into the sea.

Most summer nights an amorphous unease settles over Coney Island as apartments become too stifling to bear and the streets fall prey to the gangs and drug dealers. Options are limited: to the south is the stiff gray meringue of the Atlantic; to the north, more than ten miles away, are the Statue of Liberty and the glass-and-steel spires of Manhattan's financial district. Officially, Coney Island is considered a part of the endless phantasmagoria that is New York City. But on nights like these, as dealers set up their drug marts in the streets and alleyways, and the sounds of sirens and gunfire keep pace with the darkening sky, it feels like the end of the world.

Yet even in Coney Island there are some uses to which a young man's talent, ambition, and desire to stay out of harm's way may be put: there is basketball. Hidden behind the projects there are dozens of courts, and every night they fill with restless teenagers, there to remain for hours until exhaustion or the hoodlums take over. The high-school dropouts and the aging players who never made it to college usually show up for a physical game at a barren strip of courts by the water known as Chop Chop Land, where bruises and minutes

4

played are accrued at a one-to-one ratio. The younger kids congregate for rowdy games at Run-and-Gun Land. The courts there are short and the rims are low, so everyone can dunk and the only pass ever made is the one inbounding the ball. At Run-and-Gun, players stay on the move for another reason: the court sits just below one of the most dreaded places, where Coney Island's worst hoodlums sometimes pass a summer's evening "getting hectic," as they say—tossing batteries and beer bottles onto the court from apartment windows fifteen stories above.

The neighborhood's best players—the ones like Russell, with aspirations—practice a disciplined, team-driven style of basketball at this court by the O'Dwyer projects, which has been dubbed the Garden after the New York Knicks arena. In a neighborhood ravaged by the commerce of drugs, the Garden offers a tenuous sanctuary. A few years ago, community activists petitioned the housing authority to install night lights. And the players themselves resurfaced the court and put up regulation-height rims that snap back after a player dunks. Russell may be the only kid at the Garden who practices his defensive footwork while holding a ten-pound brick in each hand, but no one here treats the game as child's play. Even the hoodlums decline to vandalize the Garden, because in Coney Island the possibility of transcendence through basketball is an article of faith.

Most evenings this summer I have come to the Garden to watch Russell and his friends play ball. The notion that basketball can liberate dedicated players like these from the grinding daily privations of the ghetto has become a cherished parable, advanced by television sportscasters, college basketball publicists, and sneaker companies proselytizing the work ethic and $120 high-tops. And that parable is conveyed directly to the players at the Garden by the dozens of college coaches who arrive in Coney Island each year with assurances that even if a National Basketball Association contract isn't in the cards, a player's talent and tenacity will at least reward him with a free college education, a decent job, and a one-way ticket out of the neighborhood. But how does this process actually unfold? And what forces stand in its way? How often is basketball's promise of a better life redeemed? It was questions like these that drew me to this court, between Mermaid and Surf avenues.

"Just do it, right?" I glance to my left and there is Corey Johnson, smiling mischievously, eyes alight. He nods towards the court—players stretching out, taking lay-ups—and it does, in fact, resemble a sneaker commercial. "Work hard, play hard, buy yourself a pair of Nikes, young man," Corey intones. Corey is a deft mimic and he does a superb white TV announcer. "They get you where you want to go, which is out of the ghet-to!" He laughs, we shake hands, and he takes up an observation post by my side.

Corey is Russell's best friend and one of Lincoln High's other star seniors. He, too, expects to play college ball. But he specializes in ironic detachment and normally shows up courtside with his Walkman merely to watch for girls beneath his handsome, hooded eyes. Tonight he is wearing a fresh white T-shirt, expertly ripped along the back and sleeves to reveal glimpses of his sculpted physique; denim shorts that reach to his knees; and a pair of orange sneakers that go splendidly with his lid—a tan baseball cap with orange piping, which he wears with the bill pointing skyward. From his headphones come the sounds of Color Me Badd, and Corey sings along: *I— wanna — sex — you — up* ... He loops his fingers around the chicken-wire fence and says, "I tell you, Coney Island is like a disease. Of the mind. It makes you lazy. You relax too much. 'Cause all you ever see is other guys relaxing."

Although a pickup game has begun at the basket nearest us, Russell still commands the other. As the last light drains from the sky, he finishes with three-pointers and moves on to baby hooks: fifteen with the left hand, fifteen with the right; miss one and start all over again. Corey smiles at his friend's hair-shirt discipline. Russell, it is hoped, will play next year in the Big East, one of the nation's top college conferences, in which Seton Hall, St. John's, Georgetown, Syracuse, and others compete. Russell is six feet three, 180 pounds, with a shaved head and a small goatee that seems to mean business. Last spring the Lincoln team, with Russell leading the way, won the New York City public-school championship in a rout at Madison Square Garden that was broadcast citywide on cable TV. But one can never predict what may happen to Russell, because, as Corey observes, "Russell is Russell." I can guess what this means: Russell lives in one of the neighborhood's toughest projects, and misfortune often seems to shadow him. Last year a fight between Russell and his girlfriend turned violent. Terrified that his college scholarship had just been replaced by a stiff prison term, Russell climbed to the top of one of Coney Island's highest buildings. It took almost half and hour of reasoned talk by his high school coach and members of the Sixtieth Precinct to bring him back from the edge.

Russell may be tightly wound, but no Coney Island player can avoid for long the agonizing pressures that might bring a teenager with his whole life ahead of him to the edge of a roof. Basketball newsletters and scouting reports are constantly scrutinizing the players, and practically every day some coach shows up—appraising, coaxing, negotiating, and, as often as not, making promises he never keeps. Getting that scholarship offer is every player's dream—in anticipation, no one steps outside in Coney Island without a Syracuse cap or a St. John's sweatshirt. But in reality only a handful of the neighborhood's players have ever made it to such top four-year programs, most have been turned back by one obstacle or another in high school. Others who have enrolled in college never saw their dream to completion. The list is grim: there was Eric "Spoon" Marbury, who played for the University of Georgia but never graduated, and ended up back in Coney Island working construction; his younger brother Norman "Jou Jou" Marbury, who lost his scholarship to highly-ranked Tennessee because of academic problems in high school; and now David "Chocolate" Harris, a talented player who never even graduated from high school. He dropped out of Lincoln after his freshman year and became a small-time drug dealer. Earlier this summer police found him in an abandoned lot, his hood pulled over his head and a bullet through his skull. He was seventeen. Some of the players warming up at the Garden have written on the tongues of their sneakers, CHOCOLATE: R.I.P.

The orange court lights have come on now, displacing the encroaching darkness. Two players on either end of the court climb the fence and sit atop the backboards, hanging nets—a sign that a serious game is about to begin. Suddenly a ferocious grinding noise fills the air. It gets louder and louder, and then a teenage kid riding a Big Wheel careens onto the court. He darts through the playground crowd, leaving a wake of pissed-off players, then hops off his ride and watches

7

it slam into the fence. "Ah, yes, Stephon Marbury," Corey says dryly, "future of the neighborhood."

Stephen—Eric and Norman Marbury's kid brother—is barely fourteen and has yet to begin high school, but already his recruiting has begun. At least one college coach is known to have sent him fawning letters in violation of the National Collegiate Athletic Association rules; street agents, paid under the table by colleges to bring top players to their programs, have begun cultivating Stephon; and practically every high-school coach in the city is heaping him with free gear—sneakers, caps, bags—in an attempt to lure him to his school. At first glance, Stephon doesn't look like the future of anything: he's diminutive, barely five feet nine, with the rounded head and delicate features of an infant. He sports a stylish razor cut and a pierced ear, and the huge gold stud seems to tilt his tiny bald head off its axis. Caught somewhere between puberty and superstardom, he walks around with his sneakers untied, the ends of his belt dropping suggestively from his pants, and half a Snickers bar extruding from his mouth.

With Stephon here, Corey wanders onto the court. Russell, too, is persuaded to give up his solo regimen. Basketball, it is commonly said, is a game of pure instinct, but the five-on-five contest that begins here is something else. Corey and Stephon are cousins, and Russell is as good as family—the three of them have played together since they were in grade school. They seem to move as if the spontaneous, magical geometry of the game had all been rehearsed in advance. Stephon, the smallest by far, is doing tricks with the ball as though it were dangling from his hand by a string, then gunning it to his older teammates with a series of virtuoso no-look passes: behind-the-back passes, sidearm passes, shovel passes. Corey is lulling defenders with his sleepy eyes, then exploding to the basket, were he casually tosses the ball through the hoop. Russell is sinking twenty-footers as if they were six-inch putts.

The game has just begun when a crowd starts to form: sidelined players, three deep, waiting their turn. A prostitute trolling for clients. A drunk yelling maniacally, "I played with Jordan, I played with Jabbar. They ain't shit. And neither are *you!*" A buffed-out guy in a silk suit and alligator shoes arrives, swigging from a bottle of Courvoisier.

An agent? A scout? The crowd gives him elbow room. A couple of teenage mothers with strollers come by; they get less elbow room.

Basketball is so inextricably woven into the fabric of Coney Island life that almost everyone here can recite a complete oral history of the neighborhood's players. People remember the exact scores of summer tournament games played at this court ten years ago, or describe in rapturous detail the perfect arc that Carlton "Silk" Owens put on his jumper before he was shot in the elbow in 1982. Dog-eared copies of a ten-year-old University of Georgia catalogue with a picture of Spoon Marbury playing with future N.B.A. great Dominique Williams get passed around like samizdat.

Russell, Corey, and Stephon are the natural heirs to this great and vaunted tradition. But this is a complicated business: given the failures that have preceded them, the new crew is watched by the neighborhood with a certain skittishness, a growing reluctance to care too deeply. Yet Coney Island offers its residents little else on which to hang their pride. So the proceedings here have taken on a desperate, exalted quality, and by unspoken agreement the misfortunes of bygone players are chalked up either to a lack of will or plain bad luck—both of which make possible the continuance of hope. Silk didn't go pro, it is said, "because that was the year they cut the college draft from three rounds to two." Another player, the explanation goes, had that pro game, went to the hoop both ways, "but he was done in by a shyster agent."

Still, the suspicion lingers that something larger and less comprehensible may be at work. Ten years ago, the Long Island City projects in Queens produced New York's best players, but the drug industry and the collapse of that neighborhood into violence, broken families, and ever-greater poverty put an end to its dynasty. In recent years the torch has passed to Coney Island, which struggles to avoid a similar fate.

It's past midnight now, and the ambient glow of Manhattan's remote skyscrapers has turned the sky a metallic blue. Standing courtside, we can see only the darkened outlines of the projects, looming in every direction, and the shirtless players streaking back and forth, drenched in a pool of orange light. For Russell, Corey, and Stephon, the hard labor of winning their scholarships lies ahead; for now this

9

game is enough. Corey, sprinting downcourt, calls out, "Homeboy! Homeboy!" Standing under his own basket, Stephon lets fly with a long, improbably pass that Corey somehow manages to catch and dunk in one balletic leap. The game is stopped on account of pandemonium: players and spectators are staggering around the court— knees buckling, heads held in astonishment. Even Mr. Courvoisier loses his cool. Stephon laughs and points to the rim, still shuddering fearfully from its run-in with Corey's fists. "Yo, cuz," he yells. "Make it bleed!" Then he raises his arms jubilantly and dances a little jig, rendered momentarily insane by the sheer giddy pleasure of playing this game to perfection.

Gerald Locklin

the hook shot

at one time basketball was my life.
no one taught me more about the game
than don garland, my eighth grade coach.
he was a big man, firm and gentle;

only his patience exceeded the bulk
of his forearms. i never knew him to
raise his voice—but who had the
cojones to test him? he was the man.

he drilled me nightly in the hook shot:
bounce pass, step to the basket, lean
with the shoulder, brace with the elbow,
sight the glass target, and arc it up lightly.

Bill Cosby

How to Cheat at Basketball

When I played basketball in the slums of Philadelphia—outdoors on concrete courts—here was never a referee. You had to call your own fouls. So the biggest argument was always about whether you called the foul *before* the shot went in, or whether you had waited to see if the ball went in. See, if you yelled "foul," you didn't get the basket. You just got the ball out-of-bounds.

Sometimes you called a *light* foul. Like you have a guy driving in on you and you punch him in the eye a little. That's a light foul in the playgrounds.

Another light foul is submarining a guy who's driving in on you. He comes down on the concrete, and you visit him every two weeks in the hospital. Of course, there is always a pole sitting in the middle of the court. Something has to hold up the basket. So you let a guy drive in, and you just kind of screen him a little bit, right into the pole. This is where you visit him three times a week in the hospital.

There's always a big argument, too, about whether you stepped out-of-bounds or not. That's a four-hour argument. So usually you take another shot—20-minute argument. Another shot—20-minute argument. Out-of-bounds—four-hour argument. So this one game—the winner is the first team to score 20 points—can go maybe two weeks. The most important thing is to remember the score from day to day. Sometimes you argue four hours about *that*.

To play on any team outdoors, you have to have a pair of old jeans that you cut off and shred a little bit above the knees so they look like beachcomber pants. You get an old sweat shirt of some university—

mine was Temple—and you go outside to the playground, and play basketball all day, until dark, and your mother has to come get you.

Let me say something about mothers. When I was a kid, mothers were never really interested in sports. Even if you became a fantastic star, your mother was probably the last person to know. She was more concerned with you being on time for dinner.

My mother was a fantastic color changer. Whatever color my uniform was, my mother would always put it into the washing machine with different-colored stuff—the red bedspread, the green curtains, the yellow tablecloth or the purple bathroom rug. And when the uniform came out, instead of being white, it would be avocado.

I've worn a pink uniform, and I've worn a running yellow-and-blue uniform—which of course startled my teammates quite a bit. One time, I had to learn how to use karate in order to answer for a pale-lavender uniform.

Later, I graduated from playground basketball to indoor basketball. I played for a place called the Wissahickon Boys' Club along with a very famous defensive back by the name of Herb Adderley.

Well, very few teams could whip the Wissahickon Boys' Club on our own court, mainly because our court was different. First of all, the floor hadn't been varnished and the out-of-bounds lines hadn't been painted since the day the gym was built, about two weeks after Dr. Naismith invented basketball. We didn't have to see them. We could feel where they were. Our sneakers had soles as thick as a piece of paper. But it was hell on the other team.

So was the ball. We used a leather ball that had been played with outside—in the dark of night, in the rain, in the snow. It was about as heavy as a medicine ball, and just as lively. There were stones and pieces of glass stuck into it, and it never had enough air, because the valve leaked. You could wear yourself out just trying to dribble it.

Now about the basket. The rim was loose, and hanging, and shaking. And all you had to do was kind of lay that heavy ball up softly. The rim acted like a trampoline. It lifted the ball up and threw it through the center of the hoop and you always had two points.

Another thing about playing at the Wissahickon Boys' Club. We would get ol' Weird Harold, who was six feet nine and weighed about 90 pounds, to make black X's all over the backboard. Now, only our team knew what each X stood for. See, we aimed maybe two inches under a mark, and, zap, two points. If you followed our mark, you'd miss the rim. We always had something going for ourselves.

The ceiling in the gym was only 15 feet high. For those who may not know that much about basketball, that means our ceiling was only five feet above the rim of the basket itself. When other teams came to play us, they weren't aware right away that the ceiling was low. So when they shot the ball, they hit the ceiling—which was out-of-bounds. And we would get the ball. Meanwhile, we had practiced shooting our jump shots and set shots on a direct line drive. No arch, no nothing—just straight ahead into the basket. Sort of Woody Sauldsberry style.

We also had a hot-water pipe that ran around the wall, and the wall of the gym was out-of-bounds. If you touched the wall or anything, you were out-of-bounds. So whenever a guy on the other team would go up for a rebound or a jump shot, or drive into the basket, we would kind of screen him into the hot-water pipe.

At the Wissahickon Boys' Club, we had graduated to the point where we had referees for the games. We had them because they were honest and fair and impartial. Which is what they teach at boys clubs. Also because we were playing teams from other neighborhoods and had to finish the games in one day. The referees cut down on the long arguments.

We had two steady refs whom we named Mr. Magoo and The Bat. You might say they did not have Superman vision. They more or less had to make their calls on what they could hear. Like if they heard a slap, and thought they saw the ball fly out of a guy's hands, they cried "foul" for hacking. So whenever a guy would go up for a rebound or something, all we had to do was just give him a little nudge, and boom! He'd wind up against the wall and probably that hot-water pipe. His screams would tell The Bat and Mr. Magoo he was out-of-bounds.

When new teams came down to play us and saw our uniforms, which consisted of heavy old long-sleeved flannel pajama tops over below-the-knee corduroy knickers, they'd call us "turkeys" and all kinds of chicken names. Maybe we weren't cool. But we were protected from that hot-water pipe.

One time, Cryin' Charlie's mother had his PJ tops in the washing machine at game time, and we had to make him non-playing coach that day so he wouldn't cry.

In the middle of the court, we had five boards that happened to be about the loosest boards that you ever stepped on in your life. So that while dribbling downcourt on a fast break, if you hit one of those five boards, the ball would not come back to you. Many times, a guy on the other team would dribble downcourt on the fast break, and all of a sudden he'd be running, and his arm would be pumping, but there was no ball coming back up to him. All we had to do was just stand around at the loose boards, and without even stickin' the guy, let him go ahead and do his Lamont Cranston dribble, and we could pick up the ball, dead and waiting, right there. Whenever *we* went on a fast break, we dribbled *around* those loose boards.

One team I remember we lost to was the Nicetown Club for Boys & Girls. We played in their gym. They had a balcony that extended out over one side of the court about ten feet. It was almost exactly the same height as the rim of the basket. So if you went up for a jumper, the balcony would block your shot. The defense of the Nicetown Club was to force the flow of your offense to the side of the court with the balcony. When we tried to shoot from there, the Bill Russell balcony would block the shot, and the ball would bounce back and hit our man in the eye. Whenever *they* came downcourt, they would play on the free side of the floor away from the balcony.

I would say, on a home-and-home basis, the Wissahickon Boys' Club and the Nicetown Club were even.

In high school, I had one of the greatest jump shots—from two feet out—anybody ever saw. The only man who stopped me was Wilt Chamberlain.

We played Wilt's high school, Overbrook, and they had a guy on the team by the name of Ira Davis, who was a great track man. He ran the 100 in like nine-point-something, and a few years later was in the Olympic Games. Ira was great on the fast break. So Chamberlain would stand under our basket and growl at us. And when he growled, guys would just throw the ball at him—to try and hit him with it. And he would catch it and throw it downcourt to Ira Davis, who would score 200 points on the fast break. We lost to them something like 800 to 14.

My best shot was where I would dribble in quickly, stop, fake the man playing me into the air, and then go up for my two-foot jump shot. Well, I was very surprised when I found Mr. Chamberlain waiting under the basket for me. I faked, and faked and faked and faked and faked, and then I threw the ball at him and tried to hit him. But he caught it and threw it downcourt to Ira Davis: 802 to 14.

So then we tried to razzle-dazzle him. But for some reason, he could always follow the ball with that one eye of his in the middle of his forehead. And of course, the only thing we could do was just throw the ball at him.

We had one play we used on Wilt that had some success. We had one kid that was completely crazy. He wasn't afraid of anything in the world. Not even the Big Dipper. He was about as big as Mickey Rooney, and we had him run out on the court and punch Chamberlain right in the kneecap. And when Chamberlain bent over to grab our guy, we shot our jumpers. That foul alone was worth our 14 points.

Now that I'm a celebrity making a million dollars a year, we have Celebrity Basketball. I play with guys like James Garner, Jim Brown, Don Adams, Sidney Poitier, Mike Connors, Mickey Rooney, and Jack Lemmon.

In Celebrity Basketball, you pull up to the fabulous Forum in your Rolls-Royce, and your chauffeur puts you in a beach chair and wheels you out on the court. And after each shot, you have a catered affair.

And the ball. The pros wish they could find a ball this great. It's gold covered and has a little transistor motor inside, with radar and a homing device, and it dribbles and shoots itself.

A 60-piece orchestra plays background music while you're down on the court, and starlet cheerleaders are jumping up and down. After every basket, we all stop and give the guy who scored it a standing ovation.

Another thing about when I used to play basketball in the playgrounds. If you went to a strange playground, you didn't introduce yourself. You had to prove yourself first. No names.

"Over here, my man."

"Yeah, nice play, my man."

Later on, if you earned it, you'd be given a name: Gunner, My Man or Herman or Shorty or something.

Now, when we play the Celebrity games, they come out on the court and they say, "Hi, my name is such and such. I'm from so forth and so on," and the whole thing. And I say, "Oh, very nice to meet you."

But later, during the game, I forget the cat's name anyway and I just go right back to "Over here, my man. I'm free in the corner, my man." And I'm back in the old neighborhood.

Bill Keller

Apartheid Blocks the Slam Dunk

Johannesburg, Aug. 27, 1993—Visiting South Africa earlier this year, Bob McAdoo, the American basketball master, was amazed by an apartheid anomaly: a black country where the winning basketball teams are all white.

McAdoo, a five-time All-Star who now plays in the Italian league, was here advising the producers of a forthcoming Hollywood movie about an American coach who recruits basketball talent from Africa. They filmed the movie, called "The Air Up There," in South Africa, but McAdoo had to import his ball-handlers from Kenya and Zaire.

"Very strange," he recalled yesterday, after he spent the morning demonstrating layups and dribbling techniques for worshipful Soweto children.

McAdoo has returned to South Africa as part of a National Basketball Association mission to the only country in Africa where, as Hollywood might put it, black men can't jump.

"They Can Do It Here"

Along with Dikembe Mutombo, the seven-foot-three-inch Denver Nuggets center, the Hall of Fame shoo-in Alex English, and assorted coaches and N.B.A. officials, McAdoo was pushing basketball as an engine of black excellence and pride in the post-apartheid era.

"This is the message we brought to them: Don't let the dream fall apart," says Mutombo, a native of Zaire, one of three Africans in the N.B.A. and certainly the only black man these children have ever seen who earns three million dollars a year. "We did it in America, and they can do it here in South Africa. Blacks can do it."

More specifically, said Kingly Masilo, a twenty-year-old Soweto coach who came for pointers, "We don't want to see white people play basketball and black people sitting in the streets or stealing."

Basketball is generally reckoned to be the Number Two sport in Africa, after soccer. In America, basketball is so closely associated with slam-dunking black kids that, when a white team takes the court against a black team, the supposition is that the white team will get creamed.

Why in South Africa is the assumption just the opposite?

Eight Courts for Soweto

The question was put to Christopher Mahasha, a Soweto seventh grader who once saw the Chicago Bulls play the Phoenix Suns on television and seems to have memorized every flourish.

The beaming four-foot-something twelve-year-old had just won a dribbling relay race and exchanged not-very-high-fives with the towering Denver center. He drifted down from cloud nine to provide the obvious answer.

"Because," he said, "the white kids get the basketballs."

Indeed, in all of Soweto, a black metropolis inhabited, according to the census, by 837,731 people and, according to anyone who lives there, by as many as five million, there are exactly eight basketball courts. Elsewhere in South Africa every white school of any size has a gymnasium.

No hoops means no black heroes to emulate, and the white players of national stature, even when race is not considered, are not exactly the kind of titans who can excite the imagination of township kids.

As South Africa's dismal Olympics performance last year demonstrated, the country's long-segregated athletic programs have been badly stunted by the exclusion of eighty percent of the population, and by the lack of international competition during the years of international sanctions.

"Some of our better high schools would have no trouble beating the best university teams here," said Craig Jonas, the head coach of Lakeland College in Sheboygan, Wis., who has been holding clinics in South Africa. "In fact, it would be a rout."

In addition, noted Sam Ramsamy, president of the National Olympic Committee of South Africa and a spectator at the Soweto workout, basketball has a longstanding image problem with black boys because of a game called netball. Netball is a British colonial version of basketball played almost exclusively by girls.

"It's a very sissy type of a game," said Ramsamy, speaking freely about one of the few sports that is not in line for Olympic status.

But basketball's image in the townships may be changing, thanks in part to television. Bop-TV, a channel that broadcasts from the northern black homeland of Bophuthatswana, has carried N.B.A. games for years, and beginning in November a weekly half-hour show of N.B.A. highlights will be on a more accessible national station.

Albert Mokoena, who plays on a Soweto team and is vice-chairman of the amateur basketball association in the Johannesburg region, said glimpses of N.B.A. style have already begun to inspire black South Africans.

Mokoena said his team, the Liberty Center Unlimited, or L.C.U.'s, used to step on the court and emulate the white South African manner of play. Like the whites, they played a slow, methodical, everybody-in-his-place kind of game, heavy on passive zone defense. And they lost.

"Then we said, O.K., let's play our game, which is a fast, N.B.A.-type of a game, a lot of excelling from individuals but still playing as a team," Mokoena related.

This season the L.C.U.'s and another Soweto team became the first black teams to break into the upper echelon of the amateur league, the "premier division."

"I give it three years, and the eight top teams will be black teams," he predicted.

The American visitors said the conquest may take longer than that, as it did in America, where professional basketball was exclusively white until the 1950's.

"It took America about thirty years to get to where we are today," said Mutombo, "I think it will happen here, but it will happen slowly."

John Updike

from *Rabbit, Run*

Boys are playing basketball around a telephone pole with a backboard bolted to it. Legs, shouts. The scrape and snap of Keds on loose alley pebbles seems to catapult their voices high into the moist March air blue above the wires. Rabbit Angstrom, coming up the alley in a business suit, stops and watches, though he's twenty-six and six three. So tall, he seems an unlikely rabbit, but the breadth of white face, the pallor of his blue irises, and a nervous flutter under his brief nose as he stabs a cigarette into his mouth partially explain the nickname, which was given to him when he too was a boy. He stands there thinking, the kids keep coming, they keep crowding you up.

His standing there makes the real boys feel strange. Eyeballs slide. They're doing this for their own pleasure, not as a demonstration for some adult walking around town in a double-breasted cocoa suit. It seems funny to them, an adult walking up the alley at all. Where's his car? The cigarette makes it more sinister still. Is this one of those going to offer them cigarettes or money to go out in back of the ice plant with him? They've heard of such things but are not too frightened; there are six of them and one of him.

The ball, rocketing off the crotch of the rim, leaps over the heads of the six and lands at the feet of the one. He catches it on the short bounce with a quickness that startles them. As they stare hushed he sights squinting through blue clouds of weed smoke, a suddenly dark silhouette like a smokestack in the afternoon spring sky, setting his feet with care, wiggling the ball with nervousness in front of his chest, one widespread pale hand on top of the ball and the other underneath, jiggling it patiently to get some adjustment in air itself. The moons on his fingernails are big. Then the ball seems to ride up the right lapel of his coat and comes off his shoulder as his knees dip down, and it appears the ball is not going toward the backboard. It was not aimed there. It drops into the circle of the rim, whipping the net with a ladylike whisper. "Hey!" he shouts in pride.

"Luck," one of the kids says.

"Skill," he answers, and asks, "Hey. O.K. if I play?"

There is no response, just puzzled silly looks swapped. Rabbit takes off his coat, folds it nicely, and rests it on a clean ashcan lid. Behind him the dungarees begin to scuffle again. He goes into the scrimmaging thick of them for the ball, flips it from two weak white hands, has it in his own. That old stretched-leather feeling makes his whole body go taut, gives his arms wings. It feels like he's reaching down through years to touch this tautness. His arms lift of their own and the rubber ball floats toward the basket from the top of his head. It feels so right he blinks when the ball drops short, and for a second wonders if it went through the hoop without riffling the net. He asks, "Hey whose side am I on?"

In a wordless shuffle two boys are delegated to be his. They stand the other four. Though from the start Rabbit handicaps himself by staying ten feet out from the basket, it is still unfair. Nobody bothers to keep score. The surly silence bothers him. The kids call monosyllables to each other but to him they don't dare a word. As the game goes on he can feel them at his legs, getting hot and mad, trying to trip him, but their tongues are still held. He doesn't want this respect, he wants to tell them there's nothing to getting old, it takes nothing. In ten minutes another boy goes to the other side, so it's just Rabbit Angstrom and one kid standing five. This boy, still midget but already diffident with a kind of rangy ease, is the best of the six; he wears a knitted cap with a green pompom well down over his ears and level with his eyebrows, giving his head a cretinous look. He's a natural. The way he moves sideways without taking any steps, gliding on a blessing: you can tell. The way he waits before he moves. With luck he'll become in time a crack athlete in the high school; Rabbit knows the way. You climb up through the little grades and then get to the top and everybody cheers; with the sweat in your eyebrows you can't see very well and the noise swirls around you and lifts you up, and then you're out, not forgotten at first, just out, and it feels good and cool and free. You're out, and sort of melt, and keep lifting, until you become like to these kids just one more piece of the sky of adults that hangs over them in the town, a piece that for some queer reason has clouded and visited them. They've not forgotten him; worse, they never heard of him. Yet in his time Rabbit was famous through the country; in basketball in his junior year he set a B-league scoring record that in his senior year he broke with a record that was not broken until four years later, that is, four years go.

He sinks shots one-handed, two-handed, underhanded, flatfooted, and out of the pivot, jump, and set. Flat and soft the ball lifts. That his touch still lives in his hands elates him. He feels liberated from long gloom. But his body is weighty and his breath grows short. It annoys him, that he gets winded. When the five kids not on his side begin to groan and act lazy, and the kid he accidentally knocks down gets up with a blurred face and walks away, Rabbit quits readily, "O.K.," he says. "The old man's going."

To the boy on his side, the pompom, he adds, "So long, ace." He feels grateful to the boy, who continued to watch him with disinterested admiration after the others grew sullen, and who cheered him on with exclamations: "God. Great. Gee."

Jim Carroll

from *The Basketball Diaries*

Fucked up yesterday, lost our last game in the summer 15-and-under league up at George Washington High School, and that deuced us out of the championship game today. We had a good squad, mostly cats from down the block in the projects but that had a rule that no Varsity players could play. That ruined our chances of using big Lewie Alcindor even though he's from the neighborhood and all. I mean, shit, most of the teams got ringers but it's a little difficult to sneak in a seven foot All-Everything cat onto a court. He can't exactly use a fucking pair of sunglasses, dig? So I go up to watch the game today and pick up my trophy for the all-league team and what a hassle is steaming as I bop into the gym. THE SUGAR BOWL ALL-STARS, one of the teams playing, are in a rage bitching about the ringers on RUTGER'S team. So true! those cats didn't have a dude under eighteen running for them, none of them played school ball, but they were some of the best playground players in Harlem. I walked over and was rapping to a few friends, Vaughn Harper, an All-American from Boys High, and Earl Manigault, a Harlem legend of 5 ft. 10 ins. who can take a half dollar off the top of a backboard. He's invariably on and off his school team because of drug scenes and other shit. These two cats are, with big Lew, the best high school players in the city. Finally the captain of SUGAR BOWL points over to us and tells the other team and the man who runs the gig that if they're gonna use that team, that their team's gonna use Harper, "Goat" Manigault, and me. The bossman axes the idea of letting in Harper and "Goat" but says they can use me, which is fine with the other team who don't even know who the fuck this white boy is. Before I say a fucking word I get a uniform tossed in my mug and since there're bunches of chicks in the stands, my new team mates are huddling around me and I whip on the shit and start warming up. Big fucking difference I'm gonna make 'cause we need leapers for the boards and no backcourt dude like me. Anyway the slaughter starts and I'm hitting long jumpers like a fucker (I gotta say that I always burn up that gym, something about it that I just can't miss, crazy) so we're holding our own by the half and I got twenty-eight points, each move of which I make sticks out like a hard-on because I'm the only whiteman on the court and looking around, in the entire fucking place, in fact; my bright blond-red hair making me the whitest whitey this league has ever seen. So in short we made a good show for a team our age, but can't keep up with the other dudes and lose by ten, but that ain't bad and I got myself forty-seven points and at least got to play for once with these cats I've always had to play against in various tournaments since Biddy League days. Then to bust all kinds of balls, the bossman gets some college scout in the stands to testify the other team got at least three ringers he knows and we are awarded the champ bit. After the gold is handed out and all (I didn't get a trophy for the game 'cause they were one short and I had to say "fuck it," but got an outofsight plaque for All-League), we go in a corner and pose a team picture for the Harlem paper, "The Amsterdam News." We're waiting for the birdie to click when the photog calls over the SUGAR BOWL coach and whispers something to him who then walks over to me and mumbles, "Dig, my man, don't know how to say this but for, well, . . ." I cut him short and told him I got the message and stepped out of the pix. I guess I would have messed up the texture of the shot or something. Or maybe they didn't want to let the readers get to see that the high scorer was a fucking white boy.

Tom Meschery

Lowell High

Our red brick square gymnasium was an anachronism
Among the steel-ribbed, concrete muscled ellipses
And angles of the day; it was full of shadows—
The floor corduroy, the backboards wood
And the rims were bent with age
       (the relentless ricochet of basketballs)
It had none of the embellishments
Found in more modern gyms.
It was simply a no-nonsense structure
Built to house players not spectators.
Surrounded by its gray walls and wrinkled floor
We practiced two-to-six, six days a week.
And throughout that time—four years—
Our coach, who was as old as the building,
Taunted and inspired us, swore and cajoled us.
He taught us to play without frills.
We became red brick and corduroy
And learned to see through shadows.

Susan Orlean

Shoot the Moon

White men in suits follow Felipe Lopez everywhere he goes. Felipe lives in Mott Haven, in the South Bronx. He is a junior at Rice High School, which is on the corner of 124th Street and Lenox Avenue, in Harlem, and he plays guard for the school basketball team, the Rice Raiders. The white men are ubiquitous. They rarely miss one of Felipe's games or tournaments. They have absolute recall of his best minutes of play. They are authorities on his physical condition. They admire his feet, which are big and pontoon-shaped, and his wrists, which have a loose, silky motion. Not long ago, I sat with the white men at a game between Rice and All Hallows High School. My halftime entertainment was listening to a debate between two of them—a college scout and a Westchester contractor who is a high-school basketball fan—about whether Felipe had grown a half inch over Christmas break. "I know this kid," the scout said as the second half started. "A half inch is not something I would miss." The white men believe that Felipe is the best high-school player in the country. They often compare him to Michael Jordan, and are betting that he will become one of the greatest basketball players to emerge from New York City since Kareem Abdul-Jabbar. This conjecture provides them with suspended, savory excitement and a happy premonition. Following Felipe is like hanging around with someone you think is going to win the lottery someday.

At the moment, Felipe is six feet five. He would like to be six feet seven. His shoes are size twelve. He buys his pants at big-and-tall-men stores. His ears, which are small and high-set, look exaggeratedly tiny, because he keeps his hair shaved close to his skull. He has blackish-brown eyes and a big, vivid tongue—I know this only because his tongue sometimes sticks out when he is playing hard, and against his skin, which is very dark, it looks like a pink pennant. His voice is slurry; all his words have round edges. He is as skinny as a bean pole, and has long shins and thin forearms and sharp, chiseled knees. His hands are gigantic. Walking down the street, he gets a lot of attention because of his height, but he is certainly not a horse of a kid—not one of those man-size boys who fleshed out in fifth grade and whose adult forms are in place by the time they're thirteen. He is all outline: he doesn't look like a stretched-out average-size person—he looks like a sketch of a huge person which hasn't yet been colored in.

On the court, Felipe's body seems unusually well-organized. His movements are quick and liquid. I have seen him sail horizontally through thin air. High-school players are often rough and lumbering, and they mostly shoot flat-footed, but Felipe has an elegant, buoyant game. He floats around the edge of the court and then springs on the ball and sprints away. When he moves toward the basket, it looks as if he were speed-skating, and then, suddenly, he rises in the air, and shoots. His shot is smooth and lovely, with a loopy arc. Currently, he averages twenty-six points and nine rebounds per game, and he is within striking distance of the all-time high-school scoring record for New York State. He has great court vision, soft hands, a brisk three-point shot, and the speed to take the ball inside and low. He is usually the fastest man in the fast break. He can handle the ball like a point guard, and he beats bigger players defensively, because of his swiftness and his body control. When he is not on a court, though, the way he walks is complicated and sloppy. He seems to walk this way on purpose, to make light of his size and disguise his grace.

Before I met Felipe, people told me I would find him cuddly. Everything I knew about him—that he is a *boy,* that he is a *teen-age* boy, that he is a six-foot-five teen-age-boy *jock*—made this pretty hard to believe, but it turns out to be true. He is actually the sweetest person I know. At some point during our time together, it occurred to me that he could be a great basketball hustler, because he seems naïve and eager—the ideal personality for attracting competitive big shots on the basketball court. It happens that he is not the least bit of a hustler. But he is also not nearly as naïve and eager as he appears. He once told me that he likes to make people think of him as a clown, because then they will never accuse him of being a snob. He also said that he likes to be friendly to everyone, so that no one will realize he's figuring out whom he can trust.

Felipe spoke no English at all when he moved to New York from the Dominican Republic, four years ago, but he quickly picked up certain phrases, including "crash the boards," "he's bugging out," "get the hell out of the paint," and "oh, my goodness." Now he speaks English comfortably, with a rich Dominican accent—the words tumble and click together, like stones being tossed in a polisher. "Oh, my goodness," remains his favorite phrase. It is a utility expression that reveals his modesty, his manners, his ingenuousness, and his usual state of mind, which is one of pleasant and guileless surprise at the remarkable nature of his life. I have heard him use it to comment on the expectation that he will someday be a rich and famous player in the N.B.A., and on the fact that he was recently offered half a million dollars by a team from Spain to put aside his homework and come play in their league, and on the fact that he is already considered a seminal national export by citizens of the Dominican Republic, who are counting on his to be the first Dominican in the N.B.A., and on the fact that he is growing so fast that he once failed to recognize his own pants. Sometimes he will use the phrase in circumstances where his teammates and friends might be inclined to say something more dynamic. One night this winter, I was sitting around at school with Felipe and his teammates, watching a videotape of old Michael Jordan highlights. The tape had been edited for maximum excitement, and most of the boys on the team were responding with more and more baroque constructions of foul language. At one point, Jordan was shown leaping past the Celtics center Robert Parish, and someone said, "Yo, feature that, bro! He's busting the Chief's face."

"Busting his fucking face," another one said.

"Busting his goddam big-ass face."

"He's got it going on. Now Jordan's going to bust his foul-loving big-ass mama's-boy dope black ass."

On the tape, Jordan slammed the ball through the hoop and Parish crumpled to the floor. While the other boys were applauding and swearing, Felipe moved closer to the television and then said, admiringly, "Oh, my goodness."

*　*　*

Felipe on his development as a player:

"Back in my country, I was just a little guy. I tried to dunk, but I couldn't. I tried and I tried. Then, one day, I dunked. Oh, my goodness. Three months later, I was dunking everything, every way—with two hands, backwards, backwards with two hands. I can do a three-sixty dunk. It's easy. You know, you jump up backwards with the ball and then spin around while you're in the air—and *pow!* I'm working all the time on my game. If Coach DeMello says he wants me to work on my ball handling, then I just work at it, work at it, work at it, until it's right. In basketball, you always are working, even on the things you already know.

"When I come to this country, I was real quiet, because I didn't speak any English, so all I did was dunk. On the court, playing, I had to learn the words for the plays, but you don't have to talk, so I was O.K. My coach used his hands to tell me what to do, and then I learned the English words for it. There aren't too many Spanish kids at school. I know a lot of kids, though. I meet kids from all over the country at tournaments and at summer camps. If you do something good, then you start meeting people, even if you don't want to. Sometimes it's bouncing in my head that people are talking about me, saying good things, and that some people are talking about me and saying bad things, saying like, 'Oh, he think's he's all that,' but that's life. I don't like when it's bouncing in my head, but I just do what I'm supposed to do. I'm quick. I broke the record for the fifty-yard dash when I was in junior high school—I did it in five point two seconds, when the record was five point five seconds. I also got the long-jump record. It feels natural when I do these things. In basketball, I like to handle the ball and make the decisions. I can play the big people, because of my quickness. But I got to concentrate or the ball will go away from me. At basketball camp, I'm always the craziest guy—people always are walking around saying, 'Hey, who's that Dominican clown?' But on the court I don't do any fooling around. I got to show what I got.

"In life, I don't worry about myself. My brother will run defense for me. I got my family. Some kids here, I see them do drugs, messing around, wasting everything, and I see the druggies out on the street, and I just, I don't know, I don't understand it. That's not for me. I got a close family, and I got to think about my family, and if I can do something that will be good for my whole family, then I got to do it. I think about my country a lot—I want to go there so bad. In Santiago, everyone knows about me and wants to see me play. If I'm successful, the way everyone talks about that, I'd like a big house there in Santiago, where I could go for a month or two each year and just relax."

After practice one day, Felipe and I walked down 125th Street in a cold rain. First, he bought new headphones for his tape player from a Ghanaian street peddler, and then we stopped at Kentucky Fried Chicken to eat a pre-dinner dinner before heading home. He was dressed in his school clothes—a multicolored striped shirt, a purple-and-blue flowered tie, and pleated, topstitched baggy black cotton pants—and had on a Negro League baseball cap, which he was wearing sideways and at a jaunty angle. In his book bag were some new black Reebok pump basketball shoes; everyone on the team had been given a pair for the Baltimore tournament. Felipe was in a relaxed mood. He has traveled to and played in big tournaments so often that he now takes them in stride. He has become something of a tournament connoisseur. One of his favorite places in the world is southern France, where he played last spring. He liked the weather and the countryside and the fact that by the end of the tour French villagers were crowding into the gyms and chanting his name. This particular evening, he was also feeling pleased that he had finished most of the homework he needed to do before leaving for Baltimore, which consisted of writing an essay for American history on Brown v. Board of Education and the Fifteenth Amendment, preparing an annotated periodic table of the elements, and writing two poems for his Spanish class.

One of his poems was called "Los Dientes de Mi Abuela," which translates as "The Teeth of My Grandmother." Sitting in Kentucky Fried Chicken, he read it to me: "*Conservando la naturaleza se ve en aquella mesa los dientes de mi abuela, que los tenía guardados para Navi-*

dad.'" He looked up from his notebook and gestured with a chicken wing. "This is about an old grandmother who is saving her special teeth for Christmas, when she'll be eating a big dinner. The teeth are brilliant and shiny. Then she gets impatient and uses them to eat a turkey at Thanksgiving—'*GRRT . . . suena la mordida de la abuela al pavo.'"* The other poem Felipe had written was about a man about to enter prison or some other gloomy passage in his life. It is called "La Primera y Ultima Vez . . ." As he began reading it, an argument broke out in front of the restaurant between a middle-aged woman in a cream-colored suit and two little boys who were there on their own. First, the boys were just sassy, and then they began yelling that the woman was a crack addict. She balled up a napkin and threw it at them, shouting, "Why don't you respect your elders? What are you doing out at night all alone? Why don't you get your asses home and watch television or read a fucking book?" Felipe kept reciting his poem, raising his voice over the commotion. When he finished, he said, "It's a sadder poem than the one about the grandmother. I like writing poems. In school, I like to write if it's in Spanish, and I like to draw, and I like math. I'm good at math. I like numbers. How do I write the poems? I don't know how. They just come to me."

* * *

Felipe Lopez is certainly a born athlete. But he may also be one of those rarer cases—a person who is just born lucky, whose whole life seems an effortless conveyance of dreams, and to whom other people's dreams adhere. This aura of fortune is so powerful that it is easy to forget that for the time being, and for a while longer, Felipe Lopez is still just an immigrant teen-ager who lives in a scary neighborhood in the South Bronx and who goes to high school in Harlem, where bad things happen every day.

Currently, there are five hundred and eighteen thousand male high-school basketball players in the United States. Of these, only nineteen thousand will end up on college teams—not even four percent. Less than one per cent will play for Division One colleges—the most competitive. The present N.B.A. roster has three hundred and sixty-seven players, and each year only forty or fifty new players are drafted. What these numbers forebode is disappointment for many

high-school basketball players. That disappointment is dispropor-
tionate among black teen-agers. A recent survey of high-school students by Northeastern University's Center for the Study of Sport in
Society reported that fifty-nine per cent of black teen-age athletes
thought they would continue to play on a college team, compared
with thirty-nine percent of white teen-agers. Only sixteen per cent of
the white athletes expected that they would play for the pros; forty-
three per cent of the blacks expected that they would, and nearly half
of all the kids said they thought it would be easier for black males to
become professional basketball players than to become lawyers or
doctors. Scouts have told me that everyone on the Rice team will
probably be able to get a free college education by playing basketball,
and so far all the players have received recruiting letters from several
schools. The scouts have also said that it will require uncommonly
hard work for any of the boys on the team other than Felipe to ascend
to the N.B.A.

Every so often, scouts' forecasts are wrong. Some phenomenal
high-school players get injured or lazy or fat or drug-addled or bored,
or simply level off and then vanish from the sport, and, by the same
token, a player of no particular reputation will once in a while emerge
from out of nowhere and succeed. That was the case with the N.B.A.
all-stars Karl Malone and Charles Barkley, who both played through
high school in obscurity; but most other N.B.A. players were stand-
outs starting in their early teens. Most people who follow high-school
basketball teams that are filled with kids from poor families and rough
neighborhoods encourage the kids to put basketball in perspective,
to view it not as a catapult into some fabulous, famous life but as
something practical—a way to get out, to get an education, to learn
the way around a different, better world. The simple fact that only
one in a million people in this country will ever play for the N.B.A.
is often pointed out to the kids, but that still doesn't seem to stop them
from dreaming.

Being told that you might be that one person in a million would
deform many people's characters, but it has not made Felipe cynical
or overly interested in himself. In fact, his blitheness is almost unnerv-
ing. One evening when we were together, I watched him walk past a
drug deal on 125th Street and step off the curb into traffic, and then

he whiled away an hour in a fast-food restaurant where several ragged, hostile people repeatedly pestered him for change. He hates getting hurt on the court, but out in the world he is not very careful with himself. When you're around him, you can't help feeling that he is a boy whose body is a savings account, and it is one that is uninsured. But being around him is also to be transported by his nonchalant confidence about luck—namely, that it happens because it happens, and that it will happen for Felipe because things are meant to go his way. This winter, he and the Rice Raiders were in Las Vegas playing in a tournament. One evening, a few of them went into a casino and attached themselves to the slot machines. Felipe's first quarter won him a hundred quarters. Everyone told him to stop while he was ahead, but he continued. "I wanted to play," he says. "I thought, I had nothing before I started, now I have something, so I might as well play. So I put some more quarters in, and—oh, my goodness!— I won twelve hundred more quarters. What can I say?"

* * *

[*Big game, Rice Raiders v. Baltimore Southern. Baltimore Arena.*]

Felipe gets a rebound, passes off, gets the ball back, and then suddenly he drifts upward, over the court, over the other boys, toward the basket, legs scissored, wrists cocked, head tilted, and in that instant he looks totally serene. Right before he dunks the ball, I have the sensation that the arena is quiet, but, of course, it isn't; it's just that as soon as he slams the ball down there is a crack of applause and laughter, which makes the instant preceding it seem, by contrast, like a vacuum of sound, a little quiet hole in space.

Madeleine Blais

from *In These Girls Hope Is a Muscle*

Wearing a T-shirt, shorts, and her game sneakers, she pulled into the dark parking lot and backed the car up so that the headlights would throw the greatest light possible on the hoops she had used as a child.

She got out of the car and gave the empty courts and fields a sweeping look. Good: She was alone.

She walked onto the court and dribbled in a fashion that might seem aimless to an outsider; but in fact she was glancing at parts of the pavement, imagining:

This is where Jen will throw me the ball, here is where Jamila will pull up and dish it off, here is where Kathleen might miss a shot, and this is where I have to be for the rebound.

She moved carefully, methodically, trying not to stress either of her ankles. Surgery was inevitable, but she wanted to make it through the 1992–93 season first. She inched her way closer to the basket:

Eight feet is too far away; shoot from eight and Coach will put me back on the bench just like he did in that last game against Hamp. Six feet. That's better. Right side off the backboard, through the chain-metal net. Left side, rattle it through. Over and over, spin right, dribble, jump. Drop step, pivot, shoot.

Applauded only by the mosquitoes and the crickets, she would take the ball and pound it on the asphalt, and set up and shoot. Despite the noise from the bugs and the drone of traffic on Route 116, she heard nothing except the thud of the ball and the pulsing inside her chest, the steady beat of pride and exhaustion, the old brag of the athlete's heart.

*   *   *

Usually there is a buzz of cheering at the start of a game, but this time the Amherst crowd was nearly silent as the referee tossed the ball.

The Haverhill center tapped the ball backward to her point guard on the left side of the court, who drove through the lane, uncontested, past Jen. Easy layup. Amherst blinked first. Two-nothing. In the Haverhill stands, the crowd cheered. It was the only pure cheer they got.

Within a few seconds, the score was 6–4 Amherst, and something remarkable took place. The Hurricanes entered into a zone where all of them were all-Americans. It's a kind of controlled frenzy that can overtake a group of athletes under only the most elusive of circumstances. It's not certain what triggered it, perhaps it was Jamila's gentle three-pointer from the wing, or more likely, when Jen drove the baseline and she swooped beneath the basket like a bird of prey, then released the ball back over her head, placing it like an egg against the backboard and through the hoop. It might have been ten seconds later when Jamila stole the ball, pushing it down court in a three-on-one break, made a no-look pass to Jen, who just as quickly fired the ball across the lane to Kathleen for an uncontested layup. Whatever it is that started it, there was nothing Haverhill could do to stop it, and time-outs repeatedly called for by their frustrated coach only fueled Amherst's frenzy further. Jen was amazed:

It was a struggle to get up to the tempo in the first couple of minutes. We were playing even. But then as soon as we got in our rhythm, we stayed on that level. Coach always says basketball is a game of shifting momentum. It's like a car speeding up a hill and braking on the way down. You rev it up, you slow it down. But with us, right now, we hit cruise control and it is well above the speed limit. Everyone on the court is playing as close to their best every moment. It is unconscious, but it's not like sinking. Look: There's Jamila with four steals in a row, and the whole team just looking as if we won't try to catch up with her, thank you, because we just know she'll get there first. And the passing, from Jamila to me, me whipping it across the key to Kathleen, and Kathleen making the bucket. Everyone is in the right spot. Everything is clicking.

Stephen Vincent

Basketball

I never let you come to the games. I never
invited you. You never asked. You never
saw me on the court handle the round skin
of the basketball. You never came to see me
spread my warm fingers like the edges of stars
around the ball as I went like a smooth fox
down the court my tennis shoes squeaking faster
than a grasshopper through clover. At sixteen
I travelled fast
father. Lay in, set shot, jump shot, bounce pass,
chest pass, bucking, elbowing as high as I could,
reacher for what was never given, the smooth flow
of the ball arching high towards the rim, its high arc
lifting subtly down, a smooth swish through
the star shapes of the unbroken
white net. Let me play that game again. I was on the court
with Willie, Leroy, Hobo & Sam. I the only white
with four blacks. Don't get me wrong. I was scared of them
as you of me or I of you. But it began. Somebody
poked me in the eye, it stung, and I released everything
travelling up and down the court a young man
with a quick gun and a sharp elbow. For the first time
we held together like a rapid running loom weaving
up and down between the other players who held together
stiff as strings as we broke through all their empty

edges. Suddenly it was no game. Perfect harmony
of movement and song. The referee could blow no whistle.
In victory I always refused you
entry. This time
I am going to win.

John R. Tunis

from *Ain't God Good to Indiana!*

Autumn in Indiana means yellow corn stacked in the fields and country fairs from north to south. As the days grow shorter, politics rears its ugly head around Courthouse Square, and a bit later comes the thing that unites everyone: basketball.

For here is the game of the people, rich, poor, young, old, town dweller and farmer, the sport that stirs every Hoosier heart, that everyone in the state understands and responds to. Unlike some of its neighbors, Indiana is full of small towns and small homes. Here in the middle land folks are, as Dreiser said, warm, generous, hospitable, the epitome of American virtues. There are more lawn mowers per capita in this state than in any other. Indiana also has basketball.

Basketball means various things to different people. To the high school principal or superintendent, the game is a big headache. Folks besiege him for seats he hasn't got. Businessmen downtown want a winning team—or else. If the school continues to lose, the principal's head rolls. Unless that of the coach rolls first. On the other hand, victory helps the principal with the school board, and to the winning coach means more money, power, and prestige.

To the boys on the high school team—in some states girls play interscholastic basketball—this is the Great Adventure, their first chance to see the big outside world. The sport can be fun and torture at the same time with its daily drudgery of practice, elation of competition, agony of losing, and ecstasy of triumph. To folks in town, Saturday night is something to look ahead to, the high point of many a drab existence. To the men shooting pool in the rear of Joe's Steak

House on East Michigan, basketball is their bread and butter, a large part of their yearly take. (Nobody knows how many millions are bet on basketball; but far more than on any other game.) For although some teams win and some lose, gamblers are apt to come out ahead.

Throughout the state there are hoops over every garage door and above every barn. You'll find them also inside the homes—nailed up to bedroom doors or hanging in the hall. There are grade schools with no other recreational equipment; but a basketball court is a must. Not long ago a high school in a fair-sized Indiana town burned to the ground. The gymnasium was rebuilt immediately: the school not for several years. In one south-central town of 23,000, a new school, the first for thirty years, was built at a cost of $375,000. The hat was then passed around among the townspeople for a gymnasium, and more than one million dollars was raised for a magnificent structure of stone, brick, and glass, the fourth largest in the state. The high school gymnasium today in the Midwest has the role of the playhouse of the Elizabethans, the bull ring of Seville, the theater of the ancient Greeks. Indeed the Greeks would have been entirely at home watching a basketball game in Kokomo, Indiana.

Kids throughout the state play alley basketball all summer and even go to bed with a basketball. Dad gives his youngster a regulation ball as soon as he can toddle, and teaches him to toss it through his elder brother's outstretched arms. And each year comes the biggest event of all, the Tournament, usually called "The State." Eight hundred teams from high schools compete each winter, with 4,500 boys from fourteen to eighteen in action. This event has been held regularly without interruption since 1911. About a million and a half admissions, costing almost nine hundred thousand dollars, are sold every winter.

In this game, in this region, no coach ever has to worry about material. His problem is to assimilate it, to pick out the five best youngsters on the team, and get them out on that hardwood. Businessmen, housewives, kids, the president of the Merchants National Bank, the chief of police, that loafer in the booth at Hank's Bar and Grill, the farmers turning on their television sets out on the National Road, and Doc Showalter, the local osteopath, all know basketball. They know it, love it, live it.

And every single one of them could coach a team better'n that fella down at the high school, too!

Going to the game tonight, Mac?

Silly question. Of course we're going.

For this is *our* team, not just the high school's team. It's Muncie, Marion, Logansport, Jeffersonville, East Chicago, or Vincennes. We know these boys. That six-foot-four-inch center lives two doors down the street. We remember the cold January day he was born, and that hot summer he was so sick with polio; we recall the first day he went to kindergarten, and when he got well and made his grade school team. That blond guard with the crew haircut tosses the *Sentinel* up to our front porch each evening. Joe, one of the forwards, carries our groceries out from Kroger's on Fridays. Chester, the other guard, cuts our lawn each summer. We've watched these youngsters all their lives, know them and their parents.

Going to the game tonight, Mac?

Don't be silly. Of course we're going.

Who watches basketball in an Indiana town? Everyone. That means everyone who can hobble to the Gymnasium, the Field House, the Auditorium, or the Coliseum. Men, women, kids, young, old, and middle-aged, business leaders, doctors and lawyers, factory workers, machinists from the Chrysler plant, storekeepers, and the lady who runs the best beauty parlor in town on West Walnut. Everybody is there save the blind, the crippled, and the town drunk. And, of course, those unfortunates who didn't apply for a seat in time and must watch the game over television, or, worse, listen to it on the radio.

I stepped off the train at the Monon Depot that rainy February night to find my friend waiting. To him it was very meet and right that if anybody wanted to understand basketball he should come to Indiana. Across the wide Mississippi and over the wide Missouri they're nuts about basketball, too. Granted. But not the way Hoosiers are. And if a seeker for truth comes to Indiana, naturally he should first visit Springfield.

Listen to the pride in his voice. "Why, man, there's no town in Indiana for basketball like Springfield! Hurry up! First game's almost over." He chucks my bag onto the rear seat and jumps quickly in behind the wheel. "Wildcats were behind, thirty-six to thirty-eight, end of the third quarter."

Through the icy, slithery streets at a fast pace, too fast, and so to the Gymnasium, and into that hot, fetid smell of popcorn and 6,000 people cooped up together. He led me up to the balcony where a seat had been reserved in the front row. The electric scoreboard at the end showed fifty-six seconds to play and the Wildcats behind by a single point. The entire crowd was on its feet shrieking, yelling at the ten sweat-stained youngsters on the floor below.

Beside me was a little old lady in gray. She wore a faded gray dress, an especially ancient gray hat, and held in her right hand an umbrella. Down on the floor cheerleaders leaped and turned handsprings, people in the stands thumped each other's backs and screamed. An orgy of emotions gripped the place and everyone in it.

Suddenly a towhead on the floor below stole the ball. Now the noise overwhelmed us all; you found yourself on your feet yelling in that Niagara of sound. Although insulated, indifferent to the two teams you never saw five minutes ago, this fever was contagious. It conquered you until you were one with the screaming mob as the little towhead dribbled the ball down the floor, passed to a teammate, took it back again.

The tension tightened, became taut, unendurable. There was no world but this. Reality was the heated enclosure below. Space was the confines of these four walls. Time was the electric clock beating out these final seconds. Life was this thrusting surge beneath.

The boy swung the ball around adroitly, passed and received it back, zig-zagging nearer the goal, pivoting, turning, twisting. The little old lady in gray beside me could stand it no longer. Leaning over the balcony rail, she waved her umbrella.

"Get the sonofabitch!" she shrieked. "Get the sonofabitch!"

This is the Finals of the State in the Butler Field House in Indianapolis. We are in the dressing room of the Springfield Wildcats, favorites to win the title, just as the first half is ending. Now comes the last act of this drama which started four weeks ago when 832 teams hopefully began the long, hard road through the Sectionals (sixty-four teams left), to the Regionals (thirty-two teams left), to the Semi-finals (sixteen left), to the Finals (four left). Only the Wildcats and Tigers remain to fight it out this evening.

The dressing room, like all dressing rooms, is spare, square, humid, with steam pipes crossing the ceiling, and over everything that dressing-room odor of sweaty flesh, the smell of Doc Showalter's liniment mingled with that of a pile of dirty towels in one corner. Lockers stretch along the side. Opposite is a bank of showers. The walls are a dingy concrete, the floor the same. Two long benches form a kind of V. A blackboard leans against a side wall, a clothes rack with plaid shirts, windbreakers, and slacks stands near the lockers. Two wooden chairs and a table complete the furnishings, save for a large sign hung on the wall.

EVERY DAY THINGS ARE BEING DONE
WHICH COULDN'T BE DONE.

The only person in the room is Tommy Kates, the assistant manager, a chubby, bespectacled boy of fifteen in a red-and-blue Wildcat sweater. He is placing clean towels along the benches, moving the blackboard up against one locker where it will be accessible. From outside come bursts of noise. Listen! You can distinguish the hoarse, tense shouts of the players, the cheers from both sides of the arena. Then there is a sudden roar, a cry of piercing elation that penetrates the room, seems to possess the whole building.

Tommy stops, a pile of towels in his arms. He knows the first half is dying in the frenzy of exultation. He also knows what he hears isn't good for the Wildcats.

The door bangs open and a man rushes in. It's Doc Showalter, followed by Russ Davis, the assistant coach, and a couple of subs in satin jackets with WILDCATS and their numbers on them. Then a hot, dejected boy in shorts and a red jersey, a big 34 on front, stumbles in. Another enters, another, and another, all tall, for this team averages six feet two. They tromp into the room, fall slumping and sprawling onto the benches. Behind them is Jack Stevens, the manager, with the score book in one hand, and last of all Art Benson, the coach.

Art, which is what everyone in town calls him, is a youngish man with an oldish look. Gray hair is traced over his ears, there is a deep furrow above his eyes, he is tight-lipped and tense. He steps to the center of the V made by the two benches, facing the exhausted team. The assistant manager walks silently past, handing out two vitamin pills to each player. Heads come up, heads drop again. The Doc goes along the row, kneeling to adjust an ankle brace on one player, tightening a knee supporter on the next man.

The coach's voice is hoarse after all the shouting at them he has done from the bench. "Lemme see the score book." Notice how his hand trembles as the manager hands him the book, and says in low tones, "Two on Spike. One on Jerry. Three on Tom."

Now the room is silent. Not a sound, not a movement, save for the everlasting panting from the benches. No friends, no parents or school officials, no reporters, fight their way past the guard at the door. They are all in the dressing room of the other team. The dressing room of a losing team is usually empty. We are not interested in losers in the United States.

"Nice boys? Oh sure, too bad they couldn't make it. But d'ja see that Tiger forward, that boy Karson? He's fast, he's sneaky, he's shifty, all right. . . ."

The coach stands engrossed, reading the score book in agony. There in black and white is the story of disaster. All the time the boys sit, heads down, not even using the towels in their fists; necks, backs, shoulders, and shirts soaked with sweat.

At last he reaches down, picks up a basketball from the floor, slapping it back and forth in his hands, the only outward and visible sign of the nerves he tries to suppress. He looks at each boy carefully. Their heads are still down, their eyes avoid his, they gaze at the dingy concrete, miserable, panting. Suddenly he screams at them, at the lowered heads along the bench:

"Well! You got anything to say?" No response. He shrieks at them. "Have ya?"

Nobody answers. Although each man is dying of thirst, not one ventures as far as the water cooler, or even looks at him. Heads remain down.

The manager, who has been walking around handing out towels, stands immobile. Even the Doc, his arms full of bottles and adhesive tape, is motionless.

"You patted yourselves on the back too soon." Half-crazed with the agony of it, he stalks back and forth, turning the ball around and around in his palms. "Thought you'd get by the easy way, on your reputation. Won the State last year, so you were the champs, you were the best. Then you met this gutsy gang of kids from a school of ninety students, a gang that wasn't scared of you. Didn't you? Hey?"

Still no sound or movement from the benches save that everlasting panting. No heads rise. Just an awful silence over the room. "Now mebbe you realize in Indiana a team . . . cannot . . . get by . . . on its reputation. That's something. If you guys will stop reading your clippings . . . we might get back to basketball."

Heads down, they listen as they never listened before. A bench creaks ominously. The coach's tone burns them, sears everyone in the room, the subs in the background, the two managers.

Slap-slap, slap-slap, the ball goes from one hand to the other. "Got anything to say? If you have, please say it. You figgered you were safe because you had an eight-point lead at the quarter, 'cause you were the great Wildcats, you thought they'd fold. You fell asleep out there, didn't you. Hey?

"Is there anything I can do'll wake you up?"

Still they sit panting, not even using the towels, in a state of shock. With a quick glance the coach tosses away the basketball and grabs a wooden chair beside him. Swinging it around his head, he flings it hard against the concrete wall ten feet away.

It strikes with a crash and crumples into splinters.

The heads come up, the heads immediately go down. A door slams and a voice calls: "Three minutes!"

He turns back. "You played like you were glued to the floor. Joe, you didn't make six passes all evening. Tom, ain't a mite o' use chuckin' from way out there, you know that. *Move that ball!*" His voice rises to a shriek as he glares at them. "Basketball is a game of movement; move to the strong side. Swing-it-wide-and-swing-it-true. You had things sewed up, then what happened? The roof fell in. So you lost your heads, you saw you might be beaten, and you quit. Bunch of quitters. You quit cold. You got scared, you didn't pass, you acted like you had boxcars in your shoes. . . ."

Back and forth, back and forth he stalks, suffering as they suffer, sharing their agony, yet pleading, abusing, entreating. "Watch that ball. Alla time, watch . . . that . . . ball. At no time . . . take . . . yer eyes . . . offa that ball. An' get those bricks outa your britches. This isn't kindergarten, it's basketball. How you gonna go back home and face those folks if you lose? Get out there and fight."

He turned, saw the table, kicked savagely, taking out some of his rage and disappointment upon it. The table overturned, fell, clattered to the floor with a bang, and a roll of Doc Showalter's adhesive tape jangled and bounced along the concrete.

Then he was back at them again.

"This is your last chance. The bread-and-butter quarter. Every shot counts. Have you got guts? Are you a bunch of quitters, that's what I wanna know? Have . . . you . . . got the . . . guts?"

They rise together. Benches scrape on the floor. Their voices, hoarse and husky from shouting, conquer the room.

"Les' go, big team . . . les' get those guys. Les' win this one . . . ."

Together they pour out the door onto the arena floor. You can hear the sudden cheers from the Springfield side as they appear.

Sandy Robinson

Jenny

In the summer of 1976 our family left Berkeley and moved to rural Northern California. We left behind electricity, indoor plumbing, television, Chinese food, and my regular Monday night basketball game. It took us two years to decide how much we missed it all. While we were living on "The Land" a friend erected a basket for me on a long deserted slab of concrete incongruously placed in a small oak grove with a marvelous view of snow-topped mountains. It was on that court that Jenny began to play the city game. After school my little second-grader would yell from the court and I would run down from our cabin to meet her. The basket was too high for her but she wanted me to teach her. I taught her all the old games I used to play as a kid. Horse, 21, 5-3-1, poison, around the world. Her favorite was poison as that game involved little skill and lots of running. After a time we would stop to watch the hawks play with the wind and check out the sunset on the mountains. Then we'd race back to the cabin with its wood stove and kerosene lamps dreaming of hook shots and slam dunks.

Since we had no TV, the radio and the *Sporting News* became my only sources of sports events and statistics. Some nights Jenny and I would huddle under the covers, listening to an NBA game. It might be the Lakers with Chick Hern, or Bill King and the Warriors, or Bill Schonley and the Blazers. On a clear night I could get them all. Jenny was still too young to "see" the court as I did but the excitement was catching. "Six seconds left Daddy. Tie game." I would explain the options to her. Barry should take the shot because he's a great foul shooter or how Kareem will be doubleteamed when the ball is passed in bounds. Jenny didn't care. She just liked to see me nervous, pacing the small cabin as the radio would suddenly fill with static. "What happened?" I would moan to the radio and Jenny would laugh at me getting so worked up over a game.

That winter I took Jenny to a girls' basketball tournament held at the local high school. Watching those games turned Jenny on to the game. The stands filled with people cheering on the girls ("just like me") who were racing up and down the court in bright uniforms. There was a big electric score board ticking off the seconds and tallying the score and my god the noise. Jenny loved it. We sat through four straight games until I had had enough, but Jenny wanted more. This was not L.A. or Portland but Fort Jones, California, population 947.

When she was in third grade, Jenny wanted a little more from our sessions on the court. "Teach me a play." So we worked on the give and go. I taught her how to cut close off the high post, running her man into the pick, and then going to the basket. I showed her how to practice dribbling with either hand by placing oak leaves on the court as an obstacle course. In the spring of our second year she would walk down to the court through the wildflowers and play by herself, shooting with two hands but now reaching the basket. Often other kids would join her and I would take out my binoculars (the ones we had bought to watch the eagles) to see them play. Laughter floated up the hill mixed with the rhythmic pounding of the ball and I felt I could reach out and hug them all.

That summer we left the country to fly to New York and visit my parents. They still live in the same house where I grew up but the trees are bigger and the basketball court-driveway is smaller. The hours I spent on that court. There was a new backboard hanging on the garage for my nephews. Somebody placed it in the middle of the driveway, enabling a person to drive to the right without trampling the lilac bushes. "See that crack in the cement, Jenny. That's where I would shoot foul shots trying to decide if I should shoot them with two hands or one." The corner shot that seemed so hard was now a six-footer while the most difficult shot on the court—the one I used to heave like some grenade—is now a seventeen-foot jump shot.

Jenny and I played a quick game of horse and all the memories flood back. Seconds ticking off the clock, game tied. I would play both sides, all the time keeping up a running commentary as if millions were listening. It never failed to amaze me how quickly I would get lost in the story line, the drama of the moment. I would go so far as to fake injuries while playing the game. "Cousy is hurt. He's down on one knee holding his ankle. He's obviously in pain folks. Red has called a time-out as the Couz limps to the bench, Russell helping him over as a worried Auerbach checks the clock. One minute left and the Celtics are behind by one. The ref signals the teams back onto the court. The Celtics pretend not to hear the whistle, giving their injured star a few extra seconds. The crowd is on its feet, and yes Cousy is coming back to the floor, his ankle taped, and obviously limping. The Garden is going crazy!" I would hit two limping one-handers and win the game just before my mother would call me in for roast chicken. The endless hours playing a game. Larry Bird played endless games and became great. Sandy Robinson played those same games and the best he made was seventh man on his high school team.

We now live in Ashland, Oregon, and Jenny has finished fifth grade. She plays on a team in the YBA program run by the local YMCA. She has been the best player on her team (boys and girls) for two years and the best girl in the league. Once this past season she came up to me before one of her games all sweaty red-faced from the warm-ups and asked, "How do I stop Thad'?" Thad, whom I had seen the year before, was a tall blond boy in Jenny's class whose legs seemed to start from his chin. Apparently, no one had mentioned to the boy that he had a left hand because he always went to the hoop to the right. Today, Jenny was determined to shut him out. "Make him go left—overplay him to the right." And that's exactly what she did. The poor boy didn't have a chance. Later that same season I nearly jumped out of my skin when I saw Jenny steal a ball, dribble the length of the court, stop at the foul line, and pass the ball to a teammate cutting to the basket. Never mind that the kid threw the ball over the backboard. Jenny understood. The game is pure communication. It is a chance to star and solo but also a chance to say I know where you will be without looking. You are in a better position than me so here's the ball. I trust you.

I love to watch her play. She is playing my game and enjoying it. All my secret hours of fantasizing with a ball and a basket and now she loves it too. Jenny is growing old quickly. She is leaving me and yet the game binds us together. We sit in front of a TV watching the pros. Lloyd Free propels another thirty-footer off the fast break and I groan. "Should have hit the man under the basket, right Dad?" She is beginning to understand the game.

There have been times late at night underneath our down quilts when my wife and I talk about our daughter. Future and past, back and forth whispering softly, questioning our actions, our fears and hopes. "She is so beautiful," we boast to each other. "Remember the time she wandered our Berkeley neighborhood naked waiting to be toilet trained. Crying in the dark when Dumbo's mother was thrown in jail. Her first bra and her second baseball mitt." A girl changing into a woman and then in the same breath my wife will ask me quietly, "Are you sorry you never had a son too?" And every time Judy asks that question I get the same clear image of Jenny racing down the court dribbling with her left hand and then the right.

Anne Forer

After the Game

The quiet
more intense after
the overwhelming noise
a frightening silence
in the big empty gym

I crouch nervously
on the side
sometimes happy
a proud happiness
suffusing my body
sometimes sad
I feel the frustration
too
but always
always nervous
as I wait alone
in the big empty gym

Then I see him
the agility has left
his body
like a man grown
suddenly old

We hear some
boys arguing on the other side
the perennial
discussion
their voices
reverberating—as we
walk slowly across
the big empty gym

Part Two

School Daze

Jeremy Larner

from *Drive, He Said*

The trainer shaved all the hair off his upper leg, and wound a thick bandage round his thigh. Hector wouldn't let him tape his ankles.

He put his shoes on carefully. Mustn't bunch the socks or he'd get blisters.

Laced up the high tops. The socks were clean and everything felt snug. His elastic jockstrap held him at the waist and kept his balls on. The practice uniform had been washed, too, and smelt like a laundry. The sweatsuit was warm and covered up his limbs.

None of the others were there, and as he bounced up the iron steps from the lockerroom to the gym floor, the separate clanks echoed lonely metal sounds. He could feel his toes pressing him upward and the arch of his foot.

He scooped up a ball and stood there stretching it over his head, whirling it in one hand then another with his arms stiff as semaphores. Leaning over backwards to wake up his back muscles, then bouncing the ball very low and fast off the floor in little figure eights around his feet.

He liked to take some shots all alone. He had learned to shoot alone on the darkening California concrete long after the others had gone home to supper, on into the dark, when his red cat's eyes needed no help but the moon's. Silver moonshine—the ghostly silver cords flipping as an invisible ghost ball passed through.

He wasn't really warm yet—he was lazy, basically lazy, and needed the press of others to warm him. It was mostly for his fingers that he came up early by himself—his fingers had to learn the ball all over again each time in a kind of ritual remembering. When Hector was in a hurry, he was chancing it might be no go.

He took a couple of stretchy hook shots, without aiming—one with the right, one with the left hand. The cuffs of the sweatsuit felt tight and sweet on his wrists. But the bandage threw him off balance. *Damn:* he resented it like a defense that hung on his back all night. *A big train pulls so many passengers. . . .*

"Chug chug chug chug chug chug chug chug chug chug," he said to himself, as he tried a series of short jumpshots. He let the ball bounce away, and cupping his hands made a locomotive whistle, beautifully shrill & enormous in the high-beamed field house.

He stood under the backboard and tossed up hundreds of lay-ups on both sides of the basket and from the front, hardly ever bored. It was a wonder to him how infinite were the ways of angling the ball off the backboard and into the basket. And his fingers were flexing. Occasionally he would spin the ball like a globe on one fingertip, then let it roll down the arm and across his back and out into his other hand. He jumped easily off his feet and stuffed the ball down through the basket, then went back again to lay-ups. Frequently he missed, to his fascination. After about two hundred lay-ups he began bouncing the ball high off the backboard and tapping it back into the basket. There was no noise: he cupped his hand and cushioned each ball on his fingertips as he tapped it through. Everything depended on the feel in his fingertips and the control when his wrist straightened. And his timing: to get the ball at exactly the right time & place.

He could see right through the glass backboard and into the vacant stands behind. It looked almost as though the ball were stopped by an invisible hand that took his pass and made the score. But Hector had made the play so many times the board was real to him whether he saw it or not, real as the ball which he never looked at while dribbling so as to be constantly ready for the shift or the shot or the pass.

While he was working on his tips his teammates began to drift in and collect at the basket at the opposite end of the floor. It was their custom to stay clear of Hector till he was ready.

Hector knew that Goose Jefferson was at the bottom of the stairway.

He stood waiting with his back to the stairwell for two seconds, then threw the ball over his head so that it took one long bounce into the corner of the gym and would have fallen straight down the stairs had Goose Jefferson not emerged at just that instant, caught the ball without surprise, and dribbled right on to lay it in the basket.

Goose and Hector passed the ball back and forth, took lazy shots at the basket. Goose had the way of the great Negro ballplayers of going up in the air and shooting only after he had stayed a few ticks longer than anyone's nerves would have figured, the defensive man down and Goose still there, finally shooting. He seemed to hang, the result perhaps of a couple of centuries with a rope at his neck.

Hector instead of hanging seemed simply to keep going up. He could grab a rebound off the defensive boards, pivot on his way down, dribble up court while the others were turning and catch maybe one or two back on defense. When he got to the foul line Hector would take off, sailing right up over their heads, either passing off to a teammate unguarded in his wake or shifting the ball from hand to hand and cramming it through the hoop.

There were six boys at the far basket and six at a basket off to the side. They played three on three as Hector and Goose stopped to watch them. The boys played white-boss style. There are two styles of basketball in America, where the white-boss grimly prevails. The loose lost Negro style, reckless in beauty, is joyous to play if you can, but white-boss is the style that wins. Even Negroes must play white-boss to win, though the best ones can't, they end up with the Negro coming out right on top of the other. And these boss Negro players boss the basketball world, they are the ones you need two or three or six of to stay beautiful and win.

The boys were *hustling* for all they were worth: 'cause that is the first rule, see, of white-boss basketball. He who wants to relax and enjoy it is gonna be left behind, or knocked over and his ball ripped away. For white bosses play very rough. Unlike Negroes, they will not back off and let a man keep the rebound he has jumped for: they tackle him, lean on his back with slapping grabbing to jar away his prize. And before the rebound even, the grim jostling and bumping for position. Football America—deadly, brutal and never satisfied, by golly! What keeps the white boss going is the dandy little thought that he and no one else must win always, every instant. Let him win twenty games and he will sulk and sob and kick down the referees' lockerroom door because he did not win the twenty-first. So by definition there can be no enjoyment. The millions tied in by their legs know this well. They scream not for pleasure but revenge. Revenge for a crime that is committed fast as it can be wiped away. Because for every winner there is a loser, and then it is the winner who must pay, sooner or later, and on & on & on, right up to heaven vs. hell.

O sweet god, thought Hector, *this is my heaven right here!* He swished a blind hook from the middle of the floor. He and Goose played a wild hilarious one-on-one.

Kiss me, Jesus, by chance I'm still alive!

At this point Fighting Coach Jack Bullion entered the gymnasium. His blood had not the slightest drop of black. His line of scripture was, "If you don't hear from me, you're doing fine; 'cause if you screw up, you'll hear plenty!" Even the most competent ballplayers glanced at the bench each time they made a mistake, to see if a substitute were getting up. Before Hector, the players used to pass the ball through carefully rehearsed patterns for five minutes, then either take the shot they had in the first place or lose possession. Hector Bloom was the only player in Coach Bullion's career who remained absolutely unaffected by his coaching; because his ups and downs depended entirely on what went on inside him.

The boys at the other end played twice as hard and twice as bad when Coach Bullion came on the scene. They would play on ferocious, all their lives, hustling on & on, so that someone else would lose and pay and take the blame. Then truly when the final seal was lifted and the great scorer came to write etcetera, he might reveal that they'd had "winner" stamped across their bellies all the time. They might even get by.

Coach Bullion walked in with his legs spread and stood planted. He wore basketball shoes and a big baggy pair of sweatpants, a T-shirt with "COACH" on it and a silver whistle hanging down on his expansive chest and paunch. His head was getting bald and was covered by a short-peaked baseball cap, but around his neck and where the sleeves ended on his arms the black and white tufted hair crept out and rioted.

He called the team around him and explained how lousy they

looked and how badly they were going to get beaten the next night.

Then began the calisthenics. They circled the empty gym doing the good old American duck-walk, the exercise of grasshoppers that bulges the thighs and ruins the knees for life. Then the sit-ups and the stretching, with a partner clamping the feet while each in turn stretched and turned and stretched and turned in panicked time to numbers that were always just a little too fast. Then flat on your bellies, thirty push-ups, over on your backs, feet three inches off the floor. Hold it ... hold it ... now everyone running in place, faster, knees up to chest, faster faster! NOW FALL FLAT! TEN PUSH-UPS! UP AGAIN & RUNNING! FASTER!

After half an hour they were permitted to sprawl flat and rest thirty seconds, then up and twenty laps at good speed around the gym. When Luther Nixon emptied his big canvas sack and passed out the basketballs they were grateful as orphans climbing up on Santa Claus. The first drill involved sets of three men each and was designed to practice ball-handling and fastbreaking. Each man ran full speed straight down the floor, one in the middle and one on either side, passing the ball to the center and out, to the center and out with no dribbling, till they got to the end and one man took a final pass and laid it in. The whole thing took three seconds and five passes, and by the time one trio got past center court another would begin from the end line. After each man went through five runs at each position, Coach Bullion decided on a two-man defense, Hector Bloom and Goose Jefferson, as a punishment for their not hustling. Hector and Goose stood one on each side as the trios came down on them and tried to break up the play before a shot could be gotten off, or, failing that, to force a bad shot and grab off the rebound. They didn't mind, really, and began unstringing the boys with Indian whoops, small ones, whoop-whoopwhoop, and broke up eight plays in a row. But still they came, one trio after another bearing down with them having to pick themselves up and momentumless defend the same position time after time; it got wearing and they began to sag, save their breath, play it safe and let the middle man come just a little closer inside the foul line where he could score and did. "One lap duckwalk," said Bullion. Whupwhupwhup, mimicked the delighted unpunished boss boys, who knew nothing of Indians. "No," said Hector, and there was a silence, and Coach Bullion said "What did you say?"...and Hector Bloom said, "I prefer not to," and there was a long pause and Hector Bloom turned and walked into the corner of the gym and kicked a basketball into the wall with a smack while Coach Bullion switched to another drill.

Plays had to be practiced, whether or not they would actually be used in a game, to protect the team from fear of improvisation. So they split into three teams of five and dry-ran their plays for half an hour with no shooting allowed until after five passes, while a manager counted and Coach Bullion blew on his silver whistle and stopped everyone to shout at each wrongdoer.

Still not ready for a scrimmage: the first team played defense in a halfcourt game while the second and third teams tried to run off the plays they'd been practicing. Again, the five-pass rule, which usually gave the regulars time to disarm the play before it started, and again more shouting and blaming. At first some of the plays worked, but as more corrections were added and more movements inhibited, things went worse and worse, until finally a fifteen-minute stretch went by without a basket. The second and third teams duck-walked ten times around the gym and sprinted two lengths of the floor backwards while the first team took their first free shots since practice officially began.

At last the scrimmage, with the second team all ashamed and fighting. Coach Bullion played referee and smiled benevolently and refrained from blowing his whistle as the underdogs carved their revenge with elbows and fingernails, proving in capsule both the benefits of insult as education and the rightness of the educator's prediction as to how basically inept his best team would look on the following night.

"You stink!" he shouted at them. "You couldn't beat your own beavers!"

But they went right on stinking, because they were tired, and because most of them didn't care most of the time. They were sliding down a long season, and the bottom was not yet in sight. All of them carried tape or elastic on some part of their bodies, and four of the five favored an arm or a leg or a hand. Coach Bullion tried to fire them up by injecting third-string substitutes, but the eager sophomores just got in the way and things went worse than ever. The scrimmage ran on for an hour of plodding up and down the floor, shouting, cursing, giving and taking blows, two fist-fights and one disabling injury. By this time there was not a single man on the floor who had any love left in him for his body or what it was doing. As for Hector Bloom, he had been disconnected from the moment he preferred not to.

At six o'clock, three hours after practice had begun, Coach Bullion strode off the court shaking his head in disgust. But before the players could drag themselves into the showers, one hundred free-throws had to be shot by each and every one and recorded by a manager. Luther Nixon in person counted for Hector and passed back the ball, entering his score in an official book that contained the memory of every freethrow Hector had shot since his freshman year. Hector made seventy-one out of one hundred freethrows, whatever that means.

From the beginning the monkeys were howling, all 15,000 in a far faraway place: "Hector Bloom-Bloom-Bloomble—To Heck with Hector!" Looking for Olive, searching her eyes among 29,998 others searching his. It was not too far to come, *if she really.* . . .

The monkeys were dressed in sweaters and tweed jackets and special haircuts all their own.

Abruptly the warm-up was over. The whole thing had just started, yet the others were sweating and vibrating and clenching their fists ready to go. Butch Buckholder went around slapping each one on the pants hard. "Come on, fellas, let's get it on!"

"Bloom! Snap out of it!" Coach Bullion gripped at his arm.

The State five bounded out on the floor flexing their pectorals. Bronco Gibbon appeared in front of him and mangled his right hand. Hector stood staring at the back of Gibbon's head as the ball was thrown in the air and the game began.

The others had the ball . . . so the thing to do was to run back to the other end of the floor, to be accomplished by throwing the weight forward on alternate legs. Then he faced himself around and waited. State went into their tedious bob-and-weave, playing to bore the defense into letting them through. So Hector went sidestepping following his man as one Stater dribbled & handed off to another Stater who dribbled & handed off to another Stater who . . . Gibbon lowered a shoulder and dribbled straight in. Bouncing Hector for a five-yard loss, he went leisurely into his quaint version of the jumpshot, which he loosed from around his navel.

Cowbells, foghorn, & a number of carolers to the tune of "Davy Crockett":

> *Hec-tor, Hec-tor Bloomberg*
> *King of the La-zy Ass.*

Sure, ass anyone.

He was being hemmed into his corner. Bronco from behind bumped with a granite stomach; in front, backed up the cubical McCoy. When they couldn't get the ball to Hector, a teammate shot from the far corner, and when Hector tried to follow for the rebound, McCoy trailed him and held onto his pants.

"Fuckin' pretty-boy," commented Bronco. He took a short pass and barreled in again. From the floor Hector heard a whistle and saw the little man in the striped shirt go into his acrobatic routine. The foul was on Hector, and Bronco stepped to the line for two free throws.

The God of Israel is a just God: he'll miss.

Bronco poised still as a stuffed boar amid the tumult, then calmly grimly plumped the ball up. Real sergeant material—made both shots.

Behold! I am vile.

Four minutes went by before Hector even touched the ball, and he was vaguely sulky. He grabbed a loose ball in the corner and dribbled craftily out and toward the middle. His theory was that one spectacular shot might yet cool everything. Breaking back, stopping, then going full speed he lost Bronco and cut in straight for the basket. The defense rushed to fence him out and he swerved and sent up a long hook from the top of the key. It missed everything—rim, backboard, everything.

Hector was curious. Perhaps this was all very funny?

But when time-out was called and the team was muttering while Coach Bullion's pig-fat eyes were shouting up in his face, Hector felt his stomach clamp tight as an oyster. He was far away, seeing himself from the rafters, and his stomach was sending him a message of nausea. *Oh this would all be comic,* said the soul in the rafters; *but it's me, really me,* pulsed the stomach frantically. *Come quickly please please*

please! No, said Hector, *I can't accept it.*

This was how he looked to others: the clown, the chief performer. *Olive's wild lovely laugh by definition apart from me.*

Sapped with self-hate, he saw himself play out half mechanically. Closed out noise, stands, spirit; took part in back-and-forth running, holding up of hands, moving-shifting. Bumped for rebounds. Took safe play, scored two baskets when properly set up and screened. Permitted one thought—that soon it would all be over. Whatever came next could not be so endless as this.

Upset of the Year, Unsung Hero, Overrated Star . . . the typewriters clacked left & right & in a few years it was the half. On the scoreboard, Random State: 49–34. It was customary for players to go down a ramp to the sullen crowded visitors' dressing room. *4934: by that time we'll all be dead but this game will still be going on & on . . .on the moon, on Mars . . .*

Fighting Coach was angry, swelled up all red & cute. Reviled whole team so nice and added special personal nastiness for Mr. Guess-who, said to be loafing etc. Threatened. Brought out colored chalk and screeched demented across blackboard unveiling Master Plan for recoupment. Small red manager approached, tried to cram chocolate bar down Hector's yaw. Luther Nixon busy-busy feeding pure oxygen through hoses to tired warriors but not to Hector.

Hector took a lemon to suck and sat off behind the lockers in his frozen sweat. He was humiliated, only he didn't care: if it were someone else he would have felt sorry, but since it was only himself it was all right, no need.

Yet, slowly, as he sat, a rage built. His old rage, that had carried him so far. It was a rage at the whole world sitting, the world of spectators, at everything for putting him in the middle and mocking him. And at himself, too, because, beyond the weariness which he could not penetrate, he *did* care, he did he did he did. He had spent too long a life shooting balls into baskets. And so he found himself committed to the final degradation: though he no longer had use for self-respect he was forced to respect the only kind of self he knew, the self he had been given. Or else his only self must die. *Because that was me out there, really me. Like it or not I will have this game to remember me by.*

Therefore he clenched his fists and fought with all his might against his sickness of himself and his symbols and his deadly soul-fatigue, went back to the game and put his hands in the air and shot as best he could: so that when his team lost, he would not lose. *Not everything, not yet.*

And the funny thing was that later he remembered nothing, absolutely nothing.

Tom Meschery

Portrait of a Rebound

I trained for years,
tendons fixed to muscles tuned
for that particular exertion,
eyes accustomed to the
slightest variation of movement—
the exact point of departure
of ball and hand,
the decisive second of the jump.
I have even come to revel in
the stink of bodies, the bust of elbows,
the sudden spasm of the knees.

Thus, I look at the portrait and marvel.
I sit in my chair and stare,
within its black frame
two figures
leap through the painted air.

Michael Novak

Hooping It

I grew up in an era when basketball was constantly changing. Luisetti introduced the one-hand shot when I was three years old; from my first memories of playing basketball, about age eight or nine, I remember almost *everybody* shooting one-handed. I don't remember seeing baskets in the Slovak section of Johnstown where I grew up. When we moved to a suburban neighborhood, I remember being made to dribble a ball in the gymnasium for the first time. It was a humiliating effort. I remember being awkward and stiff for those early years. My family moved around a lot; I attended five different schools in the first eight grades. By the time I was twelve, I remember feeling determined and adequate and getting better. Anticipation, quickness, attentiveness could make up for the lack of special skills. Spirit reaps rewards in basketball. We played until we could scarcely see, throwing up the ball against a backboard nailed to a telephone pole on the corner in McKeesport. The games were rough, brutal even. The bodily contact was as heavy as in football. One learned not to be intimidated.

In the seminary, I grew to love the game with a passion bordering on my love for football. At Notre Dame, in high school, several of us raced during our brief hour for recreation to the smooth cement courts to shovel off the snow, scatter rock salt on the ice, and brush the slush away. We played outdoors all winter. Our hands were red and raw; the skin of our fingers split from the salt; we would bandage them. We slid, jumped over piled snow out of bounds, slapped the slush out of our tennis shoes on the pavement. Occasionally, Notre Dame varsity players dropped by to shoot a few. Leroy ("Axle") Leslie, at that time the highest scorer in Notre Dame history and a lithe, brave young man from Johnstown (a polio victim, he had never played the game until his junior year in high school, and at six-foot-two, playing center, made All-State), put on a show for us once. I had only one small pleasure: dropping in an over-the-head shot I had practiced by the hour, although Axle only laughed when it went in.

In those years, Bob Cousy was at Holy Cross in Worcester. Occasionally, we high school seminarians would get a game with one or another local team and play in a real gym—for example, with the Brothers at Dujarie Hall or the college seminarians at Moreau Seminary. Our coach didn't like my two "junk" shots—a running hook and an underhand drive—and used me as the sixth man. "Cut the cute stuff, Novak!" he would shout. "Play ball!" My greatest satisfaction was entering one game in the second quarter and hitting, by the end, for nineteen points. Still, he wouldn't start me. The next time I hit twenty-six. (All these years later, I remember the exact totals; they surprised me and pleased me so much then. I never thought of myself as a player able to score that much; several of my friends were better players. Scoring well, I felt as though I were living out forbidden fantasies, doing exactly what I had always wanted to but never thought I would. Entering the seminary had meant saying no to an athletic career.)

In college, near Brockton, Massachusetts, where we could watch Cousy on television, my cousin Jim Bresnicki and I used to stand any comers, two-on-two, every evening after dinner, no matter how hot or cold it was. Our favorite opposition were Brothers Richard, Peter, and William, religious like ourselves; we even let them have the third man. We seldom lost. "Bres" could hit from anywhere; he shot like an angel, consistent as the day was long. He loved the game more than I. He used to wink: "Wanna hoop?" I never resisted. We played at every possible free moment. We were almost insane about the game. I think it's true that I reached my peak in my sophomore year, and never again was so good. I loved, above all, to be on the weaker side, against odds, and to be losing near the end. The final rush of intensity at the end of the game was even more demanding, relentless, and exhausting than football. We used to play toward a target: fifteen baskets, winner has to win by two. Often our games went to 21–19 or 19–17. We played much more often on a half-court, with two or three on a side. I never did master the intricacies of the full-court team game. Fire the ball up, tight defense, twist and shoot. The cold scent of wintry air, or the mugginess of a summer evening, often prod my memory with images from those days.

On March 17, 1963, by now three years out of the seminary and a graduate student at Harvard, I finally persuaded my future wife to marry me. We counted the day as our engagement. I blush to recall it a little, but after dinner at Durgin Park we went to Boston Garden to see Bob Cousy's farewell game. The Garden lies in the part of the city that always made me wary, a white ghetto, rather like some scenes in novels of Boston's seedy underworld. Basketball is an indoor game, and the emotions of the crowds, on this occasion 13,000 strong, reverberate off the walls and rafters. Shouts and yells fill one's brain, seem to penetrate inside and to be heard not through the ears but through the cells within. That night, the feeling was overpowering. At the final presentation to Cousy, everyone was standing. For minute after minute, the chant was unendurably affectionate, loud, nostalgic, throbbing: "We love Cooz! We love Cooz! We love Cooz!" I shouted myself hoarse. Karen covered her ears. In the end, Cousy broke into tears. I doubt if there was a dry eye in the house. That was the first time Karen pointed out to me that during the game my hand was moist; I might as well have been playing for all I put into the game, she said. I don't think she was envious then, although with all the research "necessary for this book," she may have changed her mind.

The championship games between the Los Angeles Lakers and the Celtics in those years must constitute, it seems, the most perfectly balanced, intense, and sustained championship rivalry in the history of sports. Every year, in the midst of heavy studies and endless duties, I found myself setting aside seven entire evenings or afternoons to hear or watch every game. Unbelievably, against all odds, the Celtics won almost every time.

In the seminary, I had gone to Mass every day. We used to see many of the championship games there, too. But now sports events rivaled churchgoing in the frequency of my religious liturgies. The liturgies do not have the same worldview, of course, nor celebrate the same way of life. Yet as Aquinas said, so I found it to be true: grace exceeds, but does not cancel, nature.

William Matthews

Foul Shots: A Clinic

for Paul Levitt

Be perpendicular to the basket,
toes avid for the line.

Already this description
is perilously abstract: the ball
and basket are round, the nailhead
centered in the centerplank
of the foul-circle is round,
and though the rumpled body
isn't round, it isn't
perpendicular. You have to draw
"an imaginary line," as the breezy

coaches say, "through your shoulders."
Here's how to cheat: remember
your collarbone. Now the instructions
grow spiritual—deep breathing,
relax and concentrate both; aim
for the front of the rim but miss it
deliberately so the ball goes in.
Ignore this part of the clinic

and shoot 200 foul shots
every day. Teach yourself not to be
bored by any boring one of them.

You have to love to do this,
and chances are you don't; you'd love to be good
at it but not by a love that drives
you to shoot 200 foul shots
every day, and the lovingly unlaunched
foul shots we're talking about now—
the clinic having served to bring us
together—circle eccentrically
in a sky of stolid orbits
as unlike as you and I are
from the arcs those foul shots
leave behind when they go in.

Stanley Cohen

from *The Game They Played*

It was the big man who drew the crowd. He had been gone for a long season and now, in the first true chill of November, he was back, doing the thing he had always done best. He was playing the pivot in a schoolyard basketball game, positioned with his back to the basket and spinning left or right in the brief pirouettes of an unrehearsed choreography.

He was a big man, but he had an unorthodox shape for the game he played. His body seemed to be formed by a succession of sharp hooks and angles, except for the slightly rounded shoulders and the face, which was full and fleshy. His very presence spoke of awkwardness, but in context everything he did acquired the mysterious beauty of function. For there was to his movements the quick stuttering ease, the economy of motion, that is taught in the brightness of the big time but is refined and finally possessed in the lonely litanies of the schoolyard dusk.

The crowd had gathered slowly. They were clustered in a tight semicircle around the back of the basket, drawn in almost directly beneath the backboard. It was late in the day, and beyond the crossed wire fence, some six feet above the playing surface, twilight figures moved like shadows in the direction of the five and six-story tenements that lined both sides of the street. Except for this one small corner, the schoolyard was empty now, and it was quiet. The only sounds to be heard were the sounds of the game itself, the ball drumming against the concrete court, or rattling against the rim or the metal backboard.

There were five other players on the court. The big man was being guarded by a player of perhaps six feet two, who was giving away almost four inches in height. But he was quick and lean and very agile, and as one watched him the impression grew that his body had been wired together with catgut and whipcord. He wore a close-cropped crew cut, which was the fashion of the time, and his soft, almost casual jump shots were flicked lightly from the top of his head. The two had very different playing styles, one seemingly set against the other in the practiced medley of counterpoint.

The remaining four players formed the supporting cast. They had their own skills, some of them considerable, and on other days one or another might have stolen the game, but not today. This day, they all seemed to understand, was special because the big man was back. And so they played to the strength of his inside game, feeding the pivot and then cutting across, fast and tight, like spokes slicing past the hub of a wheel.

The pace of the game was swift and precise. The big man's team scored the first three baskets. He made the first two himself on two short spin shots, one to his right, the other to his left. On the next play he passed off for a driving lay-up. Then a shot was missed, and the crew-cut player answered back with two jump shots, fired in a flat trajectory that appeared to be short of the basket, but somehow just cleared the top and grazed the inside of the back rim before falling to the ground.

There were no nets on the baskets, and as the afternoon faded the rim seemed to lose itself against the green of the backboard. But schoolyard basketball is a game played on the accumulated instincts of one's own time and place. There were no markings on the court; no keyhole or foul line, and one learned to take his points of reference from anonymous landmarks—a jagged crack in the pavement, an imperceptible dip in the wall along the sideline, the subtle geography that is known and stored only in the private preserve of the body.

Three-man basketball is conceivably the most demanding game played in the schoolyards of America. Is it not as sophisticated as the full-court game. It does not require the same kind of speed or versatility, the almost artistic devotion to discipline. But what it lacks in complexity is compensated by the intense quality of the game. It is pressure basketball, compacted in time and space, as if a boxing match were to be held in a ring cut to half its normal size. There is no place to hide and no clock to offer respite.

The game is played by the improvised rules of the home court. In some neighborhoods ten baskets win a game, in others the point is eight, but always a two-basket or four-point, margin is required for victory. It is a game played to its own cadence, and without a referee to call fouls, it can be brutally tough. But the most important feature of three-man basketball is that the team that scores keeps possession of the ball, and so one plays always with the nagging knowledge that the game might be lost without ever having had the chance to score. It is a shooter's game, a game that is won or lost quickly on the trigger of the hottest gun.

Now, from the corner of the court, the big man sent up a one-hand push shot that cut the center of the rim so cleanly that one could not be certain it had gone through. It broke a 10–10 tie, and before the defensive team could recover, another shot, as whistling clean as the first, fell through from slightly closer range, and the game was one basket short of completion. They were the first outside shots the big man had made, and now one recalled how easily he had made those shots, and how often, on brighter nights, beneath the hundred blazing suns of big-city arenas.

That was a while ago of course, and a long season had passed since those days of early spring in 1950 when time seemed to move on private clocks, and each night was a herald to the sound of trumpets. He was not yet twenty then, a college sophomore with honors for grades and a basketball talent that might earn him All-American mention. He had not played much basketball until he reached high school, and his natural gifts were modest. He had size, of course, and good hands, and a remarkably soft touch from the outside. But the rest of it was learned. It was learned while in high school, and then honed and polished in the schoolyards of the Bronx. He worked hard at it, shooting at night-darkened rims, and in winter clearing a path through the snow so that his shooting eye would not lose its edge. Basketball was a sport without season in the canyons of New York, and the big man, who had grown to love the game, worked at it through the months and years of his teens.

He was all-scholastic in high school, and in college he joined four other all-scholastic players on a freshman squad that could have taken the measure of more than a few college varsities. A year later they moved up as a unit to a team that was deep in talent. It was a team marked early for greatness, but no one, not even its most optimistic fans and alumni, suspected that by season's end this young racehorse band of schoolyard players would beat the best the country had to offer and win both of America's major college tournaments.

They had become instant celebrities, their fame of a type seldom known to professional athletes. For they were, after all, college kids, none yet old enough to vote, and they were the local property of the neighborhoods in which they lived. It was not through bubble-gum cards or the filter of the television screen that you knew them. You would see them on the block, or at the corner candy store, and of course in the schoolyard where you would watch them play in street clothes on the Sunday after a game, and on occasion, if the available talent was skimpy that day, you might even share the court with one of them in a three-man game.

The big man was a schoolyard regular. He would arrive late on a Sunday morning, sometimes carrying a basketball under his arm, and he would shoot at an open basket while waiting his turn to take the court. He was genial and unassuming, and even on the day after his team had won the National Invitation Tournament, he came to play choose-up ball, and as he entered the schoolyard he received the applause with a diffident grace.

It had all seemed right then. The days fell together with brickwork precision, and time was the filament on which success was measured. There was not the slightest intimation then that a year later his well-ordered world of campus and schoolyard would lay in ruin. Other glories waited; the NCAA championship would be added to the NIT title within the next two weeks, but further on, around the bend of the seasons, lay the wreckage of a national scandal. He and some of his teammates would be arrested for manipulating the scores of basketball games. They would be booked on charges of bribery and conspiracy, they would be arraigned, bail would be set, they would be convicted and sentenced. Some would receive jail terms. That is what lay ahead, eleven months to the day, and that was not necessarily the worst of it.

The worst of it, they would find, was that forgiveness would be slow. They would be remembered more widely as dumpers than as the celebrated grand-slam team. Careers would be broken, their educations stunted. They would never again play big-time basketball. Culture heroes in their teens, by the time they turned twenty they would be part of the dark side of American folklore. And it would not be short-lived. Twenty-five years later their telephone numbers would still be unlisted. They were to learn something soon about one of life's fundamental truths, as relentless as it is just: that the past is not neutral; it takes revenge.

Now, as you watched him again, you had to wonder what it all meant for him, you would like to know how much of it he understood now that the legalities were done, now that he was free to do anything except what he really wanted to do. You imagined the inside of his head to be a kaleidoscope of gray-green colors, of pictures that fed one into another, whipping like wind through the tunnels of memory. And you wondered where it might stop, which frame might be frozen in view even now, as the ball snapped into the pivot, into the hands held high above the head, the ball raised like a torch against the dusk.

He stayed that way, motionless, for an instant, his back to the basket, the ball held high. Then he started to turn quickly to his right, his head and shoulders doing all of the work, and as quickly he was spinning the other way now, spinning left, the ball balanced lightly on the tips of his fingers, his arm stretching high toward the right side of the basket, and then the ball, in the air now, struck the crease between the rim and the backboard and bounced away, out of bounds.

And then something happened. It happened so quickly that it all seemed at the time to blur into the bleakness of imagination. But it would be recalled later in the finest of detail, summoned forth as if it had all taken place in slow motion to be run at will in the instant replay of the mind.

Two copper pennies were thrown out onto the court. They were tossed at the same time, in the same motion, and they hit one in back of the other with the abrupt report of two shots fired from a pistol.

You heard them hit that way, and then you saw them roll briefly and fall, and then they were lying right beneath the basket, at the big man's feet.

The game stopped now, and everyone was looking in the direction of a boy of perhaps fifteen or sixteen. He was of medium build, and he was wearing a brown suede zipper jacket above faded blue jeans. He was smiling now, a tentative smile, as if to assure that no malice was intended, but he said nothing. He said nothing and you could hear the silence as the crew-cut jump shooter walked toward the youth. He was just a few steps away, and he walked up to him matter-of-factly and with his left hand he seized the kid by the front of the jacket, and without saying a word he eased him back in the direction of the wall.

Then, with a quick, short motion, he punched out with his right hand and landed hard and clean against the side of the youth's face. You could hear the sound of the punch landing and then the kid's head bouncing lightly against the black metal door, and nothing else. The kid did not even cry out. All you heard was a muffled groan, almost inaudible, the type that follows a blow to the body. But the punch had landed flush, and the kid, making hardly a sound, sagged to the single step at the base of the door. He said nothing, and for a moment you could hardly believe it had happened.

But when the kid picked himself up you could see that his jaw was hanging loose. His jaw was dangling as if from a swivel, and on the left side of his face, where the blow had struck, there was a lump that jutted out and up in the direction of his ear. It was not the puffed-out swelling that comes with a bruise. It was, clearly, the sharp impression of a splintered bone pushing against the inside of his cheek.

The jump shooter had turned away, even before the youth drew himself up, and he walked slowly back to the court. He stopped beneath the basket, at the in-bounds line, and he waited.

"Your ball," the big man said.

Charles Stetler

Iron Duke

Joe Camic played center for the Duquesne
Iron Dukes back in the late Forties.
He was only six-four but pivoted past
puffing giants with velvet hook shots;
could also work the weave, then step back
against a zone for a lethal lengthy set
or drive for the hoop like a
peewee guard. The complete player
is the phrase.
    And on top of all this
he always moved with his chin held high
like he felt better than everyone else,
which was partly true, the reason being
an attitude that's hard (particularly
for me) to copy on or off the court.

Like other mortals, Joe would blow his
share of layups during the year.
Would he curse? Slap his forehead?
Writhe in self-demeaning agony
for that short second that allows
the opposition to get momentum going?
Never!
After each and every miss he'd
dash back down on defense with his chin

as Empire State as ever, looking
like the hero he knew he was and
would be time and time again.

Oh, that I could
Camic out the past.

Bill Russell and Taylor Branch

from *Second Wind:*
The Memoirs of an Opinionated Man

K.C. Jones took up where Giudice left off. When I was assigned a
room with him in a USF dormitory, I had no way of knowing that
we'd become lifelong friends. At first I didn't think we'd be friendly
at all because K.C. didn't speak a word to me for a solid month. Not
a *word.* He'd slap my bunk on the way out of the room in the mornings, and he'd nod at the salt or sugar during the silent meals we ate
in the school cafeteria. That was the extent of our communication,
until one day when he suddenly started talking like a normal person.
Nothing in particular had happened; he just started talking. It was as
if somebody had forgotten to plug him in before then. To my relief,
I found that he'd just been shy, even more than I was. Once he got
used to me, we became inseparable. At a Jesuit university, we were
in an alien world, so we leaned on each other. At first I did most of
the leaning; K.C. was a year older and had a slightly better scholarship, so he looked after me. He seemed to spend his money more
freely on me than he did on himself. He bought me shoes, meals,
movie tickets, and books.

K.C. was usually silent except when basketball was being dis-
cussed. The barest mention of the game would throw him into a
Socratic dialogue that would go on for as long as anyone would carry
his half of the conversation. Since I was always around, the conversations would ramble on for hours. We decided that basketball is basically a game of geometry—of lines, points, and distances—and that
horizontal distances are more important than the vertical ones. If I

were playing against someone a foot shorter, the vertical distances could be important, but in competitive basketball most of the critical distances are horizontal, along the floor or at eye level. Height is not as important as it may seem, even in rebounding. Early in my career at USF, watching rebounds closely, I was surprised to discover that three quarters of them were grabbed at or below the level of the basket—a height all college players can reach easily. (This is also true in the pro game.) Generally, the determining distances in those rebounds were horizontal ones.

K.C. and I spent hours exploring the geometry of basketball, often losing track of the time. Neither of us needed a blackboard to see the play the other was describing. Every hypothetical scene seemed real. It was as if I was back on the Greyhound, assembling pictures of my moves in my mind, except that K.C. liked to talk about what combinations of players could do. I had been daydreaming about solo moves, but he liked to work out strategies. K.C. has an original basketball mind, and he taught me how to scheme to make things happen on the court, particularly on defense. In those days almost every player and coach thought of defense as pure reaction: that is, you reacted to the player you were guarding. If he moved to the left, you moved with him, shadowing him. Whatever he did, you reacted to guard the basket. K.C. thought differently. He tried to figure out ways to take the ball away from the opponent. He was always figuring out ways to make the opponent take the shot *he* wanted him to take when *he* wanted him to take it, from the place *he* wanted the man to shoot. Often during games he would pretend to stumble into my man while letting the player he was guarding have a free drive to the basket with the ball, knowing that I could block the shot and take the ball away. Or he'd let a man have an outside shot from just beyond the perimeter of his effectiveness, and instead of harassing the player would take off down the court, figuring that I'd get the rebound and throw him a long pass for an easy basket. He and I dreamed up dozens of plays like these and fed into our equations what we knew about the weaknesses of our opponents. On both offense and defense, our plans included two or three alternatives if the primary strategy failed to work. We liked to think ahead, and before long, K.C.'s way of thinking erased my solo images. Whenever I got the ball near the basket,

I tried to have two of three moves in mind in advance. They didn't always work, but at least they were there. I found that such planning cut down on my mental hesitation on the floor and generally reduced the number of times I messed up teamwork. I began to daydream about sequences of moves instead of individual ones.

Gradually, K.C. and I created a little basketball world of our own. Other players were lost in our conversations because we used so much shorthand that no one could follow what we were saying. Most of the players weren't interested in strategy anyway. Basketball talk was mostly an ego exercise in which they flapped the breeze and pumped themselves up over their last performance or in preparation for the next one. The prevailing strategy was that you went out, took your shots and waited to see what happened. It was not considered a game for thinkers. K.C. and I were thought to be freaks because of our dialogues on strategy, which were fun for us but dull to everyone else. I used to get a kick out of a remark by Einstein, who said that his most difficult thinking was enjoyable, like a daydream. We were inspired rocket scientists in sneakers.

Only after a game, would K.C. and I appreciate certain things that had happened out on the court—at least that's the way it felt. We shared an extra fascination for the game because of the mental tinkering we did with it in our bull sessions. For example, K.C. was instantly aware of what I thought was the best single play I ever made in college. We were playing Stanford in the San Francisco Cow Palace, and one of their players stole the ball at half court for a breakaway lay-up. He was so far ahead of us that nobody on our team bothered to chase him except me. As he went loping down the right side of the court, I left the center position near our basket and ran after him as fast as I could. The guy's lead was so big that he wasn't hurrying. When I reached half court I was flying, but I took one long stride off to the left to change my angle, then went straight for the bucket. When the guy went up for his lay-up in the lane, I too went up from the top of the key. I was flying. He lofted the ball up so lazily that I was able to slap it into the backboard before it started down. The ball bounced back to K.C., trailing the play.

Probably nobody in that Cow Palace crowd knew anything about how that play developed. They didn't see where I came from, and they saw only the end of the play. But to K.C. and me, the sweetness of the play was the giant step I took to the left as I was building up speed. Without that step the play would have failed, because I'd have fouled the guy by landing on him after the shot. The step to the left gave me just enough angle coming across to miss him and land to the right of him without a foul. K.C. was the only guy in the Cow Palace who noticed that step and knew what it meant. I noticed similar things about his game, and they were the starting points of our daydreams.

There always seemed to be new lessons to make the game more interesting. In my sophomore year, Coach Woolpert gave us a lecture on peripheral vision. People have a line of focus on whatever they're trying to see, and objects outside that line are blurry. In fact, they lose sight of the objects within their peripheral vision unless they train their eyes to pick them up. K.C. and I became fascinated with this and practiced for hours. We stood near each other day after day, focusing straight ahead at different distances while trying to keep track of each other peripherally. Eventually we discovered that under certain conditions you can hide on a basketball court. With no one on the floor but ten players and two referees, you can still position yourself so that a player facing you will not see you. It's possible because everyone has a blind spot in each eye, about fifteen or twenty degrees on either side of straight ahead. Most people are not aware of this.

K.C. had such a bad case of appendicitis that year that he could not play, but he could talk and experiment with me. I'd stand still a few feet away, and he'd rotate slowly until part of me faded into his blind spot. Once we convinced ourselves that it really existed, our experiments began. We discovered that the blind spots seem larger when the eyes are tilted. A player who dribbles with his head down, adjusting with the tilt of his eyes, will tend to have a larger blind spot. Also, a dribbler will have more of a blind spot on the side where the ball is. He won't lose sight of you completely, but his impression may be so dimmed that he won't react the way he should. This was our theory, anyway, and it had some practical effects. I found that if I positioned myself in a player's blind spot as he drove toward the basket, he'd be more likely to charge right into me or to take a shot easily within my blocking range. When K.C. could play again he found that he was more likely to succeed in a steal if he tried to make his move through a player's blind spot.

K.C. and I also talked a lot about jumping. If an opponent goes up for a jump shot and you're trying to block it or just harass him, you have to come as close as possible to the arc that the ball makes between the opponent's hand and the basket. Since the ball usually climbs rapidly after it leaves the shooter's hand, your hand must intercept it as it travels through the first one or two feet of that arc—the earlier the better. Therefore your hand must be close to the plane of the shooter's body. In other words, you've got to be close to a jump shooter in the air to have a chance of blocking his shot. That's why there are so many fouls called in the act of shooting.

K.C. and I noticed that most defensive players got close to a shooter by jumping toward him and then reaching up for the ball. We figured that you wouldn't lose as much reach toward the arc of the ball if you jumped straight up and reached out instead, so we tried not to jump toward our opponents, for often you commit a foul with your body. It's also the way you get hurt, because your body is unstable when it's leaning in the air. The vertical technique—jumping straight up and reaching out with your arm—puts a premium on long arms and high jumps; it was made for people built the way I am. After I worked on it I could get rebounds even when I was screened, because I could jump straight up and reach out over the screener for the ball. I could also block shots that could not be stopped with any lateral motion in the jump. In one game against Marquette University, for instance, I found myself standing right behind a player as he went up for a jump shot facing the basket. He was already in the air when I went up behind him, reached over his shoulder and batted the ball in the direction it was already going. The shot missed, the ball bounced off the backboard. Blocking shots this way made jumping even more fun.

K.C. and I were to keep our dialogues going for many years with the Boston Celtics, as my lucky streak continued. I can think of no coach other than Red Auerbach who could have made me feel as comfortable or work as hard as I did, and I was lucky to play with teammates who had such compatible ideas about how to have fun and win.

Bill Reynolds

College Basketball Gains a Spokesman

There is a white towel draped over an empty chair in the middle of the Georgetown bench. The Hoyas, ranked number three in the country with the loss to Seton Hall the only blemish on their season, are set to play Boston College in the Capital Centre. But their coach has already walked off to the locker room, surrounded by cameramen.

He is protesting Proposition 42, the new N.C.A.A. edict that if a high-school student doesn't score at least 700 on the SAT, he is no longer eligible for scholarship.

Proposition 42 is an extension of the controversial Proposition 48, which was passed by the N.C.A.A. in 1986. Prop 48 states that any high-school student who does not have either a 2.0 in the standard high-school core curriculum or a combined total of 700 points (out of a possible 1600) can receive a scholarship but is not eligible to play in games or practice with the team the entire freshman year of college. Now Prop 42 is taking away the scholarship, and John Thompson believes it discriminates against inner-city kids.

"The events of the past week at the N.C.A.A. Convention in reference to Proposition 42 are disquieting and disturbing because they affect a group of individuals who are least able to defend themselves. I felt I had to personally take a stand in reference to Proposal No. 42.

"Many of the proponents of Proposal No. 42 may have laudatory academic and athletic goals in mind. However, this proposal fails to take into account the significant detrimental effect that it will have on socio-economically deprived students. They will no longer have the opportunity to show that a poor test score in the SAT or the ACT is not a result of the lack of native intelligence but is a result of the cultural bias of the test and the deprivation that has existed in their lives because of socio-economic and racial issues that are, unfortunately, inherent in our society today.

"In an effort to rekindle discussion in this proposal and to highlight the inequities inherent in it . . . I will not be on the bench in an N.C.A.A.-sanctioned Georgetown game until I'm satisfied that something has been done to provide these student-athletes with appropriate opportunity and hope for access to a college education."

* * *

There is no question that John Thompson is a complicated man.

He is a child of racism, yet he has been accused of being a racist in that he has no white players. He is criticized for being overly protective of his players while also criticized for not doing more for the black community in Washington. He has browbeaten many a reporter through the years, but when he discovered Katha Quinn, the St. John's sports-information director, was battling cancer, he was always sensitive and caring.

For such a public figure, his family life has remained remarkably private. He has always been better after losses than after wins. He can be an arrogant and belligerent bully, but he has also displayed a tender side. In the N.C.A.A. finals in 1983, a player of his named Freddie Brown panicked in the last seconds and gave the ball to North Carolina's James Worthy, a play that lost Georgetown the national title. Thompson embraced Brown after the game and went out of his way to protect his player from the press.

Over the years some of his former players have been quoted as saying that Thompson's overriding message is that no one is ever going to give you anything, whether it's on the basketball court or in life. He also strongly believes that economic power is a way of overcoming racism. Thompson told the *Washington Post* last summer that he tells young people, "Put yourself in a position of power where you create a need for yourself that has enormous effect on somebody. The world is not black or white as much as green. And I think our kids have to understand and learn that."

In a story last summer in the *Washington Post Magazine,* writer Juan

Williams recounted the story of the day Thompson stood in the door-
way of McDonough Gym and talked fondly about James (Jabbo)
Kenner, who was the coach and counselor for the Metropolitan Police
Boys and Girls Clubs in the District for forty years. Thompson recalled
that in the mid-70's some bureaucrats began questioning Kenner and
eventually cost him his job.

"I saw what happened to Mr. Jabbo," Thompson told Williams,
jabbing his finger into the air, "and I said to myself, 'I'm never going
to let this happen to me—I'm going to stay in control.' "

Certainly, Thompson's coaching career has been marked by his
propensity for keeping control. Practices are always closed. Requests
for interviews go through Mary Fenlon. The locker room is open for
15 minutes after games and not a minute more. Everything is done
the way John Thompson wants it done, to the point that Georgetown
no longer plays other schools in the D.C. area because John Thompson does not want to play them. With the ones whose basketball
programs are inferior to his, he figures he has nothing to gain and
everything to lose by playing them. With the University of Maryland,
the ACC school that's only a long jump shot away and one Georgetown traditionally played, he ended that relationship in the early
eighties after a dispute with Lefty Driesell, whom he once called a
motherfucker in front of several thousand people in the D.C. Armory.

One former player has said that one of Thompson's favorite say-
ings to them is: "I am Georgetown basketball. I built this program.
I made it. I am Georgetown basketball."

In the Providence Civic Center four days later, facing his alma
mater, he is still missing. He had ended the suspense the day before
by walking into the sports-information office at Georgetown and
telling one of the people there, "Tell anyone who needs to know that
I'm not going to Providence."

He also said that he wasn't sure how many more games he would
boycott, only that he had to talk to some "people we feel are of influ-
ence," and "I have to feel sincerely we are moving in the right direction." He reiterated it was now a day-by-day decision on when he
would be back, and while he had been at practice with the team, he
wasn't coming to Providence.

The chair in the middle of the bench remains empty except for the white towel draped over it.

Thompson returns to the bench for Saturday afternoon's game against Connecticut in the Capital Centre, a close game the Hoyas win by four. After traveling to Kansas City to meet with N.C.A.A. officials, Thompson says that although there hadn't been a complete solution to the problem, he was satisfied enough that everyone was moving in the right direction to return to the bench.

"I would like to make it clear once again that I am in support of core curriculum, I am in support of cumulative 2.0, but I am opposed to the misuse of standardized testing, which fails to consider the individual's opportunity or situation. There is nothing more unequal than the equal treatment of unequals. . . . I am grateful to all those who lent their support to change this legislation, and I am presently satisfied enough to end my protest and return to the bench."

Thompson told the *Washington Post*, "I was glad to get back because this is what I do. I'm not a protester. I'm a basketball coach."

Charles Smith said later that Thompson's spirit was with the Hoyas even if he wasn't, and Jaren Jackson said, "I don't think other players on other teams have experienced such things the way we have with Coach Thompson. You never know what's up. You never knew Prop 42 would come up. You never knew Coach Thompson would depart from the court. You never know what's going to happen. But whatever happens, you know it will be in the best interests of all of us. And that's why I'm here."

Jackson was asked if it really made that much difference to have Thompson on the sidelines.

"Everyone knows Coach Thompson's presence." He smiled. "There's always a difference."

John Maloney

Good

The ball goes up off glass and rebounded
down the court, outlet flung to the quick guard
like clicking seconds: He dribbles, hounded
by hands, calls the play, stops short, looking hard
for a slant opening, fakes it, passes
into the center—he lobs to the tall
forward, top of the key/a pick: asses
crash (the give & go), he cuts, bumps, the ball
reaches him as he turns, dribbles, sends it
back to the baseline, forward back to him
Jump—& In mid-air, twisting, he bends it
over a tangle of arms—SHOOTS, the rim
gives as it jerks against the back joints
and into the net, trippingly, drop two points.

John Feinstein

from *A Season Inside*

Nowhere in the country do they enjoy October fifteenth more than in Lawrence. There are a number of reasons for this, not the least of which is the absolutely horrific record of the Kansas football team. In 1987, the record was 1–10 and the victory was 13–12 over Southern Illinois. By October, everyone is more than ready for hoops to begin.

It goes beyond that, though. This is one of the great traditional basketball programs in the country. Phog Allen Field House, named for the legendary Kansas coach, is one of the great old arenas in the country, a place that reeks with memories and rocks every time the doors open.

In 1985, Mark Friedinger, then a Kansas assistant, suggested to Larry Brown the notion of opening the season with a 12:01 AM practice. The idea was hardly original. Kentucky has done it for years and many others also do it now. But Friedinger and Brown came up with a twist of their own. They decided to call it "Late Night with Larry Brown." On a college campus filled with David Letterman watchers, this was bound to get some attention.

The first "Late Night" was that October and more than eight thousand people showed up. The Jayhawks were coming off a 26–8 season and with Manning just a sophomore, expectations were high. It was also a novelty. People wondered how the second year would go. It went even better. This time twelve thousand people showed up. The Kansas Athletic Department was so excited that it wanted to charge admission for the third year. Brown wouldn't allow it. But there were "Late Night" T-shirts ($10) and pizza for sale.

Allen Field House was packed. All 15,800 seats were filled, most of them by 10 PM, an hour before the pre-practice festivities were to begin. While the players were gathering, Brown sat in his office with a friend watching game seven of the Cardinals-Giants playoff series. Already, the annual rumors that he would leave Kansas at the end of the season had started—especially with Manning graduating.

Brown had thought about leaving the previous spring to coach the New York Knicks. At the same time, Manning had thought about leaving to turn pro. Both were still in Lawrence, however, for reasons of their own. Maybe that was why the T-shirts said "Still Late Night, Still Larry Brown."

The party began at 11 PM with a look-alike contest. The guy doing Larry Brown walked with a noticeable limp, a tribute to the hip surgery Brown had undergone the previous spring. "I thought I got rid of that thing," Brown said, watching. "Pee Wee Herman" beat out "Letterman" to win the contest and got booed. All seemed right with the world.

Then came a search for the missing Jayhawk, the KU mascot for seventy-seven years. A contest was held to replace the Jayhawk. Just as the girl in the white hot pants and black heels was about to be declared the winner, the Jayhawk showed up. Can't win 'em all.

Finally, just before midnight, the players showed up dressed in sunglasses and raincoats. The seniors were the last to arrive. Only one of them—Manning—wasn't in sunglasses. To thunderous cheers, he led his teammates in a truly atrocious version of "My Girl." That Manning was willing to lead the song was a tribute to how far he had come since he had been an almost painfully shy freshman.

That his voice was lousy didn't matter. Brown shrugged. "I'd rather be his agent as a basketball player than as a singer," he said, laughing.

Finally, with all the lights turned out, the clock struck midnight, the Jayhawks took of their raincoats and practice, in the form of a scrimmage, began. Kevin Pritchard scored the first basket of the season, Manning gave him the first high-five, and everyone partied well into the night.

As the Jayhawks left the floor an hour later, the band played—what else?—"Kansas City." One hundred and seventy-three days later, they would be in that city. But no one in the building could even begin to imagine the journey that would take them there.

The Champions
April 4, 1988 ... Kansas City

For a split second, he didn't move. The ball was cradled in his hands the way a doctor might hold a newborn; the grip firm, yet soft and clearly full of love, with just a touch of wonder. Danny Manning loved this moment, perhaps more than any other in his entire life. He had fantasized it thousand of times and now, when it was real, he wasn't quite sure whether to believe it.

But his eyes and ears told him it was true. He looked at the Kemper Arena scoreboard and there it was: Kansas-83, Oklahoma-79. And the clock said :00. The questions had all been answered. The basketball was his to keep and so was this feeling. If it had been tangible, Manning would have gripped the feeling so tightly he might have choked it. Instead, he had the ball.

When a full second had passed and he still hadn't jolted awake in bed to realize it was just another dream, when he heard the cheers of joy still ringing in his ears and understood that it was 10:09 PM on a warm April night in Kansas City and he, Daniel Edward Manning, had become a part of history, he reacted. His face exploded into a look of utter ecstasy and he began searching for people to hug.

He didn't have far to go. Chris Piper was running toward him, arms in the air, his head back, screeching something that was unintelligible to Manning. It didn't matter. Piper had been there all four years at Kansas with Manning. They had suffered together, living through all the near-misses and the key injuries, wondering often if there was such a thing as a happy ending and holding each other as if the other were a life raft when it seemed so often that their epitaph would be, "If Only ..."

Now, there would be no epitaph, just a legacy—and a happy ending. And so, as was only right, Manning and Piper fell into each other's arms, living a moment so filled with happiness that, later, it hardly seemed real. Then their teammates were climbing on them, clutching and grabbing at them, each player a part of this because no one—not even their coaches—among the thousands in the arena or the millions watching on television could understand how this felt. For that brief moment, before fans and officials and TV types and newspaper people interrupted, it was just the Jayhawks, piling on one another, sharing a feeling that was theirs and theirs alone.

They had won a national championship. They had beaten 290 other teams and they had beaten the odds. They had beaten their own self-doubts and they had beaten a season that seemed to have beaten them on a couple dozen occasions. The coaches had put in the hours too and felt the pain, but for coaches it was different. Ten years from now they would still be coaching. College basketball players have a brief lifespan. They are freshmen one minute; alumni, it seems, only seconds later.

Within minutes of Manning's grabbing that last rebound, the rest of the world would intrude on them. Manning and Coach Larry Brown would be hustled in front of the television cameras. The others would find microphones and cameras and pencils surrounding them. They would all look into the stands for family and for friends to begin to share the joy with them. But those first few seconds belonged to them and to no one else. No one.

C. Fraser Smith

Dreams

Len Bias felt a rush of panic as he opened his eyes. The time flashed at him like an accusation.

An event he had dreamed of most of his life was starting without him. He was due at Madison Square Garden's Felt Forum. The 1986 National Basketball Association draft, his draft, was beginning, and he wasn't there.

"Oh, no," he must have thought. "I'll never make it."

He tore out of the sheets, scrambled into his clothes and ran into the street. No cabs. He started to run, turning down one street and then another and another. But he seemed to be running in place. He ran faster. He ran until he was gasping for air.

Then he woke up.

It was 6 AM. Still early. Plenty of time to make it. Plenty of time for the dream to come true.

Bias and his father, James, had checked into the Grand Hyatt Hotel in New York City the night before. The young man was excited and apprehensive. Though his basketball future had been carefully scripted down to the finest detail, he could hardly believe how fortunate he was.

The star basketball forward knew he would be taken by the Boston Celtics. He was the personal choice of Celtics General Manager Arnold "Red" Auerbach, the patriarch of professional basketball, builder of the National Basketball Association's most storied franchise and one of the best evaluators of talent and character. Auerbach didn't pick losers. The legendary coach had been watching Bias from the time he was in junior high school. He had been available, and clearly anxious, to advise Bias's parents and Bias's coach at the University of Maryland, Charles G. "Lefty" Driesell. And he had plotted to be sure Boston could draft Bias, the University of Maryland forward. The Cleveland Cavaliers had traded for the first choice and they would take the University of North Carolina's center, Brad Daugherty. Auerbach, whose Celtics had won the No. 2 pick in the N.B.A.'s lottery, would take Bias. All the moves had been planned.

A few hours after his nightmare, which he mentioned to several reporters, Bias walked into the arena with his father. The star wore a light gray suit with dark stripes and a dark tie loosely knotted. Fathers and sons sat in rows of chairs in front of a small stage. They were a most exclusive group. Not many of America's basketball dreamers have this moment: Only one in 10,000 high school players makes it to college and into the pros. The odds of going first or second in the draft, of being chosen by Auerbach, of being in Len Bias's shoes, were hardly calculable.

Cleveland followed its part of the script, taking Daugherty. Then it was Boston's turn. With excitement barely suppressed in his voice and a smile flickering over his round face, Auerbach said, "The Boston Celtics, after five seconds of deliberation, draft from the University of Maryland, Len Bias." Auerbach was laying the cornerstone of yet another disciplined Boston powerhouse, finding and signing another key player for another generation of haughty, intimidating and talented Celtics.

"We feel like Len Bias can make us a better team than we were this year, and that's saying something," Boston assistant coach Jimmy Rodgers told reporters. A few weeks earlier, Larry Bird, Dennis Johnson, Kevin McHale, Robert Parrish, Bill Walton, and their teammates had taken Boston to its 16th N.B.A. championship.

After Auerbach spoke for Boston, N.B.A. Commissioner David Stern beckoned Bias to the stage, and before he got there, someone handed him a bright, Kelly green baseball cap with Celtics splashed across the front in white script. He carried it onto the stage in his left hand. Later, for the photographers, he put it on the back of his head and turned at a kid-like angle. The picture ran in papers throughout the country. As the audience applauded, Stern congratulated him.

Bias turned his head away slightly as if the words were too flattering. Stern found him poised and gracious.

Bias was living a modern American dream. He was the latest in basketball's series of Horatio Alger stories. A black kid of modest means who works hard and makes millions in the N.B.A. His name was being added to a list of stylish players that included Walt Frazier, Julius Irving, Magic Johnson, Michael Jordan, great players with bankable images. There were enough of these success stories, and the stories were so well-known, so widely communicated by games and by television commercials, that even fans may have assumed that good basketball players usually got jobs in the pros.

But only about 150 of the thousands of eligible collegiate players are drafted each year and no more than fifty are signed by N.B.A. teams. Those who want young men to know those odds are in conflict as they preach the lesson of overcoming odds, of "making it," of turning big dreams into goals. The players that make it are young, elegant and often well-spoken. They buy houses and expensive cars for their mothers and mansions for themselves. They wear championship rings, floor-length fur coats, gold chains and suits from the pages of *Gentleman's Quarterly.* Life is good. They are in control. No one was more in control than Len Bias.

By the time he was a twenty-two-year-old senior at the University of Maryland, Bias had sculpted himself into a striking physical presence. Even among basketball players, athletes with superb bodies, he was extraordinary, a David of hoops. He was 6 feet 8. He weighed 205 pounds. He had hard-muscled arms and shoulders as wide as a door. He could bench press 300 pounds. His vertical leap from a standing position was 38 inches, higher than a kitchen table, and almost half his own height. With a running start, he seemed to neutralize gravity.

Len Bias had fancied himself an N.B.A. star for some time. He called his '77 Cutlass "my Porsche." For an official U.M. team photograph, he wore a gold choker as thick as a garden hose and he gave expensive jewelry to his girlfriend, including a necklace featuring his Maryland number, 34, and his last name spelled out in gold letters. He had borrowed $15,000 that summer on the strength of his impending pro contract. And he had leased a Datsun 300 ZX sports car, cobalt blue, with a T-top. On the wall of his dormitory room, he had hung pictures of a Porsche, a Lamborghini, and a full-sized photograph of himself in a Maryland Terrapins uniform—three high-powered machines, Sally Jenkins, a *Washington Post* sportswriter, had observed. There was a sense of omnipotence about him, a growing self-image that, occasionally, must have made him feel invincible, indestructible.

When opponents or hecklers in the stands tried to distract him, he would smile at them, unaffected. He was above it.

"Too good," he would say, sinking shot after shot. "Nothing but cake and ice cream."

Part Three

Chasin' the Game

Rick Telander

from *Heaven Is a Playground*

May

Coming around the corner of Foster and Nostrand at dusk, I see a ten-foot fence and the vague movements of people. Men sit on car hoods and trunks, gesturing, passing brown paper bags, laughing. Stains on the sidewalk sparkle dully like tiny oil slicks in a gray ocean. Garbage clogs the gutters. At the main entrance to Foster Park, I step quickly to the side to dodge a pack of young boys doing wheelies through the gate. When I came out of the subway, I had asked directions from an elderly woman with a massive bosom like a bushel of leaves, and while she spoke I had involuntarily calculated the racial mix around me—ten percent white, ten percent Latin, eighty percent black. Now, as I walk into the park I am greeted by a lull in the noise, pulling back like musicians fading out to display the rhythm section at work: a million basketballs whack-whacking on pavement.

Rodney Parker is there on the first court, standing still thirty feet from the basket, slowly cocking the ball. He is wearing red sneakers, sweat pants, and a sun visor that splits his Afro like a line between two cumulus clouds. His tongue is pointed out the side of his mouth, and as he shoots, he tilts his entire body sideways like a golfer coaxing home a putt.

The ball arcs up and through the iron hoop and Rodney bursts into laughter. "Oh my God, what a shot! Pay up, Clarence. Who's next, who's got money?"

In 1966, Rodney, his wife, and two children moved from the East

New York district of Brooklyn to the Vanderveer Homes, the housing project that cups Foster Park like a palm on the north and east sides. At that time the area was a predominantly Jewish, Irish, and Italian neighborhood of tidy shops, taverns, and flower beds. The Parkers were among the very first blacks to move into the Vanderveer and Rodney, a basketball fanatic since childhood, became one of the first blacks to hang out at Foster Park.

Never one to maintain a low profile, Rodney was soon organizing games between the white neighborhood players and his black friends from East New York and Bedford-Stuyvesant. On weekends he would preside over these frequently wild contests, usually from his vantage point as fifth man on a team that might include several college stars and pros. He would be everywhere, screaming, refereeing, betting money on his thirty-foot shots, with two hundred, three hundred, or more people whooping it up on the sidelines. For identification purposes some people began referring to the playground as "Rodney's Park."

Then as now, Rodney's occupation was that of ticket scalper, a freelance bit of wheeling-dealing that took him to all the big sporting events in the New York area, and put him in contact with most of the sporting stars. He already knew several basketball heroes from his neighborhood, among them, pros Lenny Wilkens and Connie Hawkins, and with the connections he made through scalping, it wasn't long before Rodney was giving reports on Brooklyn players to interested coaches and scouts and anyone else who might be interested.

Rodney, whose education ended in ninth grade and whose basketball abilities were never better than average, derived a deep sense of personal worth from his hobby. "I can do things that nobody can," he liked to say. He helped boys get scholarships to college, he pushed them into prep schools, he got them reduced rates to basketball camps, he even arranged for two of the local white baseball players to get tryouts with the New York Mets. He became known around the park as somebody who could help out if you played ball and weren't getting anywhere on your own. Kids said that Rodney knew everybody in the world.

Now, seeing me by the fence, he comes over and demands that I play in a game immediately to help me get acquainted with "the guys."

He charges into the middle of the players and throws commands right and left. This is the rabble—the young men who populate every New York City playground all summer long. Faceless, earnest, apathetic, talented, hoping, hopeless, these are the minor characters in every ghetto drama. They move, drifting in and out in response to Rodney's orders.

The ball bounces away from one of the players and is picked up by a small boy on the sidelines. He dribbles it with joy.

"Gimme that ball 'fore I inject this shoe five feet up your black ass and out your brain," hollers a somber-looking player named Calvin Franks.

The boy dribbles, wriggling his hips and taunting; Franks lunges at the boy who drops the ball and sprints through a hole in the fence into the street.

Franks retrieves the ball and begins talking to himself. "Calvin Franks has the ball, oh shit, is he bad. He takes the man to the base. . . . No, no, he shakes one! . . . two! . . . he's on wheels . . . the crowd stands to watch the All American . . ." Franks shoots and the ball rolls up and around the rim like a globe on its axis, then falls out. "He's fouled! Butchered! They gots to send him to the line . . ."

The sun is gone now, passed behind the buildings in a false, city sunset. Old women with stockings rolled to their ankles doze near the slides.

A boy locates his younger brother who had errands to do at home and pulls him from a card game. "I'll kick yo' ass!" he shouts, slapping his brother in the face. The boy runs out of the park, blood flowing from his nose. The friends at the game laugh and pick up the cards. Crashes of glass rise above the voices, forming a jagged tapestry interwoven with soul music and sirens.

I am placed on a team with four locals and the game gets underway. Rodney walks to the sidelines and begins coaching. He hollers at the players to pass the ball, not to be such stupid fools. Do they want to spend their whole useless lives as nobodies in the ghetto? Pass, defense. "You're hopeless! Fourteen-year-old Albert King could kill you all," he shouts.

"Rodney, my man, my man! This is pro material," screams Calvin Franks. "Kareem Jabbar come to Foster Park."

There are no lights in the park and vision is rapidly disappearing. The lights, I learned last summer, were removed several years ago to keep boys from playing basketball all night long.

"What? What's happenin' here?" says a young, stocky boy named Pablo Billy, his eyes wide in mock surprise as he dribbles between his legs and passes behind his back.

"Boom! She go boom!" yells Franks.

"You done now, Skunk," answers Lloyd Hill, a skinny 6 feet 3 forward with arms like vines and large yellowish eyes.

"Here come the street five! Jive alive. Loosey goosey."

"Look at him!" shrieks a player named Clarence, apparently referring to himself, as he spins out of a crowd. "His body just come like this."

The fouls become more violent now, with drive-in lay-ups being invitations for blood. I don't consider myself a bad basketball player, a short forward who at twenty-five could probably play on a few mediocre high school teams, but out here I pass the ball each time I get it, not wanting to make a fool of myself. Players are jumping over my head.

"Gonna shake it, bake it, and take it to the . . ." A boy named Eddie has his shot batted angrily out to half court. "Reject that shit," says someone called "Muse" or "Music," I can't tell which.

The Vanderveer project rises on our left like a dark red embattlement against the sky, TV's flickering deep within like synchronized candles. The complex covers part of four city blocks and houses nearly ten thousand people, a small American town. At one time—no more than ten years ago—the Vanderveer was totally white. Flatbush itself (a name coming from the eighteenth-century English bastardization of *Vlacke Bos* which is Dutch for wooded plain) was a haven for the working and middle-class whites who had fled Manhattan and inner Brooklyn, believing no city problems could reach this far.

By settling in the neighborhood, Rodney and the other first blacks started the chain reaction again. Within days, white residents began leaving. Apartment for Rent signs went up as fast as the rented vans carried families and belongings out further to Canarsie, Sheepshead Bay, or Long Island. The exodus continued in an unbroken stream until by 1970 the Vanderveer and surrounding area was less than half white. By 1974, whites had become a small minority and the Van-derveer Homes had turned entirely black, the number being split fairly evenly between West Indian immigrants and "native born." Soon, the real signs of decay began to appear—the broken glass, graffiti, garbage, and battered buildings that had been predicted by the doom-sayers all along.

If, indeed, there was any plus side to the degeneration, it showed itself on the Foster Park courts where a new grade and style of basket-ball was developing. Premier leapers and ballhandlers appeared almost overnight. Patterned play and set shots dissolved to twisting dunks and flashy moves. Black players seemed to bring more of themselves to the playground—rather than follow proven structures they exper-imented and "did things" on court. Soon they controlled the tempo on the half-block of asphalt between Foster and Farragut, and the whites, who came as visitors the way the blacks once had, seemed ponderous and mechanical in comparison.

To Rodney it was simple justice. "Blacks own the city," he said. "They should own the game, too."

But as the talent escalated, so did the problems. Almost every boy now came from a broken home and was, or had been, in some kind of trouble. The athletic potential had multiplied but the risk had doubled.

I think about this as I attempt to guard my man, wondering if he's had it bad, if he has dreams. He blocks me and I push off, feeling his heart through his jersey like a butterfly against a screen.

There is almost total darkness now. Yellowish speckles from a street light fan through a tree at the other end but do not come this far. Teammates and opponents have merged and the only thing I can do is hold on to my man and not let him disappear. Rodney is still hollering, "Pass, dammit. Pass like Danny Odums. Hit the boards! Looking for another Fly! Who's gonna fly out of the ghetto?"

Passes have become dangerous, starting off as dark orbs which do not move but simply grow larger and blacker until at the last sec-ond hands must be thrown up in protection. The first ball that smacks dead into a player's face is greeted with hoots.

Lloyd Hill unleashes his "standing jump shot" and the ball dis-appears into the night. It reenters, followed by a sharp pop as it whacks straight down on someone's finger.

"Oooh, god day-yam! Pull this shit out, Leon. Thing's all crunched up." The damaged joint is grabbed and yanked. There is a similar pop. "Eeeeee! Lorda ... ahh ... there, now she walking around a little ..."

"Where's Franks?" shouts Lloyd Hill. "Where'd he went just when I'm shooting the rock in this eyeball."

Franks reappears from the side. "It's gone."

"What's gone?" Lloyd asks. "The bike." "What bike?" "My bike."

"You ain't got a bike, fool."

"Friend gave it to me. Had it right over there."

The ball is punched out of Rodney's arm as little kids appear like phantoms out of the darkness to shoot and dribble during the break.

"Shit, Franks, that ain't funny."

"It's terrible."

"Can't laugh. Heh, he he."

"Five seconds, gone. Man walks in and rides out."

"Hee ga-heeeee."

"It's terrible and I ain't laughing."

"Hooo hoo ooooohhhh ... they steal things in the ghetto."

"Niggers ... hoo hooo ... they take your shit."

"Some little spook halfway to Fulton Street ..."

"Hoo ha hoo haaa ... peddlin' his ass off in the motherfuckin' ghetto ..."

"In the for real Ghet-toe ..." Franks is now laughing hysterically, doubled up and slapping palms.

The darkness is complete. The old people have gone home. Slow-moving orange dots point out groups of boys smoking reefers under the trees. Two other basketball games are going on, but the farthest can only be heard. I start to wonder what I'm doing here, in this game, under these conditions. Playing basketball in total darkness is an act of devotion similar to fishing on land. Soon, I know, someone will rifle a pass and shatter my nose.

"Come on now, let's be serious," says Eddie. "We down, twenty-four, twenty-one."

The ball is returned and the contest starts again. Laughter fades and the bicycle is forgotten. Everything is in earnest and yet I am blind; I cannot follow the game with my ears. Rodney shouts but does not exist. Quietly, on an inbounds play, I walk off the court.

"Hey, hold it," says Lloyd. "Where's that white dude we had?"

"Yeh, we only got four men." Someone counts. "Where'd he go, Rod?" The players look around.

"He went to get some water, I think. He's not used to this shit, he's quitting. Just get another man."

"Come on, little brother," says the tall player called "Muse" or "Music" to one of the hangers-on. "Put the weight to this dude and keep him outta the sky."

From thirty feet away on the bench, I can barely see the occasional sparkle of medallions as they catch the street lights along Foster Avenue. I'm exhausted and relish the chance to wipe my face with my shirt and rub my sore knees. I can hear the players' voices, and it sounds to me like they'll go all night. . . .

Mid-June

At 9:30 PM the park is dark and nearly deserted. Standing by the fence is an old man wearing a green cap, a German who comes to the park frequently to watch the games, carrying a radio from which wafts the classical music of Wagner and Beethoven. He seldom speaks, indeed there is no one for him to talk to. He is always alone, content to watch.

Under the first basket there is a bit of commotion as Cameron, a fifteen-year-old park regular with legs as thick as stove pipes, is being taught the rudiments of stuffing. Eight or nine other boys are all trying to explain their personal techniques for palming the ball, approaching the basket, hooking over the rim, returning to the pavement.

Cameron listens to each intently, nodding his head as the points become clear. When the last man is finished Cameron backs up, wipes his hands, and runs at the basket.

At 5 feet 8 he is an exceptional leaper, but on his first attempt the ball slams into the back of the rim and bounces ten feet in the air. Cameron remains above, hanging on the rim.

Lloyd Hill, who has been walking down the sidewalk, steps through the hole in the fence onto the dark court. He looks up at the body dangling above. "Get off there, boy," he orders. Cameron drops.

Lloyd points back to the free-throw circle, "Now try the dunk again."

Being the master leaper and stuffer of Foster Park, Lloyd's word is a solemn and valuable thing. Cameron backs up and snorts like a bull before charging down the lane. Though he seems to rise beyond all normal boundaries for a man his size, Cameron's second attempt is a repeat of the first, with him again hanging like wash on the rim.

"Don't be scared," says Lloyd. "Man, that first time you gots to overcome. The dunk is something, specially for a little man." He pats Cameron paternally on the head.

"Now I know you is kinda scared of falling over ass-backwards and smacking your head on the floor. But it ain't gonna happen if you just let the ball go once it's over the hole. See, you doing the two-handed power stuff, which is cool because you kinda squatty and all, and so you make the run a little different than if you was hook-dunking or behind-the-head dunking."

Lloyd simulates a takeoff without leaving the ground. The other players begin dunking the ball to show how it's done, and soon they form two lines as in pregame drills. Cameron joins the group and gets closer than ever to dunking but is not quite smooth enough to flip the ball down.

The boys become earnest, silent except for loud "aahs!" as they jump into the night air. "Yeh, I hear you!" they shout to each other, sweating and tossing off their shirts. "In his face!"

There is an atmosphere of ritual surrounding the event, as though Cameron is in the company of braves, with Lloyd a chief watching from the perimeter. What I have seen of dunks in playground games has made me realize their importance: a man can leave his opponent behind with fancy dribbling or he can embarrass him by blocking his shot or stealing the ball, but nothing makes a statement of dominance better than a resounding stuff shot.

After one shot the ball bounces into the street and one of the players chases it, nearly getting run down by a bus. "That's the spirit Leon," they yell. When the player returns Lloyd asks for the ball. He takes it and saunters to the front of the line. "You just not cool enough, Cameron," he says.

Carefully removing his shirt and folding it into a square which he places on the sidelines, Lloyd palms the ball and looks at the basket ten yards away. He puts the ball down and reaches into his pockets, pulling out an Afro pick, some change, and a dollar bill. He places these things on top of his neatly folded shirt and then picks up the ball. He rolls his shoulders two or three times and starts loping toward the basket. When he is close enough, his skinny legs uncoil and he sails into the air, cradling the ball in the crook of his elbow before casually smashing it through the hoop.

He slowly returns to the front of the line. A boy hands him the ball again. This time Lloyd runs in a little faster. While in midair he waves the ball around his head like a pendulum before dunking. Again, he returns.

On his third approach he cocks his arm back like a pitcher in his windup and throws a strike straight through the rim at the pavement.

For his final attempt Lloyd walks back an extra ten paces and blows on his hands. He grasps the ball in front of him and takes an all-out sprint at the basket. He cuts sharply through the row of silent boys like a halfback turning upfield and then, nearly ten feet from the hoop, flings himself into the air. As he floats slowly to the rim he rubs the ball on the back of his neck like a man with an itch under his collar and then slams it through the rim so hard it caroms wildly off to another court.

Lloyd walks silently back to the sideline. He picks up his comb and change and puts them in his pocket. He picks up his shirt and puts it on, buttoning it as carefully as he removed it.

The lines start moving again, with added energy and a sense of respect. But Cameron has peaked and will not dunk tonight.

From the shadows the old man is laughing and shaking his head. "Ooooh, that was great," he says, clapping his hands quietly. "How high they go and hang there."

I walk over and sit next to him because I'm a little excited myself. The middle chords of Schubert's *Unfinished Symphony* weave from his radio.

"They're just like flies, eh, buzzing. Different bodies—see, the short one and the long one with his shirt on—like the green flies and the blue ones and the big horseflies. They come right out of the pavement, that's what I say. Flatbush was never like this, but now there is such a pretty game and so good to watch. Flies all summer...."

107

Late July

Bad happenings seem to be in the air, all of a sudden. Two days ago DeMont, Pontiac Carr, and I had taken the bus to the sports shop in Bedford-Stuyvesant where our Subway Stars shirts were being made. One of the heavy plate glass windows on the side of the store was boarded up and there were bloodstains on the pavement.

"What happened?" DeMont asked the clerk.

"Some boys tried to break in last night."

"Didja catch 'em?"

"Yeh, the police caught 'em. The alarm went off. One of them nearly lost a finger."

"Wow!" said DeMont.

"What were they after?" asked Pontiac.

"Got me. We don't keep any money here."

The boys looked around at the store's contents. Basketballs, posters of Julius Erving and Abdul-Jabbar, sneakers, tube socks, sweatbands, shorts and bags, uniforms. A paradise.

The man followed their eyes.

"Maybe some Pro-Keds." he said. "Seems funny to do five years for that, though."

Despite the incident our shirts were ready. I paid the man the balance due, approximately fourteen dollars. The players had all paid me their share, a dollar apiece. Yanking a shirt out of the box DeMont held it up and began yipping with joy.

"Oh, man, look at my jersey! Number thirty-two! Dr. J! That's me. Number thirty-two!"

Back at the park the shirts were instant sensations. Red with black stars and the logo: "Subway Stars, Foster Park, All-City, Brooklyn, N.Y.," they drew boys out of every nook and cranny like a pied piper's flute. Pontiac had to fight to hold onto the box, but within minutes each team member had arrived and gotten his own shirt. Personally I was quite pleased with the shirts, enjoying the sight of the red splotches spreading through the park as the boys made the rounds.

It was in that same spirit of enthusiasm the next day, Sunday, that I suggested the team take a trip to Manhattan for a ball game. The players were all for it and immediately began shooting craps for subway fare.

"Where we going, Rick?" Pablo Billy asked.

I didn't really know. Someone had told me there was a park with a few decent courts on East 18th Street. On Sunday, I figured, there was bound to be some action, and if we wanted to get a game it should be easy.

We got on the subway at Newkirk, with Pablo Billy, Mark, and Sgt. Rock, hopping the turnstile and diving through the train doors as they closed. The man in the booth shook his fist in anger. At West 14th Street in lower Manhattan we got off.

"Where did you say those courts were on 18th Street?" Pontiac Carr asked.

"Eighteenth and Lexington, I think the guy said."

"Well, goddamn, Rick, we're on Eighth Avenue."

It was a bright day and there were artists and sculptors and dogs scattered along the sidewalk. The paintings hanging on the fences resembled skylines done in a hurry and the sculptings looked to have been welded from hangers and spoons and carburetors. The dogs were mangy and half-rabid-looking, but there was a cheerfulness lingering over the area as tourists came and went and the bells in a nearby church chimed the hour.

We started walking crosstown, a loud defiant group openly evaded by pedestrians. DeMont jogged in the front, kicking cans and rattling car doors. I wasn't sure how far we had to go but I wanted it to be short; I felt this could be a strong, unifying day if conflict was meticulously avoided.

Pontiac Carr walked on my left, and Doodie, his large ball peen head trembling with excitement, clung to my right arm.

"Rick, we gonna donut 'em," he yelled in my ear, "put the skunk on their ass! They ain't gonna believe it when we walk in, they be so petrolized, all these nasty niggers, jackin' and jivin' ..."

He got on my nerves sometimes, all eagerness, malapropisms and stupidity. And his gawky body only added to the effect. All of the boys were growing but Doodie seemed to be haphazardly elongating, like a rubber figure grabbed at each end and stretched. I worried that some day his threadlike neck would no longer support his head and the entire affair would simply wilt on his shoulders like a bloated sunflower.

Doodie did not have an easy time of it at Foster Park, and his jab-berings and false cockiness were mostly reactions to his lowly status there. Under the basket he was pushed around by much shorter play-ers; on the bench he was the brunt of the jokes.

"Hey, you cross-eyed motherfucker," they teased him. "What's it look like outta that eyeball." In the photos I had begun taking of the park boys Doodie always tried to hide half of his head behind another player or under a towel or jersey in an attempt to keep from looking ridiculous.

His one hero was Fly Williams, whom he called "my man" and imitated both on and off the court. He worked endlessly at "finger-rolling" the ball and dribbling through his legs and other useless tac-tics which he equated with Fly's court prowess. In all debates Doodie defended Fly's behavior with his own honor. Whenever Fly came to Foster Park Doodie followed like a shadow, grinning with reverence. Whenever Fly drove off Doodie, watched the departing car until it vanished. Fly, for his part, never noticed the boy.

We reached 17th Street and Second Avenue but there was no basketball court in sight. This made me nervous. En route the boys had demanded we stop in a candy store and had then proceeded to shoplift the place blind. Now, after the long walk they were in a rather volatile humor. Without stopping I turned left. At 18th Street, where the park was supposed to be, there was nothing. "You on your own now, coach," Pontiac Carr whispered to me.

At 19th Street I could see an asphalt treeless park a block away on First Avenue, and I led the boys there without a hint of the relief I felt. The players in a basketball game on the far court turned to watch us file in through the fence.

"Who you guys?" a small Puerto Rican boy asked as the players changed into their shorts and red T-shirts.

DeMont told him we were a basketball team from Brooklyn look-ing for a game, so why didn't he go find some suckers for us to play.

The boy ran off and within moments we had our challenge. The entire park and its mixed Puerto Rican, black, and Italian popula-tion mobilized into a unit, putting together a ragged squad of ten players varying in age, I estimated, from thirteen to thirty-five. The remaining locals stood at one end of the court and shouted out insults. One of the Manhattan players, a barrel-chested black man about thirty years old with a razor scar from his nose to his ear, came up to Sgt. Rock and said, "We don't lose in here."

I gathered the stars together and told them to go out and play team ball, to hustle on defense, to pass the ball and wait for the good shot on offense. "Just like we worked on in practice," I said. "If you get a chance to run, go ahead and run." I was amazed at how easily the clichés rolled out of my mouth. I was a little scared. I sent the first five out: Martin and Pablo Billy at guard, Vance and Arthur at forward, and Sgt. Rock at center.

The game started and soon passersby began drifting up to the fence to watch the action. Cabbies pulled over to look, and men in suits and ties stepped up, shading their eyes with newspapers.

The Stars, unable to figure out the swirling air currents or the bounce of the unfamiliar rims, quickly fell behind. They made only five baskets before crumbling completely and being swept away. From the park crowd came a din of humiliating catcalls. "Subway assholes!" they chanted. "Go play on the D train!"

Attempting to regroup, the Subway Stars stood in a cluster yelling at each other. Lloyd Hill, who had come along as assistant coach, tried to calm them down while I went over to the other team and asked hesitantly if they'd like to play another game.

"Hell, yes," said a tall red-haired kid. "We'll send you back to Brooklyn in baggies if you want."

As the game began the Subway Stars seemed to realize they had little to lose by playing as hard as they could. I'd told them as much, asking them to perform as though they were back in the confines of Foster Park. DeMont had looked worried. "I'm gonna break some bottles," he said, tugging on my belt.

For a while the boys played wildly, taunting the other team and elbowing them under the boards. Pablo Billy opened his eyes wide and shook his head back and forth as he stutter-dribbled through a fast break. Sgt. Rock and Vance combined to block a shot so hard that the entire rim, backboard, and pole spun around in its foundation. Mark, talking all the way, threw in a blind reverse lay-up.

But soon the disorder returned.

Doodie attempted a Fly-style whirlybird which disintegrated pathetically in midair like a watch exploding. Then Mark got so disgusted with Pablo Billy's dribbling that he stood statue-like in the corner, facing the street. I called time out and told Mark to start playing or he'd sit on the bench. "Man, how'd *you* like to play with that yo-yoing punk nigger?"

Lloyd held Pablo Billy, but I knew the day was lost. Shortly after that, Champagne, still uncertain of the rules, called time-out while the other team had the ball and then watched from the sidelines as his man went in to score.

By the end, with the game again turning into a rout I could hear crashes of glass against pavement as DeMont started breaking bottles. "They gonna fight, I know it," he said, slipping the necks over his fingers like claws.

But there were no fights. While I placated the Manhattan team in my most diplomatic voice, Arthur, the quietest of all the Stars, grabbed Sgt. Rock who was muttering about "caving someone's chest in," and Martin grabbed Doodie, who was squaring off with a bow-legged Puerto Rican. Lloyd Hill directed the squad out the gate and I quickly joined as we beat an angry and embarrassed retreat toward the subway.

Back at Foster Park, Rodney Parker watched as the Subway Stars entered their territory. He was feeling sorry for himself of late, I knew, but his words were even more contemptuous than usual. "Look at them, every one of them an attitude case and not one of them a ballplayer. The scum."

He closed his eyes and feigned deep thought. "Don't tell me. I bet they just got their asses kicked by a team half as good as them, but if you ask them they'll say the game was stolen, the refs were crooked, everybody cheated." I said nothing, but he was very close.

Yusef Komunyakaa

Slam, Dunk, & Hook

Fast breaks. Lay ups. With Mercury's
Insignia on our sneakers,
We outmaneuvered the footwork
Of bad angels. Nothing but a hot
Swish of strings like silk
Ten feet out. In the roundhouse
Labyrinth our bodies
Created, we could almost
Last forever, poised in midair
Like storybook sea monsters.
A high note hung there
A long second. Off
The rim. We'd corkscrew
Up & dunk balls that exploded
The skullcap of hope & good
Intention. Bug-eyed, lanky,
All hands & feet . . . sprung rhythm.
We were metaphysical when girls
Cheered on the sidelines.
Tangled up in a falling,
Muscles were a bright motor
Double-flashing to the metal hoop
Nailed to our oak.
When Sonny Boy's mama died
He played nonstop all day, so hard

Our backboard splintered.
Glistening with sweat, we jibed
& rolled the ball off our
Fingertips. Trouble
Was there slapping a blackjack
Against an open palm.
Dribble, drive to the inside, feint,
& glide like a sparrowhawk.
Lay ups. Fast breaks.
We had moves we didn't know
We had. Our bodies spun
On swivels of bone & faith,
Through a lyric slipknot
Of joy, & we knew we were
Beautiful & dangerous.

Pete Axthelm

from *Two Games:*
The Challenge of Basketball

The Rucker Tournament is actually not a tournament but a summer league in which teams play one another through the weekends of July and August. Established in 1946 by a remarkable young teacher named Holcombe Rucker, it was originally intended mainly to keep kids off the streets and in school by encouraging them in both studies and basketball. Rucker's idea was to give dignity and meaning to pickup games by adding referees, local publicity, and larger audiences; it worked, and gradually the Rucker Tournament expanded to include divisions for young athletes from junior high school through the pro level. A project that had begun with four teams and one referee began to offer basketball from morning until dark in various Harlem parks, before crowds estimated as high as five thousand. When Rucker died of cancer in 1955 at the age of thirty-eight, a well-known Harlem player named Bob McCullough and pro guard Freddie Crawford, now with the Milwaukee Bucks, took over the direction of the tournament. It remains the pinnacle of playground ball in New York, annually attracting stars from both pro leagues, members of touring teams such as the Harlem Globetrotters, as well as the best players of the regular pickup games of the city.

The pro section of the Rucker Tournament had long since been moved to another storied playground, at 155th Street and Eighth Avenue, but the lure of a decade-old game remained in that Seventh Avenue park for Pat Smith. Outside the ragged fences, the quiet Harlem Sunday was interrupted by the sounds of the women on the ubiquitous church steps, straightening uncomfortable dresses and pushing veils away from their faces as they chatted feverishly, in the weekly ritual escape from rat-infested kitchens and endless labor. Near the knots of women, grown men in boys' uniforms joined small children in formation for one of the minor parades that still serve some Harlemites as straggly symbols of unity and pride. Young, educated, and militant, Pat Smith had very different ideas about black dignity; moments earlier he had been depressed by the Sunday delusions of some of his people. But under the tree that had once been his reserved seat, he occupied his mind with loftier drama, recalling a game of street basketball at its best.

"It was the kind of game that established citywide reputations. Clinton Robinson was playing. Jackie Jackson was there. So was Wilt Chamberlain, who was in his first or second year of pro ball at the time. . . ." He savored each name as he spoke it; this was a very special honor roll. Some of the names, like Robinson's and Jackson's, would be familiar only to the ghetto kids who once worshipped them; others, like Chamberlain's, would be recognized by every basketball fan. But to Smith and many others they were all gods, and their best games were Olympian clashes.

"Chamberlain and Robinson were on the same team along with some other greats, and they were ahead by about 15 points. They looked like easy winners. Then, up in the tree, I heard a strange noise. There were maybe four, five thousand people watching the game, and all of a sudden a hush came over them. All you could hear was a whisper: 'The Hawk, The Hawk, The Hawk is here.' Then the crowd parted. And the Hawk walked onto the court."

The Hawk was Connie Hawkins. When you ask ghetto basketball fans to cite the very best players ever to come out of New York, you find much disagreement; but a few names are invariably included, and one of them is The Hawk. Yet for years he seemed fated to become one of those virtually forgotten playground stars who never earn the money or fame they deserve. Connie made his reputation at Brooklyn's Boys High in the late 1950s, but when he was a freshman at the University of Iowa in 1961, he was linked to a gambling scandal. His chief crime had been naïveté in talking to glad-handing gamblers, and he had never been indicted or even accused of trying to shave points or fix games. But his college career was shattered and for almost a decade he was an outcast, barred from the NBA, laboring in the short-lived American Basketball League and then in the American Basketball Association as it struggled for survival.

In 1969, after a prolonged legal battle, Hawkins won a million-dollar lawsuit and readmission to the NBA as a member of the Phoenix Suns. He quickly justified everything the playground kids had been saying about him for years. At the time of the game Smith described, Hawkins was a year or two out of Boys High, a man without a team or league. Yet he was the most magnetic star in Harlem.

"The crowd was still hushed as they called time out," Smith continued. "They surrounded the man. They undressed the man. And finally he finished lacing up his sneakers and walked out into the backcourt. He got the ball, picked up speed, and started his first move. Chamberlain came right out to stop him. The Hawk went up—he was still way out beyond the foul line—and started floating toward the basket. Wilt, taller and stronger, stayed right with him—but then The Hawk *hook*-dunked the ball right over Chamberlain. He hook-dunked! Nobody had ever done anything like that to Wilt. The crowd went so crazy that they had to stop the game for five minutes. And I almost fell out of the tree.

"But you didn't get away with just one spectacular move in those games. So the other guys came right back at The Hawk. Clinton Robinson charged in, drove around him, and laid one up so high that it hit the top of the backboard. The Hawk went way up, but he couldn't quite reach it, and it went down into the basket. Clinton Robinson was about six feet tall and The Hawk was six feet eight—so the crowd went wild again. In fact, Clinton had thrown some of the greatest moves I'd ever seen, shaking guys left and right before he even reached The Hawk.

"Then it was Chamberlain's turn to get back. Wilt usually took it pretty easy in summer games, walking up and down the court and doing just enough to intimidate his opponents with his seven-foot body. But now his pride was hurt, his manhood was wounded. And you can't let that happen in a tough street game. So he came down, drove directly at the hoop, and went up over The Hawk. Wilt stuffed the ball with two hands, and he did it so hard that he almost ripped the backboard off the pole.

"By then everybody on the court was fired up—and it was time for The Hawk to take charge again. Clinton Robinson came toward him with the ball, throwing those crazy moves on anyone who tried to stop him, and then he tried to loft a lay-up way up onto the board, the way he had done before. Only this time The Hawk was up there waiting for it. He was up so high that he blocked with his chest. Still in midair, he kind of swept his hands down across his chest as if he were wiping his shirt—and slammed the ball down at Robinson's feet. The play seemed to turn the whole game around, and The Hawk's team came from behind to win. That was The Hawk. Just beautiful. I don't think anybody who was in that crowd could ever forget that game."

John McPhee

from *A Sense of Where You Are*

Bradley has a few unorthodox shots, too. He dislikes flamboyance, and, unlike some of basketball's greatest stars, has apparently never made a move merely to attract attention. While some players are eccentric in their shooting, his shots, with only occasional exceptions, are straightforward and unexaggerated. Nonetheless, he does make something of a spectacle of himself when he moves in rapidly parallel to the baseline, glides through the air with his back to the basket, looks for a teammate he can pass to, and, finding none, tosses the ball into the basket over one shoulder, like a pinch of salt. Only when the ball is actually dropping through the net does he look around to see what has happened, on the chance that something might have gone wrong, in which case he would have to go for the rebound. That shot has the essential characteristics of a wild accident, which is what many people stubbornly think they have witnessed until they see him do it for the third time in a row. All shots in basketball are supposed to have names—the set, the hook, the lay-up, the jump shot, and so on—and one weekend last July, while Bradley was in Princeton working on his senior thesis and putting in some time in the Princeton gymnasium to keep himself in form for the Olympics, I asked him what he called his over-the-shoulder shot. He said that he had never heard a name for it, but that he had seen Oscar Robertson, of the Cincinnati Royals, and Jerry West, of the Los Angeles Lakers, do it, and had worked it out for himself. He went on to say that it is a much simpler shot than it appears to be, and, to illustrate, he tossed a ball over his shoulder and into the basket while he was talking and looking me in the eye. I retrieved the ball and handed it back to him. "When you have played basketball for a while, you don't need to look at the basket when you are in close like this," he said, throwing it over his shoulder again and right through the hoop. "You develop a sense of where you are."

Bradley is not an innovator. Actually, basketball has had only a few innovators in its history—players like Hank Luisetti, of Stanford, whose introduction in 1936 of the running one-hander did as much to open up the game for scoring as the forward pass did for football; and Joe Fulks, of the old Philadelphia Warriors, whose twisting two-handed heaves, made while he was leaping like a salmon, were the beginnings of the jump shot, which seems to be basketball's ultimate weapon. Most basketball players appropriate fragments of other players' styles, and thus develop their own. This is what Bradley has done, but one of the things that set him apart from nearly everyone else is that the process has been conscious rather than osmotic. His jump shot, for example, has had two principal influences. One is Jerry West, who has one of the best jumpers in basketball. At a summer basketball camp in Missouri some years ago, West told Bradley that he always gives an extra hard bounce to the last dribble before a jump shot, since this seems to catapult him to added height. Bradley has been doing that ever since. Terry Dischinger, of the Detroit Pistons, has told Bradley that he always slams his foot to the floor on the last step before a jump shot, because this stops his momentum and thus prevents drifting. Drifting while aloft is the mark of a sloppy jump shot.

Bradley's graceful hook shot is a masterpiece of eclecticism. It consists of the high-lifted knee of the Los Angeles Lakers' Darrall Imhoff, the arms of Bill Russell, of the Boston Celtics, who extends his idle hand far under his shooting arm and thus magically stabilizes the shot, and the general corporeal form of Kentucky's Cotton Nash, a rookie this year with the Lakers. Bradley carries his analyses of shots further than merely identifying them with pieces of other people. "There are five parts to the hook shot," he explains to anyone who asks. As he continues, he picks up a ball and stands about eighteen feet from a basket. "Crouch," he says, crouching, and goes on to demonstrate the other moves. "Turn your head to look for the basket, step, kick, follow through with your arms." Once, as he was explaining this to me, the ball curled around the rim and failed to go in.

"What happened then?" I asked him.

"I didn't kick high enough," he said.

"Do you always know exactly why you've missed a shot?"

"Yes," he said, missing another one.

"What happened that time?'

"I was talking to you. I didn't concentrate. The secret of shooting is concentration."

His set shot is borrowed from Ed Macauley, who was a St. Louis University All-American in the late forties and was later a star member of the Boston Celtics and the St. Louis Hawks. Macauley runs the basketball camp Bradley first went to when he was fifteen. In describing the set shot, Bradley is probably quoting a Macauley lecture. "Crouch like Groucho Marx," he says. "Go off your feet a few inches. You shoot with your legs. Your arms merely guide the ball." Bradley says that he has more confidence in his set shot than in any other. However, he seldom uses it, because he seldom has to. A set shot is a long shot, usually a twenty-footer, and Bradley, with his speed and footwork, can almost always take some other kind of shot, closer to the basket. He will take set shots when they are given to him, though. Two seasons ago, Davidson lost to Princeton, using a compact zone defense that ignored the remoter areas of the court. In one brief sequence, Bradley sent up seven set shots, missing only one. The missed one happened to rebound in Bradley's direction, and he leaped up, caught it with one hand, and scored.

Even his lay-up shot has an ancestral form; he is full of admiration for "the way Cliff Hagan pops up anywhere within six feet of the basket," and he tries to do the same. Hagan is a former Kentucky star who now plays for the St. Louis Hawks. Because opposing teams always do everything they can to stop Bradley, he gets an unusual number of foul shots. When he was in high school, he used to imitate Bob Pettit, of the St. Louis Hawks, and Bill Sharman of the Boston Celtics, but now his free throw is more or less his own. With his left foot back about eighteen inches—"wherever it feels comfortable," he says—he shoots with a deep-bending rhythm of knees and arms, one-handed, his left hand acting as a kind of gantry for the ball until the moment of release. What is most interesting, though, is that he concentrates his attention on one of the tiny steel eyelets that are welded under the rim of the basket to hold the net to the hoop—on the center eyelet, of course—before he lets fly. One night, he scored over twenty points on free throws alone; Cornell hacked at him so heavily that he was given twenty-one free throws, and he made all twenty-one, finishing the game with a total of thirty-seven points.

When Bradley, working out alone, practices his set shots, hook shots, and jump shots, he moves systematically from one place to another around the basket, his distance from it being appropriate to the shot, and he does not permit himself to move on until he has made at least ten shots out of thirteen from each location. He applies this standard to every kind of shot, with either hand, from any distance. Many basketball players, including reasonably good ones, could spend five years in a gym and not make ten out of thirteen left-handed hook shots, but that is part of Bradley's daily routine. He talks to himself while he is shooting, usually reminding himself to concentrate but sometimes talking to himself the way every high-school j.v. basketball player has done since the dim twenties—more or less imitating a radio announcer, and saying, as he gathers himself up for a shot, "It's pandemonium in Dillon Gymnasium. The clock is running out. He's up with a jumper. Swish! . . ."

The depth of Bradley's game is most discernible when he doesn't have the ball. He goes in and swims around in the vicinity of the basket, back and forth, moving for motion's sake, making plans and abandoning them, and always watching the distant movement of the ball out of the corner of his eye. He stops and studies his man, who is full of alertness because of the sudden break in the rhythm. The man is trying to watch both Bradley and the ball. Bradley watches the man's head. If it turns too much to the right, he moves quickly to the left. If it turns too much to the left, he goes to the right. If, ignoring the ball, the man focuses his full attention on Bradley, Bradley stands still and looks at the floor. A high-lobbed pass floats in, and just before it arrives Bradley jumps high, takes the ball, turns, and scores.

If Princeton has an out-of-bounds play under the basket, Bradley takes a position just inside the baseline, almost touching the teammate who is going to throw the ball into play. The defensive man crowds in to try to stop whatever Bradley is planning. Bradley whirls around the defensive man, blocking him out with one leg, and takes a bounce pass and lays up the score. This works only against naïve opposition, but when it does work it is a marvel to watch.

To receive a pass from a backcourt man, Bradley moves away from the basket and toward one side of the court. He gets the ball, gives it up, goes into the center, and hovers there awhile. Nothing happens. He goes back to the corner. He starts toward the backcourt again to receive a pass like the first one. His man, who is eager and has been through this before, moves out toward the backcourt a step ahead of Bradley. This is a defensive error. Bradley isn't going that way; he was only faking. He heads straight for the basket, takes a bounce pass, and scores. This maneuver is known in basketball as going back door. Bradley is able to go back door successfully and often, because of his practiced footwork. Many players, once their man has made himself vulnerable, rely on surprise alone to complete a backdoor play, and that isn't always enough. Bradley's fake looks for all the world like the beginning of a trip to the outside; then, when he goes for the basket, he has all the freedom he needs. When he gets the ball after breaking free, other defensive players naturally leave their own men and try to stop him. In these three-on-two or two-on-one situations, the obvious move is to pass to a teammate who has moved into a position to score. Sometimes, however, no teammate has moved, and Bradley sees neither a pass nor a shot, so he veers around and goes back and picks up his own man. "I take him on into the corner for a one-on-one," he says, imagining what he might do. "I move toward the free-throw line on a dribble. If the man is overplaying me to my right, I reverse pivot and go in for a left-handed lay-up. If the man is playing even with me, but off me a few feet, I take a jump shot. If the man is playing me good defense—honest—and he's on me tight, I keep going. I give him a head-and-shoulder fake, keep going all the time, and drive to the basket, or I give him a head-and-shoulder fake and take a jump shot. Those are all the things you need—the fundamentals."

Bradley develops a relationship with his man that is something like the relationship between a yoyoist and his yoyo. "I'm on the side of the floor," he postulates, "and I want to play with my man a little bit, always knowing where the ball is but not immediately concerned with getting it. Basketball is a game of two or three men, and you have to know how to stay out of a play and not clutter it up. I cut to the baseline. My man will follow me. I'll cut up to the high-post position. He'll follow me. I'll cut to the low-post position. He'll follow me. I'll go back out to my side position. He'll follow. I'll fake to the center of the floor and go hard to the baseline, running my man into a pick set at the low-post position. I'm not running him into a pick in order to get free for a shot—I'm doing it simply to irritate him. I come up on the other side of the basket, looking to see if a teammate feels that I'm open. They can't get the ball to me at that instant. Now my man is back with me. I go out to the side. I set a screen for the guard. He sees the situation. He comes toward me. He dribbles hard past me, running his man into my back. I feel the contact. My man switches off me, leaving the pass lane open for a split second. I go hard to the basket and take a bounce pass for a shot. Two points."

Herbert Wilner

Whistle and the Heroes

It is only basketball, yet twice a week, in the early night, Marvin Wessel lives the life of a man. He doesn't play before the Garden crowds, and even the time of club ball is far behind, yet Wednesdays and Fridays are the best days of his week. The community center is open on Monday evenings too, but on that night he drives his mother for her injection. It's a sacrifice for Marvin, and they both know it. She might change the day of her appointment, but he never presses her to. Next to the nights that he plays basketball, giving it up on Monday is the other big thing in his week.

His mother alludes often to a devil, and when the doctor first explained her child's cleft palate, she always spoke of it as more of Satan in her life. As a boy, he knew what she said had something to do with him, and he understood no more of it than that. But now he no longer thinks of it. He tries to think of little that is in the past: basketball on the two nights and his job satisfy his idea of time.

Whistle—as his friends have always called him—works as a packer in one of the city's largest department stores. Before that, four years ago, he worked for a button company, but his present job is better. The building is huge and he is shifted among departments often enough to overcome the monotony of his work. The frequent changes make it unnecessary to get too friendly with anyone, and this, also, satisfies Whistle. He feels no need for new friends, and his speech makes it difficult to talk to people he doesn't already know. When the work gets too dull, he thinks ahead to his two big nights.

On a Wednesday or Friday, Whistle is always nervous. This happens as early as breakfast. He fries an extra egg and has milk instead of the usual coffee. He is grateful at these times that his mother always sleeps late and he can manage the mornings for himself. On the subway, he pushes back against the jostling with a little more force, although he is careful to avoid argument. If he is close to a window, he peers at his face, which is trapped in the window against the darkness of the tunnel. He thinks he hardly looks the part he will play that night, and the deception gives him some kind of advantage over the others in the car. At work, when he walks from the packing table for empty cartons, he pushes hard against the balls of his feet. He can feel his calves tighten, and he has to fight the impulse to run a few steps. Even when he packs, the work is not enough to wear away the energy that builds inside him. He is almost pained by the sense of his body, and he is able to isolate parts of it: the weight of an arm, the tension in a leg, the bunching behind a shoulder. This impatience for violent movement compels his mind to wander as he packs, and he lapses into a familiar image of himself. They are jumping under the backboard for a loose ball, and he suddenly angles in from the corner of the court and finds an opening. He cuts in cleanly and leaps with the power of his run to snatch the ball out of the air and come down without contact some fifteen feet away toward the other corner, already dribbling quickly downcourt. The picture excites him, and he works with more conviction at the carton on his packing table.

At lunch, he runs the short distance to the cafeteria, finding little spaces in the hurrying noon crowds. He runs with his feet wide apart and his legs bent slightly at the knees so that he might veer sharply through any sudden opening. Though he can tell himself he runs to get a window seat, he doesn't care to understand why this seat isn't so important on other days. He eats quickly, again having milk instead of coffee, and spends the rest of the hour smoking cigarettes and staring out the window. He can usually guess which of the girls that pass are models, and he can even decide between those who work in the high-price houses and the cheaper ones. He has heard enough stories to know they are all tramps, and he has seen it himself when he worked in a dress house. But when one walks by who is beautiful, yet clean—like the fragile girl in a perfume ad—he finds the stories and what he knows hard to believe.

In the afternoon his mind wanders again, and the time passes quickly. If he grows too conscious of his straying thoughts, he works at the packing with a renewed vigor. When it gets toward quitting time, he is pleased by the energy that is still in him. At five o'clock he turns in his slips, knowing that he has packed more than he does on the ordinary days. Men in the same department mutter goodbye to him, and he nods his head and smiles in return. Three middle-aged women work there, but they say nothing to him, though they joke with the other men. In the crowded street he runs again to the subway—the feet wide apart, the knees slightly bent.

When he gets home on Wednesdays or Fridays, he takes the stairs to their first floor Bay Ridge flat two at a time. His mother knows the community center opens at seven, and supper is always ready for him. She finds it a nuisance to have her time fixed this way twice a week, and she complains bitterly about it. She often tells him that he must stop playing ball, that he is no longer a boy, that were his father alive he would have to toe the line. But she never forces an argument because she has come herself to depend on these two nights. When he hurries out the door with his gym clothes in a traveling bag, she begins to mutter about her devil as she rubs a hand across her chest.

On the gym floor, Whistle moves with a bird's grace. He uses the game as a gull does the wind, tacking toward the basket in what is almost flight. He is slender and not more than five-ten, and though all the fellows he plays with are much younger than he, many of them are taller and stronger. Some of them, swelling in their late teens, strip to their shorts so that the sweat will shadow the contours of their bodies. But Whistle wears a grey fleece-lined sweater and track pants.

They play on only one basket, yet Whistle rarely stops moving. If there is a loose ball—no matter how far away—he chases for it. If someone is about to shoot, he is already moving toward the backboard for the rebound. Even when he crouches to jump for a ball that has not yet begun to drop, there is so much tension in his poise that there is no apparent halting of motion between the wait and the leap. Yet with all his running, there is a great economy to Whistle's movement. He possesses a flawless instinct for knowing where to be. Despite the smallness of the court, he never collides with the other five who play. There are many such collisions in this unrefereed game, but

Whistle is seldom involved in the tangle. The kids, often desperate with his near perfection, claim that his one shortcoming is a fear of the rough stuff, and they try to provoke him. But Whistle knows this is not a part of his game, and he is able, by the certainty of his movements, to avoid it.

It does not matter to him that he is twenty-eight and most of the boys he plays with are still in their teens. Nor does it matter that there is no great audience and the game is only a pick-up affair. It is enough that he performs well and the sweat is on his body. But more than other things, there is that fine chemical change as he plays. Sometimes he will put a hand to his abdomen, as though to feel it. Things inside of him—hard things he is unaware of during the day, but feels now he should be able to touch—loosen as though parts of his body had begun to dissolve. After a few minutes on the gym floor, he can almost hear himself unwinding, as though there were some connection between running and health. When he leaps in from the corner of the court to steal a ball from the taller fellows under the backboard, he may—as he begins to dribble away—raise his head slightly and look back toward the players with a curiously defiant stare in his eyes, a thinning of the lines in his already taut face. Aside from this one lapse, he is all but oblivious to place and time. He does not think once while he plays how much better it all is than his work as a packer, or his life at home. He runs with pursed lips and never speaks, but neither is he aware that he has not spoken.

Yet in his mind there are the impressions of a long time ago. There are many people and various days, but if he were to remember well there would be only one night, there would be the girl and Bernstein. It was eight years ago and a good time in Whistle's life.

It was a winter evening that came with a heavy snow. He would remember that because the girl sat on his lap and he wouldn't help when the car settled on the ice and the fellows got out to push. It was winter, too, because the last he'd ever seen of Bernstein was after the game when the kid had thrown a snowball at the lamppost outside the school, threw it so well that he hit not the post but the lamp fixture, and when it came down it made a splattering thud in the soft snow. Then Bernstein and his gang ran off around the corner, shouting, and Whistle stood there. He looked into the darkness where the lamp had been, looked up at the falling snow, and listened to the echoes of Bernstein's laughter.

It was the winter of the year. Even with the car as crowded as it was, they made vapor funnels with their breathing, and they passed the bottle around often. She swallowed from it along with the other girls, and when she finished and gave the bottle to Whistle, he saw her shoulders shudder and felt her squirm on his lap. She was broad and thin, and her name was Alice. When she turned her face to hand him the bottle, the edge of her profile was rimmed in a soft light. Whistle thought she was very pretty.

It had been Dox's idea that they take the girls to the game. Whistle worked with Dox in the dress house, and Alice worked there too. Dox's date was a model in the place, but Alice worked in the office. Dox insisted she was too thin to be a model, but Whistle thought she was clean and would not be one. He had never spoken to her, and it was Dox who had arranged the date. That made Whistle angry, but he could not understand why. For weeks he had wanted her to see him play. At nights, the desire had made him restless with a new excitement.

After work they went to the New Yorker for dinner. Flip and Artie met them there with their girls, and it was almost a party. They had drinks before dinner, but Artie kept insisting about the game, and so none of the fellows had more than two. Whistle wanted to drink more, but he felt himself tighten when Artie mentioned the game, and he held back.

But in the car when the bottle Dox had bought went around and she would swallow from it and then turn to hand it to him, Whistle was afraid she would hear the beating in his chest. There was the soft light on her face, and she said, "Here, Whistle," without even a smile. But there was an edge to her voice that startled him. He did not think from seeing her at work that she would drink the way she did, and he believed she was doing it because the other girls were. But she didn't say anything or even change the expression on her face when Dox's girl started to curse, and Whistle felt the blood inside him to the ends of his fingers. He wanted to take a long swallow when she said, "Here, Whistle," but Artie still kept on about the game, so he ran a little of it over his lip and passed it on. She sat well back in his lap, and he had a hand on her shoulder. He thought ahead to when he would be running on the gym floor and she would be watching him. Thinking of that relieved the sense of his awkwardness. It would be much easier for him after the game. He could look forward to the party in Dox's basement. He was almost not afraid to think of taking her home by himself afterwards.

But suddenly, even the thought of the game was strangely frightening. She might not know anything about basketball. She might not care at all about how he played. He remembered he had not spoken a full sentence to her since the evening started. That terrified him now. The others were all making noise in the car. When he listened, he could hear Dox's girl laugh loudly. But Alice was quiet. Maybe Dox had spoken to her before the date. Quickly, without thinking, his fingers—as though they were apart from the anguish inside him— tightened about her shoulder. He waited for her to protest, wanting now to be out of the car, not caring anymore about the game. But she didn't speak. She didn't even move. She just sat there on his lap looking out through the opposite window, the light shading the edge of her fine profile. He felt his fingers loosen on her shoulder.

Then Flip, sitting in front with his girl on his lap, twisted his head toward the corner where Whistle sat in the back. Looking past Alice, Whistle could see Flip's thick neck wrinkle in two ugly folds.

"It's awful quiet back there," Flip said. "They must be having fun. Whistle didn't even get out to push." Dox's girl laughed. Whistle thought hard for something to say, but Alice was quiet too. Then Artie's girl, sitting next to Whistle, spoke.

"Nothing's going on. You take care of your own troubles."

"What did I say?" Flip called back. "I thought I was being nice. I was looking out for Alice."

"I'm fine, thank you," Alice said without moving. Her voice, clear, brittle, sounded in Whistle's ear like the tapping of metal. It came upon him quietly—as though the thought had been in his mind for years—that he was going to love her. They were on the bridge now, and the water below them was dark in the twilight. Looking out between the massive, bolted girders at the river, at the boats, at the snow, and at the lights that beamed their narrow yellow tracks across the water, Whistle lost himself for a moment in a surprising calm. It was as though he had done all this—Alice on his lap and his hand on her shoulder—many times before. He thought he would ask her, after the party, when they stood before her door, to go on a boat ride with him when the warmer weather came. When he turned away from the window, he saw that she had raised a hand to her face to touch precisely with a finger near the corner of her eye. The nail was long and polished lightly, in pink.

"There won't be much for us to do at the game, just watching you guys run around," Dox's girl suddenly said.

"Anxious to get to the party?" Dox asked. Whistle knew Dox had smiled.

"It'll be better than the game," she said.

"I suppose it will," Dox said.

"You girls can bet on that," Flip said.

"There he goes again," Artie's girl said.

"For Christ's sake, what the hell's eating you?" Flip answered.

"Oh, can it already, will you," Dox said. It grew quiet and Whistle wondered why Alice hadn't said anything when they spoke about the game. Then Dox looked quickly at his girl.

"You watch Whistle during the game. That'll give you enough to do."

"Why? Is he something special?" She turned a little to look toward Whistle. He bit his lip to stop the childish grin.

"The best basketball player you ever saw," Flip said.

"So what?" she laughed.

"This one's got the giggles," Flip said. "Listen kid, if girls were basketballs Whistle would have you all screwed by tomorrow." Flip laughed, and Dox's girl laughed. A small knot of breath caught in Whistle's throat. Then Alice laughed, louder than the others, filling the car with the sound of it, tilting her head back so that her hair fell against his face. She jerked on his lap as she laughed, and then began to cough and laugh at the same time. Whistle heard himself mumble, "Take it easy. Take it easy." When she stopped at last, they were all quiet again. Whistle listened to the continuous grinding of the snow beneath the tires.

"It's going to be a rough game," Artie said, breaking the silence.

"Quit worrying," Dox said.

"Is this a very special game?" Alice asked. Whistle shrugged, then nodded toward Artie. "He thinks so," he heard himself say.

"They're only kids," Artie said, "but they play high school ball together. They got this guy Bernstein on the team. He's got offers from colleges already."

"Oh, is that the kid who plays for Madison?" Alice asked. Whistle looked up eagerly at her. Her mouth was half-parted in surprise. It was small, pretty. He turned his head away.

"How did you know?" Flip asked.

"He lives on my block. I used to date his brother."

"No shit?" Flip said.

"Bernstein's a nice kid," Alice said. "I've seen him play."

"You watch Whistle tonight," Dox said.

"Are you really that good, Whistle?" she asked, turning her face down to him. He could not see her face except for the shadows, but he thought surely she must hear the beating of his heart. He wanted to be out of the car and on the gym floor. He wanted that very much. He opened his mouth to say something, not knowing what he would say. But then Dox began.

"He ought to be that good. Hell, even I might be if I worked at it like him. Hey Artie, you remember when we were kids and it was ass-cold outside. Below zero, remember? We were going to a movie— *Captain Blood,* wasn't it? You nearly lost an ear on the way. And when we passed the schoolyard, there was Whistle running around in a sweater and steaming like the fourth of July. He even shoveled the snow away from the backboard, remember?"

"I ought to," Artie said. "I had to go to the doctor on account of my frozen ear. Whistle, you were a crazy kid."

Whistle smiled.

Flip began to sing a song, and his girl joined in. Then Dox and Artie sang, and Alice hummed. Whistle thought confidently of the game. He had hardly spoken to her, had not really touched her. It would be different afterwards. He would sing with them on the way to Dox's place. The words were almost in his mouth now. He liked the light weight of her on his lap, but he wanted to be in the game already. He thought of it longingly, saw himself angling in from the corner for that free ball. But it was hard for him to think only of the game. He got it mixed in with the metallic ring of her voice: "Here, Whistle. Here, Whistle."

When the car pulled up before the community center, Whistle thought he should help Alice out, but she was on his lap and had to leave first. Inside the building, they all lingered for a while at the steps to the locker room.

"You girls keep together," Flip said. "We'll see you after the game." Then, looking at Alice as the fellows started down the stairs, Flip added, "Having fun?"

"Terrific," she said flatly. Whistle, already hurrying down the steps, did not look back. The word, the sound of it, terrified him. He'd been a fool with her. He should've said more in the car. He should've maybe touched her arm now before leaving her. He should've held her hand when they were going through the snow. The steps had been icy too.

"You got a big mouth, Flip," Dox said, as he pushed open the door to the locker room.

"Say, what the hell is all this?" Flip complained. "I ain't said one word tonight when everbody didn't come jumping on me."

"Then shut up!" Dox said.

"Cut it, will you guys. Think about the game a little," Artie said. "It ain't going to be a breeze with that Bernstein kid."

They met the rest of the team in the locker room, and as they dressed Whistle outlined the way they'd play. But even as he spoke, he heard the single sound of her sweet voice. He urged them all to hurry.

When they were finally on the gym floor for the pre-game practice, Whistle moved like a diving gull, as though an idea of his body had become dependent upon it. His teammates sensed the urgency of Whistle's motion, and believing he was being driven only by the thought of Bernstein, their own movements became gracelessly self-conscious. The kids and girls and men of the neighborhood who had come to watch talked in low voices, looking from one end of the court to the other, from Bernstein to Whistle. But Whistle, even up to the moment when the ball was about to go into the air between the two centers, and Bernstein crouched beside him, thought only that she was watching, that her eyes—with the brows arched curiously—were on him. And a second later, when he moved quickly and the ball was in his hands, he thought of nothing when the ball went through the basket. He indistinctly heard the clamor that rose up from the shot he had made, feeling now only the tremendous uncoiling inside him, as though a wall of air had finally burst from his throat. A moment later when he was under and then past the basket and had scored again, his temples beat with the image of his body that had twisted itself between two men, had gone beneath an outstretched hand and angled the ball against the backboard, all in the motion of an instant. He had no thought that he had twice within a minute's time outmaneuvered Bernstein.

So lost was he in the sensation of his running that he could not say when Bernstein first moved in on him, to be no more than six inches away, no matter where Whistle turned or how fast he ran, to stay there continuously as long as Whistle or his team had the ball, hawking him that way with his adolescent face, his eyes bulging, his mouth open, but with no sweat on his body. He did not even know at first that it was Bernstein who had begun to cling to him, and did not know until he had spent the deliberate effort of minutes in trying to shake him off—who would not be shaken—that the stalking figure always inches away was the Bernstein who'd been spoken of so much, who was the high school star, who had the pop-eyes and open mouth and no sweat and who was to be the way of measuring him. It was against this recognition that Whistle made—when he next got his hands on the ball—his first desperate effort to overcome the kid who was taking him. With a violent wrench of his body that feigned movement in a direction he did not go, Whistle got a foot ahead of Bernstein and drove toward the basket. He left his feet, raising the ball for the shot, and then saw, too late, the blur of the hand that came over his shoulder without touching him to hit the ball cleanly from his grasp. Whistle knew without turning it had been Bernstein's hand. He ran wildly to retrieve the ball he had lost, his body colliding against others. When the foul was called against him, and Bernstein, unperturbed, went to the line and quickly made his throw, Whistle began, for the first time, to think not in the images he always made, but of himself against Bernstein; began to think in advance even of what movements he might make with the other hounding him so. With his mind working feverishly as he ran, Whistle lost possession of his game. When he began himself to sense the loss, his thoughts went past Bernstein, went to Alice who was watching him from somewhere in the crowd. Then Bernstein, almost from the center of the court, soon after the foul, lofted a long set-shot that he turned his back on even before he could see it drop cleanly through the basket. Whistle felt an unfamiliar panic as he ran. He even looked for a second toward the crowd, trying to find Alice where he could not see one face in the blur that was before his eyes.

During the time-out that Artie called, Whistle could hear the words, but he did not listen to what the others said to him. He stared across the floor to where Bernstem stood among his teammates, nonchalant, unsweating, listening and talking. Whistle could see now that Bernstein was not even tall, that he was comically thin, with a sunken chest and no spread at all to his shoulders. Bernstein put a finger to his side and scratched slowly, and Whistle—his eyes hot with anger—thought he would like to drive his fist through the ribs where Bernstein's finger picked indifferently. When they began to play again, Bernstein started to move as he had not before. Something close to fright tore at Whistle as he tried to keep up with him, to try sometimes even to find him. And always, when Whistle had the ball himself, Bernstein was on him, never touching him, but never more than six inches away, his face thrust out to Whistle's so that Whistle saw, whenever he turned, the popped eyes, the open mouth, the dry skin. Whenever he could get close enough to raise his hands for the shot, there was the other hand raised to the same height, blocking or worrying the ball. Whistle swore at himself for his clumsiness, angry with the body that would not move as he wanted it.

At half-time, on the way to the lockers, moving through the crowd, he passed next to Alice, suddenly, unexpectedly. He lowered his head. He was grateful she had not seen him, that she was talking with Sonny who kept score for them and did not play. But when he moved on and heard the brittle pitch of her laughter come after him, he felt anew the weight that had fallen on his heart since the first moment after work.

In the locker room, Whistle sulked and the others left him to himself. He ran his hands nervously over his knees, and the legs felt insensitive to the touch. He began to think then that he was ill, or having a bad night, and then began to believe that, and believed too—as he remembered the two quick baskets he'd made at the beginning of the game—that it might be only a bad stretch. The name Bernstein came to him from all parts of the room, the words "great" and "what a ballplayer" and "what can you do with him," so that Whistle blurted out, "I'm on to the sonofabitch now. I'll get him this half." He spoke so hurriedly and with so little expectation from the others, that they could not understand the words. But they took from the tone what he had meant, and when they ran from the locker room to the gym, they called encouragements to each other.

A minute after play had started again, Whistle was in the corner of the court, and there was a ball loose in the air under the backboard. He angled in quickly toward the ball, feeling the oppressive weight fall out of him as his feet came off the ground with his leap, his hand outstretched under the ball he was about to seize. And then it was not there and his fingers clutched against the empty space. When he turned his head the thin, no-shouldered, unsweating Bernstein was dribbling quickly downcourt. Whistle felt the air go out of him—as though from a blow—then ran wildly after Bernstein, finally leaving his feet in a desperate lunge for the ball. He came down with a thud against the hard floor. He could feel his fingers claw against the smooth, hot wood. Even in the sudden darkness before his eyes, he knew that he was rolling, felt the joints of his knee and elbow grate against the hardness. Then he knew he was on his feet again and trying to run, but Dox had him by the arms, shouting, "Take it easy, Whistle. Take it easy." They called a foul and Whistle watched Bernstein calmly make it good, watched him while he felt his legs trembling and the blood running from his knee. But he would not leave the game and he was glad about the blood. He began looking once more to the sidelines. He ran wildly after that, not even knowing that Bernstein had begun to ease off, and he fouled freely. He could not hear Dox telling him during the time-outs that it was only a game, that he would be in no shape for the party afterwards, that Alice would get sore.

When they were undressing after the game, Whistle did not know by what score they had lost, nor did he try to think of how many points Bernstein scored and how many he made himself. He started to complain about his knee, and Dox said he would drive him home. But Whistle said no and Dox assumed he would go the party and went with Flip to find the girls. But Whistle got out of the room later and left the building. He stood for a moment on the corner in the snow that was still falling and saw Bernstein throw a snowball and heard the laughter as they ran away. He started to walk home, not knowing now why he had left. He knew he must have played better than any of the others. Certainly better than Flip. The crowd had clapped when he stayed in the game with the bloody knee. It hurt him now. It hurt a lot. He should get home and clean it out. He wondered if the blood might be staining the snow, but he did not look to see.

He did not go to work the next day, or the day after, then finally quit, telling Dox to say he'd torn the ligament in his knee and the doctor had said to lay off. He learned that Sonny had taken Alice to the party. He could not believe and tried not to care when they told him Sonny had made out.

It was hard to be with the fellows afterwards. No one spoke of Alice to him. He did not want them to talk of her, though it made him uncomfortable to have them say nothing. But they all talked to him of Bernstein. He'd gone on to college and was the leading scorer on the freshman team. He had scored less against Whistle than he did against some college players. They told Whistle this often, but they could not make him care. He tried never to think again of Bernstein. He tried not to think at all about that night. And sometimes, most often at night, late and in bed, he'd shut his eyes tight when he heard the brittle, metallic, "Here, Whistle. Here, Whistle." He continued to play at the community center, but the club team had broken up and none of the fellows were there. Flip had bought a car and Artie had married. They had parties almost every Saturday night in Dox's basement.

When Whistle's mother some months later insisted they move closer to her relatives, she had—against Whistle's indifference—to abandon unused the many arguments she had prepared.

The three hours are over quickly for Whistle, and only while he takes off the sweated suit in the locker room does he begin to feel the punishment of his body. But under the needling spray of the shower, the fatigue leaves him, and he knows only the pleasant splash of the cool water. He thinks of nothing as the shower breaks against the nape of his neck and, clinging, wets the length of his back. He takes no part in the horseplay, but the others are not angry at his aloofness. They think of Whistle as older and funny, but they never accuse him of playing the hero.

Always, after the shower, the close night air of the city lingers on his face with a fragrance it does not really own. When a high breeze slants occasionally from the bay through the rows of houses, Whistle is glad he does not bring the car on the nights he plays. He walks the half mile to home in a measured, predictable stride, and there is inexpressible assertion for him in the small weight of the traveling bag he carries. He has a choice of streets, but he walks along the busiest one, though he pays no need to the night-noises. The exhaust from a bus, the shouting from a window, a distant, muffled knock are provoking sounds, but Whistle is not trapped in their loneliness. He is conscious only of a fine freedom released inside him, of a restored balance in his body. Occasionally a group gathered idly on a corner will begin to suggest things, but only vaguely, and the impressions are already abandoned by the time he crosses the street. Even on other days, it is hard for Whistle to think back in any specific way. The few fellows that haven't married go their ways, and months pass before Whistle will bother to look up any of them. Even on the Mondays that he drives his mother to the doctor, he prefers to sit in the car and wait for her, looking absently out the window, stirred only by the annoyance of having the night at the gym taken away from him.

When Whistle gets home his mother is already asleep. He takes one of the picture magazines that always lie about the kitchen and goes into his room. Undressed, in bed, by the dim light that hangs from the ceiling, he scans the pages, unmindful really of what he sees. When he puts the magazine away and flicks the light switch, he smokes a cigarette. The taste of it sharpens his ease. In the bright glow of the cigarette's end, there is a hypnotic focus for his sleep. Whistle's mind begins to make pictures. He thinks ahead to the weekend and the possibility of driving to Scranton once more, or maybe this time to Fall River. Since he has bought the car, he toys frequently with these trips, but he does not often go. For he always, afterwards, hates the clumsy, unusable violence he feels toward the women.

When he feels the heat of the cigarette on his fingers, he drops it, still lit, into the ash-tray on the night table. His mind lingers on the impressions of shots he has made that night, of rebounds he has grabbed by angling in that way from the corner of the court. He thinks of Scranton again, and then of the next night that he will play. The poise—so fine before in his enervated body—begins now to crack. Whistle feels once more the dangerous soaring of his anticipations as he waits for sleep.

Fred Gardner

Song: Take Who Takes You

Ice Man, Magic, Bird and McAdoo
Cliff, Kevin, Jamie and Lou
In the real world
just like the schoolyard game:
You Take Who Takes You

Somedays no way they're gonna fall
Play good D and move the ball
in the real world,
just like the schoolyard game:
don't call every call

Any pick-up game I ever been to
any pick-up scene of any kind
you will find they're easy to get into
if you only bear in mind that

You take who takes you
it's a basic principle and true
in the real world,
just like in the schoolyard game:
You take who takes you

No, me and my old lady, Heaven knows
It was a good match-up I suppose

But in the real world,
just like the schoolyard game:
It's good if it goes

     (Oh no it ain't)
It's good if it goes
     (Oh no it ain't)

IT'S GOOD IF IT GOES!

Philip Singerman

Playing Doctor

Shortly after the first Saturday-morning game began, Satisfaction Guaranteed caught an elbow square in the mouth. One of his teeth skittered across the concrete court and came to rest between David-son's leg and an empty bottle of Guckenheimer's rye whiskey. David-son picked up the tooth and studied it with mild professional interest. Davidson was a six-foot, thirty-year-old dentist. "Cuspid," he said to the stranger sitting beside him against the chain link fence. In the tra-dition of schoolyard basketball, Davidson had "called winners" when he arrived at the West 4th Street court. He needed four other men, and the guy sitting next to him looked like a ballplayer. "I got next game," Davidson said. "You want to play?" "Yeah," the man said.

The two of them watched in amazement as Satisfaction Guaran-teed, blood dripping from his chin, pulled down a rebound and, shed-ding defenders with a number of forearm shivers, drove the length of the court, slam-dunked with his right hand, grabbed the rim with his left, and swung for a moment or two before dropping lightly back to earth. Satisfaction Guaranteed was five feet ten inches tall and his dark, shaved head glistened with sweat. A thin scar ran down his right side from his armpit to the base of his rib cage. "That," he said through a mangled grin, "makes it three-nothing, ours."

"That basket don't count, man," screamed Spice. "I'm callin'. You can't play that way, man. You crushed my lung."

"You callin'? You callin' what, Spice? I be missin' a tooth and I ain't callin'. Somebody get me a ice cube so we can play basketball."

"Oooweee!" shouted a spectator from behind the fence. "Get a football. It's going to be *physical* out there today."

The game resumed. Satisfaction Guaranteed played with a wadded napkin and an ice cube stuffed into his mouth. Baskets were traded back and forth until Long Enough, a man with no expression on his face, came down the middle, double pumped, and went behind his back to a skinny blond kid in the corner where the court dipped toward the steel grating of a drain. The kid took a jump shot, but six-foot-six-inch Arthur Pope, his red and white satin shorts sparkling in the sunlight, picked the ball off in midair and, still soaring above the ground, hooked a blind pass to Spice for a quick bucket.

"Goal-tending," yelled the blond kid. "Man, that was goal-tending. The basket counts."

"No way, sucker. I blocked your J on the way up. Only basket counts is the one down the other end of the court." Pope gave the kid a broad smile.

"You ever play here before?" the stranger asked Davidson back on the sidelines. Davidson shook his head. "Games go fifteen baskets. You think they arguin' now you wait'll they get up around twelve, thirteen baskets each. Me, I just like to play ball. I never argue. I play some here, some there, every weekend, all over the city. Get lots of variety that way."

The man named Kenny was in his mid-twenties, had finely chiseled features and a short Afro. He wore a white T-shirt and red warm-up pants.

"They say you called next, man. You got your squad?" Davidson turned around. The two guys behind him were about Davidson's height and both wore yellow jerseys with the words "169th Street All-Stars" in black across the front. The one who spoke had a neatly trimmed moustache and tough eyes. The other one was bearded, with a sad, kind face. "I got next," said Davidson. "And so far it's just me and Kenny here, so with you two we got four." "Take Pope," the bearded man told him, "for the boards. I'm Tony Chiles and this is my main man, Stack."

Davidson was slightly dizzy when his team took the court, but as soon as he began to sweat he felt better. Floyd, the man guarding him, was built like a bull and had the wild eyes of a shaman. The first time Davidson drove for the basket he was clouted in the forehead and jammed in the ribs, but the shot fell so he didn't say anything. The second time he faked a drive, but before he could pass he found himself crumpled against the fence. He called a foul, took the ball in under the hoop, and shuffled crabwise along the base line waiting to make his play. Stack took a long jumper that hit the front of the rim and caromed off the metal backboard. When Floyd went up for the rebound Davidson was firmly planted on his foot. Tony picked the ball off the board and laid it in. "I'm callin', I'm callin'," screamed Floyd. "No basket. The dude was standin' on my foot, man."

"Shit, Floyd," hollered Satisfaction Guaranteed from over by the water fountain, "you don't know your foot from your asshole."

"He wasn't standin' on my asshole, turkey, he was standin' on my foot. No basket!"

"The basket counts," said Stack. "You come down here for the run, Floyd, or some sympathy?"

Back and forth they went, man to man, each wild move answered by another even more outrageous; then slowly the chaos of tangled arms and legs and careening steamroller charges for the hoop dissolved into smooth, patterned basketball. Stack, cool and steady, set the plays from the top of the circle with Pope underneath, Davidson and Kenny in the corners, and Tony outside. The score was six apiece when Tony began to fire twenty-foot jump shots that slipped silently through the netless rim. "Okay. Okay," yelled Pope. "Get that man the ball. His J's are bound to fall."

Tony hit seven in a row, Kenny scored on a drive from the corner, then Pope stole one and went over his man for a two-handed slam-dunk.

"No, no, no. I got pushed," said Pope's man.

"You never got pushed, sucker."

"Then what'm I doin' on the ground, man?"

"You must've slipped, turkey."

"The game's over," said Stack. "What you wanna argue for after the game's over?"

"There you go," said the man on the ground. "You dudes got the shots, you got the boards, you got the passes, and you got the lawyers. How you going to lose?"

"Gotta have the lawyers on Fourth Street," said Stack.

144

After his team won its third game in a row Davidson collapsed on the park bench next to the water fountain. "C'mon, man," said Tony. "We just warmin' up. Now's the time for some serious runs."

"That's forty-five baskets we just scored, Tony," Davidson said. "Ninety points, man. My body's on fire. I gotta rest."

"Stack'n me played on a team down here one time won thirteen runs in a row," Tony told him.

"You ain't goin' no thirteen today, T," said a man named Dennis. "You look like your heart's about to collapse."

"Bullshit," said Tony. "I play all day, party all night, I'm still all right."

"I'm thirty-two years old," said Stack. "Tony's twenty-nine. Basketball's what's keeps us young. Tony played till eleven last night up at the gym. I played till nine-thirty, then I was in the recording studio until quarter to two. We be here all day today, up at the gym again tomorrow. It's the only way to go, man." They grabbed Dennis and ambled back onto the court, leaving Davidson sitting on the bench.

Three days earlier, as darkness settled over Long Island, Davidson, his accountant, Big Fred, and Ira "Spider" Rosenbloom, a drapery manufacturer, were hot and heavy into their final half court, three on three at a county park twenty minutes' drive from Davidson's house. They'd been at it for just over two hours with only one break when they lost and had to sit out a game. Their opponents were two schoolteachers in their twenties and a gangly kid who could scratch his calf without bending over. It was eleven baskets to win and the score was five apiece as Rosenbloom put the ball in play. Davidson took the pass, flipped it back to Spider, then took it again as the two of them worked a weave on the teachers. The only sounds were hard breathing and the slap of Converse All Stars on cement. Spider, looking the other way, slipped the ball to Big Fred at the high post for a give-and-go, but the tall kid's hand was glued to Fred's nose so he dribbled twice, fed the kid a hip, and bounce-passed back out to Davidson. Davidson faked a drive, caught his man off guard, and let go his soft "Bill Bradley" jump shot. Six to five.

Again Spider took it in with a pass to Davidson. One dribble and the same jumper. Seven to five. "Okay. Okay. Dr. H you got the range, baby," hollered Fred as Davidson pumped in another. Then a fake instead of a fourth jump shot and a quick pass under the hoop to Spider for an easy layup. "All right, Spidah! All right, I." The tall kid still dogged Big Fred with conviction, but the teachers, sensing the end, began to lay back. Rosenbloom caught his man flat-footed with a change-of-pace dribble, went in for the lay-up but faked instead and, floating under the hoop, got the bucket with a reverse-spin, left-hand hook shot over his head. "Yes! Yes! It's the Jewish Earl Monroe!" screamed Big Fred. "Whooee!"

They got the last basket on another Davidson jump shot off a quick pick set by Spider. "We'll let you have it," said one of the teachers, "but that was a moving pick."

"Moving pick, my ass," said Spider.

"Face it, turkey," said Fred. "You boys been trounced."

An hour later the three of them sat in the backyard of Davidson's $70,000 ranch-style home, drinking beer. "Kids keep growing taller and taller," said Big Fred. "That guy on me in the last two games must've been six six easy, and he couldn't have been more than sixteen." Big Fred was thirty-one, stood six three and weighed two forty-five. He had been a shotputter and second-string linebacker in college. He pulled the hood of his sweat shirt up over his head against the cool night breeze rolling in off the shore. Davidson leaned back in his chair and propped his bare feet on the ledge of the brick barbecue pit. "You held that kid good, Fred," he said. "He only scored once in the last game. And, man, did you catch Spider's move to the hoop on the next-to-the-last play? You must'a been in the air a good five seconds."

"Thank you. Thank you," said Spider. "I just keep getting better with age." Spider was thirty-four years old.

"In the winter we play full court indoors twice a week over at the local high school," said Davidson. "Five man. But I'll take three on three, half court, anytime. It's more scientific, you know. More teamwork and less one on one. When the weather's nice the three of us'll play together once a week, like tonight, and then I usually find a game somewhere else one other night or on a weekend morning, just for variety. This Saturday I'm going to play down in the Village. I never played ball in the city. I hear it's pretty crazy."

"You're what's crazy," said Spider. "Those spades are going to hand you your head. And you a dentist with a wife and two kids. For shame, Howie, for shame. You wait. Come Sunday morning you'll be buying a sailboat."

"Shit, Spider. I grew up playing street ball in Philly. Only difference between that and New York is that in New York the winners take the ball out in half-court games."

"Winners keep the ball," said Big Fred. "Ain't that just like New York."

"Big Fred's from Omaha," said Davidson. "He played a lot of basketball as a young man, only it was stockyard ball instead of schoolyard ball, huh, Fred? Wore hip boots instead of sneakers."

"You watch your mouth, boy, or the I.R.S.'ll own this house come next April."

"Fred's really not from Omaha," said Spider. "He's from Texas. But who'd hire an accountant from Texas?" "A goddamn fool, that's who," said Fred, choking on his beer.

"Where you from, man?" Davidson jumped. He had been dozing, and for a moment he didn't remember where he was. The kid next to him on the bench was shirtless and had a round, dark face. He looked to be around fifteen. "Where you from?" the kid repeated.

"From Philly, originally," Davidson told him.

"No shit," said the kid. "Oxford Circle, right?"

"How'd you know?" said Davidson.

"Man, I got people in Philly. My cousin played for Overbrook. Played with Wait Hazzard'n' them. All the Jewish ballplayers came from Oxford Circle."

"How'd you know I was Jewish?"

"Man, you *moves* Jewish. You went to Northeast High, right?"

"Right."

"All *right,* man." The kid held out his hand, palm up, to Davidson, who slipped him five. "You play ball for Northeast?"

"Nope," said Davidson.

"Just schoolyard?"

Davidson nodded.

"You play a lot of schoolyard?"

"Every day, when I lived in Philly."

"Where you live now?"

"Out on the Island."

"What do you do, man?"

"I'm a dentist."

"Smokin', man. Hey, Satisfaction Guaranteed, the dude's a dentist, man. Maybe he put your tooth back in."

Davidson held his palm out to the kid. "All *right,*" said the kid, and slipped him five.

"Hey, dude, you ready for one more run? Dennis split and we short a fifth man." Davidson looked up and saw two rivulets of sweat running from either side of Stack's moustache. A tiny muscle twitched uncontrollably in the black man's thigh. "Why not?" Davidson said, getting up off the bench to stand beside Stack. His chest and shoulders were sore, a lump had formed above his left eye, and both his hipbones throbbed; but he was no longer tired. He loped carefully to the far end of the court as Tony brought the ball down. The familiarity of the sport and the plays, worn and comfortable as an old slipper, warmed Davidson in a way he could never explain. In the corner, in the depression over near the drain, he took a behind-the-back pass from Pope and dribbled out around the foul circle, sliding off a pick to shake his man; then, leading with one lowered shoulder, he made his move, accelerating toward the hoop.

Dennis Trudell

The Jump Shooter

The way the ball
hung there
against the blue or purple

one night last week
across town
at the playground where

I had gone to spare
my wife
from the mood I'd swallowed

and saw in the dusk
a stranger
shooting baskets a few

years older maybe
thirty-five
and overweight a little

beer belly saw him
shooting there
and joined him didn't

ask or anything simply
went over
picked off a rebound

and hooked it back up
while he
smiled I nodded and for

ten minutes or so we
took turns
taking shots and the thing

is neither of us said
a word
and this fellow who's

too heavy now and slow
to play
for any team still had

the old touch seldom
ever missed
kept moving further out

and finally his t-shirt
a gray
and fuzzy blue I stood

under the rim could
almost hear
a high school cheer

begin and fill a gym
while wooden
bleachers rocked he made

three in a row from
twenty feet
moved back two steps

faked out a patch
of darkness
arched another one and

the way the ball
hung there
against the blue or purple

then suddenly filled
the net
made me wave goodbye

breathe deeply and begin
to whistle
as I walked back home.

John Edgar Wideman

from *Brothers and Keepers*

When you're in the prison visiting lounge, you never know who you might run into. It's like returning to Homewood. I'd been away from my old neighborhood over twenty years, beginning in 1959 when I left Pittsburgh to play basketball at the University of Pennsylvania in Philadelphia. Since then Homewood has been a place to visit, with visits sometimes separated by years. The visits have been more regular lately, a day or two at a time twice a year, usually at my mother's house, visits taken up with family business and family socializing; so I'd lost touch with high school friends, the people in the neighborhood where I'd grown up. My parents had twice moved to other sections of Pittsburgh—East Liberty, Shadyside—before they finally separated, so my only constant link to Homewood has been my grandmother's house on Finance Street.

I'd never called my grandmother, Freeda French, anything but Freed. The house on Finance was always known by the kids in the family as "Freed's." Finance Street parallels the railroad tracks that form the southern boundary of Homewood. I'd logged many hours on my knees, leaning on the backrest of Freed's overstuffed couch in front of the living-room window, gazing up the hillside at the trains passing through the sky of Homewood. Following the railroad tracks to Homewood Avenue would take me to Westinghouse Park, where there were swings, trees, open green space, and later a swimming pool, basketball courts, a ball field, and girls. I learned to daydream through Freed's big window. Learned to play basketball during summers on the tiny, enclosed cement court adjacent to the pool I was never allowed to go swimming in because my mother believed people caught TB from the questionable water.

Walking down a Homewood street or more likely riding through in a car, I had the habit of looking for people I knew. Faces I'd think I recognized usually turned out to be somebody else. Faces just *seemed* familiar. On closer inspection, after the obligatory wave and the mutual checking out, I'd have to admit it wasn't Reggie or Punkin Mallory or Brother Allen or Bobbi Jackson. Took me years to figure out what I was doing wrong. When I'd take my wife and kids to Freed's, I was looking for the Homewood I'd left twenty years before. Vaguely familiar faces I'd glimpse in the crowd probably belonged to the sons and daughters of my old crowd. All along I'd been skipping a generation, acting as if time stood still in Homewood.

My grandmother's been dead ten years but when we exit the parkway and turn onto Braddock Avenue, and Braddock intersects Finance just after the low train bridge, I think: Freed's, and she's sitting in her rocker beside the mantelpiece, her glasses down to the wings of her nose, her long, bony fingers worrying an edge of the sweater draping her thin shoulders. Loose wisps of gray escape the neat thickness of her hair, parted in the middle and piled atop her head. She'll sound as if she's beginning to cry when she says *Spanky,* the old nickname she's never stopped calling me. The first time she sighs *Spanky* is when the journey of three hundred miles from Philadelphia or seven hundred miles from Iowa City or three thousand miles across an ocean really ends, when I'm really home again. I can't wait to see her, to see the smile break across her features and hear what first sounded like crying become crinkly laughter. She'll seem frighteningly old and distant behind the blank moons of her glasses, till I find her eyes. I anticipate the cold bump of the metal rims against my cheek when I bend down to kiss her. Memories of time collapsing, of being a kid at the window, of running away to play college ball, of losing Homewood and finding it again race through my mind in the instant it takes to locate the bent Finance Street sign out the car window. I tell myself: Don't turn here. Keep straight on Braddock to the traffic lights on Bennett. Freed's not here anymore.

The prison lounge is like returning to Homewood because you never know who'll you see, who will pop up and in what disguise.

Like Homewood because you must teach yourself to read faces, decipher them, keep in mind how long you've been away. You must remember that the present moment is a tightrope you're negotiating and an unexpected face can terminate your act abruptly. You lose the illusion that *now* is anything more than the thinnest strand stretched over the immensity of what you were and always must be.

In the visiting lounge two or three years ago I'd asked Robby who that guy was. The old white guy over there with the priest.

That's Murphy, man.

Does he have nickname? Does anybody call him Reds?

Don't nobody like him or talk that much to him. Might be Reds for all I know. He's Murphy to me. Used to be a cop. Lucky ain't nobody killed him. Cops ain't too popular in the joint. You know what I mean. Lotta guys in here love to get they hands on a cop. Wouldn't think no more of offing a cop than stepping on a roach. Once a cop, always a cop. All of em snitches. But old Murphy been here a long time. Don't nobody bother him much no more. He's just another con now.

It had to be Reds. The elongated, pale face. Big hands. His thick body softer now, going to fat, but that aggressive forward hunch still in his shoulders. *Tyrannosaurus rex.* Arms short for his body, hanging limp but bent at the elbows, coiled, ready to receive a pass or snap into position for a two-hand set shot.

Reds was nearly bald except for a few strands of thin, reddish hair combed back over the steep crown of his skull. Like my grandmother, Reds had called me Spanky, my Homewood name. He had played high school ball against Maurice Stokes and Ed Fleming, legendary Homewood heroes who'd gone on from Westinghouse High to college, then the N.B.A. To hear Reds tell it, he was better than both of them. They were good, strong kids, but raw. He could shoot and pass rings around them. His team won every match against Westinghouse when Reds was big gun at Central Catholic.

Real shootouts when the public school champs played the Catholic league winners for the city title. Stokes and Fleming were tough, real tough, but Reds didn't mind admitting he was the best. If he'd gotten a chance at college ball like they did, no telling how far he'd have gone. But it wasn't in the cards.

Reds was one of the kings of the playground, an aging king but still on top when at thirteen or so I first had ventured away from my home court—a single wooden backboard on a pole in Liberty Elementary School's dirt left field—to Mellon Park, where good players from all over the city congregated. For some reason Reds liked me. Maybe he remembered me, even younger, watching the games in Westinghouse Park. I remembered him. He was one of the few white players there, and maybe I reminded him of those summer days in Homewood, of the wide-eyed peanut gallery that always gathered to watch the big guys play. Whatever, he took me under his wing. Made sure I got a chance to play every now and then in less high-powered Mellon games. He also guaranteed my safe passage through the white neighborhoods I had to cross walking to and from Mellon Park. *Spanky's okay. He's a good kid.* That was all Reds had to say.

Reds wasn't a cop then. He drove a bread truck for National Biscuit Company. Coincidentally, Nabisco sponsored my favorite radio show: "Straight Arrow." I'd always identified with Indians more than cowboys, and the song that began each "Straight Arrow" episode—

> *...N - A - B - I - S - C - O*
> *Nabisco is the name to know*
> *For a breakfast you can't beat*
> *Eat Nabisco shredded wheat ...*

—was a magic formula that transmogrified me into one of my Indian heroes.

Not that the white kids in the neighborhoods bordering Mellon Park posed any actual danger to life or limb. More a matter of harassment. Nigger this and nigger that and maybe a stone or two at your feet kicking dust off the asphalt, or a gang of six or seven kids with nothing better to do than block the sidewalk so I'd have to go around them and worry for the next fifty yards or so whether they'd decide to chase me or not.

Reds looked out for me. Then, over the years, as I grew bigger and stronger, Reds gradually became less of a fixture at Mellon. His skills declined. The deadly two-hand, over-the-head set shot that began when he slid one foot behind the other, stopped being automatic. His leaning jumper, which had always looked awkward because it was propelled with two hands like his set shot, dated Reds. Young sky-walkers grinned and swatted it back in his face.

When Reds sprinted or touched down after the jumper, you could hear coins crashing in the deep front pockets of his chinos. The jin-gle-jangle was out of place; Reds sounded as if he didn't belong on the court, as if he were just passing through on his way to work. I remember wondering why he always carried pocketfuls of change, remember the shock of seeing his pale white thighs when he turned up one scorching Sunday afternoon in Bermuda shorts.

As a new generation of ballplayers—blacks from Homewood, East Liberty, and the Hill, whites from Point Breeze, Morningside, and the suburbs—rose up, I battled them on even terms. My rep was established and I didn't need Reds or anybody else. Reds would show up occasionally, a faded star in the background still spinning stories about the time he outscored Stokes and Fleming combined. He took his turn with everybody else rehearsing his glory days and drinking sweet wine in the weeds behind the cyclone fence that surrounded the court. Reds wasn't a wino; but winos, hangers-on, and players sit-ting in the shade waiting for winners—when you could find shade at Mellon—were his audience.

I always greeted Reds, but as I became a king in my own right, we had less and less to say to each other. I began avoiding him when I could. He'd embarrass me, the way he'd holler Spanky. I didn't like it, but let it slide. Reds was Reds and always would be. To him I'd always be Spanky, always a kid who needed his running commen-tary on passes I should have made and shots I shouldn't have taken.

Playing Big Five and Ivy League ball in Penn's Palestra kept me busy and sometimes happy. But college basketball lacked the spon-taneity, the free-form improvisation and electricity of the playground game. Remember the early sixties before Texas Western's all-black five defeated Adolph Rupp's lily-white Kentuckians. Most coaches designed offenses more suitable for corn-fed, Big Ten linemen than for the high-flying whippets and greyhounds the city game was begin-ning to breed. "Playground move" was synonymous with bad move. Not *bad* move, but something undisciplined, selfish, possibly immoral. Twenty years later, coaches are attempting to systematize and teach the essence of the game invented on the playgrounds.

At Penn I became a better player, but I paid a steep price for that and other cultural improvements. Teachers, coaches, nearly everyone important in the white university environment, urged me to bury my past. I learned to stake too much of who I was on what I would become, lived for the day I could look back, look down on Reds and everybody else in Mellon Park, in Homewood.

If Reds was around Mellon when I returned home from college to play during summer vacations, I can't recall. On the court I wouldn't have answered to Spanky. That I do know. I resented any reference to my punkhood when I had to be protected from punks. The past was incriminating. The past was skinny legs, a silly nickname, a pickaninny potbelly that wouldn't go away till I was fifteen.

Yet Mellon Park continued to be a special place in my imagination. When I balked at the regimen, the monotony, the blue-collar ethic of practice, practice, practice, the prospect of beating Princeton or Yale was seldom incentive enough to inspire more effort. To keep hustling in practice and school, I'd imagine how lame I'd sound trying to explain to the older guys from the playground—men like Delton and Smitty, Reds and Rudy and George Brown—why I blew the chance they never had. I'd anticipate the golden summers at Mellon, the chance to show off my new skills and prove that I hadn't forgotten the old ones, the ones that mattered in my heart of hearts.

Mellon remains a magnet on summer weekends for Pittsburgh's high school, college, pro and playground royalty. The court's run down now. Scarred backboards, rims bent and loose, two cracks in the asphalt just beyond one foul line so driving down the lane is like walking up steps. Neglected, going to seed, the buckling, gray rectangle is a microcosm of the potholed city. Tradition and location conspire to preserve Mellon's uniqueness. Over the years Pittsburgh's best have always played at Mellon. And since the park's not really in anybody's neighborhood it's a no-man's land, the perfect place for a battlefield, one of the only inner-city basketball courts where white and black players confront one another.

At Mellon a few summers a go I learned what it felt like to be a ghost. A bunch of older guys (I had ten or fifteen years on most of them) were waiting for winners and reminiscing about Mellon's good

'ole days. I listened to them talk about this dude went to Peabody
High. He was bad, yeah. Played in college. Won some kind of scholarship or something. Had a nice game. What was his name? I said
my name, and one or two nodded. Yeah ... yeah. That's the dude.
He could shoot the ball.

When Robby had said Reds was a cop, a memory had been tripped,
but I couldn't contextualize it. Maybe I was creating it after the fact,
but I saw Reds in his city cop uniform, two-tone blue like the pris-
oners wear. He sports shiny boots, a Sam Brown belt across his chest,
a holster and cartridge belt slung gunfighter-low on his hip. The leather
squeaks. It's Red's face under the polished black visor of the cap but
somehow different, ominous, even though he's smiling and basking
in all the attention his uniform gets, out of place in Mellon Park.

I was trying to explain Reds to my brother. The problem was, I
wasn't sure myself. Years and years since I'd thought of Reds in any
connection, then suddenly there he was across the visitor's lounge,
his long torso and big head, the bow of his belly, his hands still poised
and ready for a pass.

What's he in for?

Chopped his wife up in little pieces.

He used to look out for me at Mellon.

Say he caught her with another dude. Went crazy and wasted his
old lady.

Reds passed by later. He shook my hand. *Spanky.* Nodded at my
brother. An incredulous look, a few mumbled words; but he was
remembering everything, and everything was too much. Neither of
us wanted to linger, or to deal with it, so off he went again with the
priest and an older woman, his sister, mother, cousin, whatever.

Robby told me during a subsequent visit that Reds had bragged
about how tight he was with the Widemans. And Widemans included
my brother, so Reds figured he had gained an in with the black guys
among whom Robby was a leader. Reds traded on that association,
boasting, carrying himself a little taller, straighter, bumming cigarettes till he carried it a bit too far, got too familiar, and Robby had
to tell him to cool it. A strange sort of payback, a false neatness round-
ing off my relationship to Reds. For a month or two, I had been Reds'
safe passage through one black corner of Western Penitentiary.

Roy Blount, Jr.

47 Years a Shot-Freak

World's Greatest (and doubtless only) Freak Shot Expert Wilfred Hetzel, who was discharged from the Army in 1943 "for nervousness," is nervous now. In the assembly program at Ladysmith (Va.) High School this morning, the kids were a little restless, and his performance a little ragged. True, he hit over seventy percent of his gallimaufry of shots—with eyes shut, with legs crossed, with legs downright entwined, on the bounce off the floor, from one foot, from one knee, from both knees, from behind the backboard (frontward and backward), from up on his toes, from back on his heels (toes in the air) and in various combinations of the above. The kids responded with a gleeful shout, as he says they almost always do, to his "goofy series," in which he suddenly assumes a fey, exaggeratedly knock-kneed or bow-legged stance and then lets fly.

But the days of his 60-foot and 70-foot peg shots, which he used to make off ceilings or over rafters or simply from one end of the court to the other, are gone. Now, fifty-eight years old and weakened by an operation for TB, the man who bills himself as "Thrice Featured in *Believe It or Not* and Twice in *Strange as It Seems*" can shoot the ball only underhanded (except on his bounce shots) and seldom from farther out than the foul line. And in fourteen tries at Ladysmith, his 18-foot dropkick, his most spectacular remaining shot, was in and out once but never quite swished. The kids cheered frequently and came up for autographs afterward but, as Hetzel says, "If I can't impress them as the *best*—well, that's the point."

Now, sitting in the boys' dressing room of Louisa County High

School in Mineral, Va., thirty miles from Ladysmith, he is shaking, and drinking his fifth cup of coffee to counteract "spots of fatigue." He got only four hours of sleep last night because the pills he has been taking for his sciatica since 1949 keep him awake in spite of Sominex. The principal of this just-integrated 580-pupil school has consented to move Mr. Hetzel's performance up from 2:30 to one o'clock so he won't have to sit around getting tenser.

"Nothing terrifies me more," Hetzel says, "than for the ball to be falling just short by inches—because these students don't know, they don't realize the handicaps. And then maybe some of the students start laughing, and I try harder. What some people can't understand is that I'm governed by averages, too."

With that he sheds his suit, revealing himself in the maroon shorts, the gold shirt lettered WILFRED HETZEL on the front and FREAK SHOT SPECIALIST on the back, the worn black-top shoes and the straggly strips of tape on his knees (kneepads shift too much when he kneels to shoot) that constitute his working uniform. He has worn this outfit underneath his clothes on the road since 1962; he had read that Esther Williams kept her bathing suit on underneath for quick changes during her appearance tours. Distractedly, Hetzel proceeds to the gym and takes a few practice shots as the kids file in. Then he presents himself and relates, in an absorbed, recitative voice, a brief history of his involvement in freak shooting.

Not the comprehensive history, because he hasn't the time. If he were to include all the material he is more than happy to bring forth in conversation, he would go back to 1924, when, in Melrose, Minn., at the age of twelve, he nailed a barrel hoop to the side of the family woodshed and took his first shot. If you start counting then, Hetzel has said, "and if you include all the times with a baseball, a kitten-ball, a soccer ball, a rag ball, some socks tied together in the form of a ball, a tennis ball, a football—I had to learn to shoot the football end over end so that it would nose down at just the right moment and pass through that small hoop"—if you count all those shots, along with the 30,000 hours he estimates he has spent shooting a regulation basketball through a real basket, says Hetzel,—"I have probably shot more goals than any man in history."

In his backyard there by the woodshed he shot them year-round, in rain, snow, in tricky gusts of wind ("It was a thrill to have the wind pick up the ball and blow it six or seven feet through the hoop") and in temperatures down to 20° below. He pretended he was the University of Minnesota and also its opponents, which meant, since he did his best for both sides, that Minnesota lost half the time. He would plan out a complete schedule in advance, but when the Gophers had lost too many games to hope for a Big Ten crown, he would start over. When he tells audiences this, Hetzel says, it gives the coaches present a good laugh "because they wish they could start a season over. Of course, it's so much easier the way I do it, all make-believe."

The first time young Wilfred tried shooting with a real basketball, "it went straight, three feet under the basket, like a pass."

"Gee whiz," remarked an unkind neighborhood boy who was watching, "if I couldn't do any better than that, I'd quit."

"He was one of those boys," recalls Hetzel, "who move away a few years later, and you don't know what happened to them." One of those boys, in other words, who do not go on to become the world's greatest anything.

Somewhat later, Wilfred started doing a little shooting in the local gym—but it wasn't easy. "There were some boys there, after school, who were good at clever fakery, dribbling, passing and that, and they would hog the ball. I might have to wait two hours, from 3:30 to 5:30, until they went home and I could get in five minutes of shooting before the janitor locked the ball up. Or maybe he would lock it up as soon as they quit. I'd think nothing later of shooting 5,000 times, because I'd been deprived of it for so long."

There was no question of Hetzel's going after one of those clever-faking boys one-on-one and taking the ball away, because ball handling has never been his forte. It has never even been a part of his portfolio. The truth is that Wilfred Hetzel, who has made 144 straight foul shots standing on one foot, who bills himself as "One of Basketball's Immortals," has never learned to dribble.

"I realized I would never be good at the game one day in PT class when I was a freshman in high school," he says now. "We were supposed to do what they called a figure-eight drill. I'd be a forward, and the center would pass it to me, and I would pass it to the other forward and then I wouldn't know where to go. They never explained it to me in detail, never diagramed it or anything. After I fouled it up twice, I knew I'd never play. I was too slow and kind of awkward in other ways."

Hetzel did serve the high school team briefly as a scrub, and "I made a few shots against the first team, and I'd pass it pretty well, but I never did dribble. And I'd be open for a shot and very seldom would anyone pass it to me. There were cliques on the team—they'd pass it to their friends."

He got into one unofficial game against a local telephone team, didn't shoot and committed two technical fouls by neglecting to check in with the timekeeper each time he went in. The year before, his uniform was stolen twice. He decided to quit organized basketball forever (except for a brief exhibition game appearance with Western Union College in Le Mars, Iowa many years later, when he was inserted to shoot two foul shots and hit one).

In fact, young Wilfred found that he had no great knack for any competitive sport. In baseball he could hit fungoes with precision and catch fly balls gloveless in his big, long-fingered hands, but he was too slow to play the outfield and couldn't get the bat around fast enough to hit pitching.

But that just meant more time for shooting basketballs by himself every day, including the day his father, a Bavarian immigrant and railroad man, was killed. The water tank for which the elder Hetzel was responsible was out of order, and evidently he went up to its rim to investigate. No one saw him fall in through the layer of ice, but when sixteen-year-old Wilfred came in for lunch, his father's hamburger was overcooking on the stove. Finally Mrs. Hetzel took it off. "The ice froze back over," as Hetzel tells it, "and they had to get special permission from division headquarters to go in and see if he was there. And he was."

It is easy enough to see a fateful symbolism in the mode of the father's death—the son doomed to act it out with a basketball over and over again—but Hetzel says he has never seen any irony in it. By the time his father died, at any rate, he had already devoted hundreds of hours to what was to become his vocation.

Pretty soon Hetzel was making ninety-eight out of a hundred from the free-throw line. But he never had any witnesses, "and people thought if I really had a talent like that I would be on the team." So one day as a high school senior, he put on an impromptu lunch-hour exhibition in the school gym. That was his first show, in 1929. "I've thought about writing Ed Sullivan," he says, "and saying they're all talking so much about the sports stars of the Golden '20s—Red Grange and so on—and here I am, out of the '20s and still performing."

But in those early days he had no tricks, just free throws, performed at no charge. Upon graduation from high school he moved with his mother, who had remarried, to nearby Sauk Centre, Minn., and began to do some sportswriting for local daily and weekly papers. In the line of duty, he would attend Sauk Centre games, and while the players were dressing he would seize the opportunity to take the floor in his street clothes and shoot before a crowd. He went so far as to write himself up in one of the papers, in the third person: "Wilfred Hetzel of Sauk Centre, in a recent practice session, hit 467 free throws out of 500."

Meanwhile, the local team was doing well to hit 40 percent from the foul line—and he reported that, too. "The fans in Sauk Centre were so hateful to me in those years," he says. "Maybe it was my fault because I slammed their team in the paper. Maybe I was like a prima donna. But once I made 120 of 122 before a game, eighty-two straight, and I-walked off the floor, and there wasn't a single handclap. But you know, they've never had a bad team since? It kind of woke them up when I slammed them."

And then one night, in the visiting cheering section, someone woke up to Wilfred Hetzel. "This very beautiful girl came down and made such a fuss about me," he recalls. "The home people never made any fuss. The principal's son would take a couple of shots before throwing my ball back to me, and they would laugh at my embarrassment. But this beautiful girl raved about how good I was. Well, the next night Sauk Centre was to play at that girl's school, and I planned to ride with the team over there in hopes of seeing her again. But at the last minute they took only one car and didn't have room for me."

"So, rather than waste the day, I got in through the window of the gym in Melrose and practiced. I'd make seventeen in a row several times, and then I'd miss. I got disgusted. 'I could do better than this with my eyes closed,' I told myself. So I just tried it that way. I shot a hundred with my eyes closed and made seventy-four. That was my first trick. I never did see that girl again."

Gradually Hetzel's reputation spread, and he was able to talk several area schools into letting him put on a free-throw show before a game or at the half. The Depression bore down, and he couldn't find much work, so he lived at home and kept on practicing his shots. When he was twenty he tired of pretending he was the University of Minnesota and began to work more on variety. He practiced for seven or eight years. After a few fans complained that free throws tended to grow monotonous, and after he lost a free-throw contest to an expert named Bunny Levitt who was traveling with the Harlem Globetrotters, he introduced his eyes-shut trick and a couple of other "unorthodox shots" to the public.

In 1937 Hetzel enrolled in the University of Minnesota and was able to work out in the gym and book himself, occasionally for a two-dollar or five-dollar honorarium, into shows at high schools, colleges and military bases throughout the state and beyond. He hitchhiked from place to place, persuaded sixty businesses in Sauk Centre to chip in on a sweat suit with SAUK CENTRE, MINNESOTA on the front and WILFRED HETZEL, STUNT SHOT SPECIALIST on the back, and it was not long before he was popping up in *Ripley's Believe It or Not* and in *Strange as It Seems*. "Wilfred Hetzel, Minneapolis Basketball Star, Shot 92 Baskets Out of 100 Tries with One Hand, Standing On One Leg and Blindfolded!" right alongside "Mrs. M. J. Wellman, Oklahoma City, Has Worn the Same Set of False Teeth for 45 Years." "Wilfred Hetzel Shot 66 Straight Basketball Foul Shots From His Knees!" right alongside "Musical Teeth! For 4 Months After Having Dental Work Done, Mrs. Fred Stutz, Indianapolis, *Could Hear Radio Programs Without Having the Radio Turned On!* Her *Teeth* Formed a Receiving Set!"

Then, in the early '40s, after he mastered the long peg shot and the dropkick, Hetzel's career reached its fullest flower. In those years, aside from ten months in the Army during which he experienced severe trouble with his teeth (though he heard no radio programs over them) as well as with his nerves, he spent September through May traveling the country, performing for around twenty-five dollars a show, sometimes four or five times a day. In 1941 he appeared at the Clair Bee Coaching Clinic at Manhattan Beach, N.Y., and was invited by Ned Irish to perform in a clown suit in Madison Square Garden, but that latter deal, to Hetzel's great regret, fell through. In the 1943–44 and '44–'45 seasons alone, he traveled 42,000 miles and performed over 150 times. He remembers all his best performances from this heyday in detail, especially the ones in Oklahoma. "I've done an extraordinary amount of spectacular things there," he says. "In Davis, Okla., on Feb. 29, 1944—which I remember because I thought at the time, 'This is an unusual day, it comes along once in four years, I wonder what feat I'll accomplish that will make me remember this day?'—I hit 40-foot, 50-foot and 70-foot shots, all on the first try. All straight through. In fact, I lost the thrill of the 70-footer because the netting moved so barely, I thought at first the ball had just brushed it underneath. In Okmulgee, Okla., on a 60-footer, the ball hit the inside of the rim, bounced way back up diagonally, hit the junction of a rafter and the ceiling, rebounded right back to the goal, bounced around the rim and went in. That was for a girl's gym class. It was funny. I had told them my superduper was coming up.

"In Miami, Okla., I made a shot over two girders at once that the coach remembered there 10 years later. In Jenks, Okla., there was just a narrow opening to throw the ball through to get it over two crossbeams. I tried it eight times before I even got the ball through, and then it missed the basket by a foot. But I've always thanked my lucky stars that I had guts. I kept at it, and on the very next try the ball went through the opening and right down into the basket. Fifty feet. Unbeknown to me, Mickey Mantle was in junior high school in Commerce, just a few miles away, that very year."

During these cross-country tours, Hetzel would book himself for three weeks in advance. As he traveled he would write to other schools, advising them to address their replies to him in care of the school where he would be performing at the end of that period, and when he reached the school he would check his mail and map out another three weeks.

It was a grueling routine, traveling by bus or train at night (he had no car, and anyway he finds that driving impairs his touch), often getting too little sleep, lugging around his two bags (one containing clothes and the other his ball and pump), casting about in each town for a room "in some respectable place," struggling through snowstorms so as not to miss a date.

Albuquerque; Dodge City, Kans.; Forest Grove, Ore.; Homer, N.Y.; Ferndale, Mich.; San Luis Obispo, Calif.; Augusta, Ga.; Manassas, Va.; Muncie, Ind.; Louisville; Leechburg, Pa.; Ogden, Utah; Akron; Morgantown, W. Va.; Hagerstown, Md.; Maywood, Ill.; Tombstone, Ariz. It was a thorough way of seeing the country, but it paid Hetzel only about enough to keep him going, and the travel took its toll on his health. Not until years later did he realize that he had contracted tuberculosis, which lingered until his operation—the removal of a rib and part of a lung in 1968—but he knew he did not feel up to any more full-time barnstorming, so when he found himself in Washington in the spring of 1945, he decided it was time he got a regular job. In 1942 he had applied for a defense-plant job in Chicago but "they watched me for a while and then they rejected me. I asked why and they said I didn't have no coordination. Well, if they'd known that coordination was one of the things I was famous for! I've always attributed my success to the three Cs—confidence, coordination and concentration. But then, you can be coordinated in one thing and not in another. I never did learn to dance." This time, in '45, his touch qualified him as a civilian typist for the Marine Corps, a job he holds to this day.

Settling down in Arlington, Va., where he lives now as a roomer in a private home, Hetzel kept up his shooting career through the '50s and '60s by spacing out his leave time in bits and pieces of two or three days. His job has not paid enough to support a wife—or so he concluded after meeting the girl of his life, a toe dancer, on a bus. He confessed to her in a letter, "I kissed you when you were asleep on the bus," and she confessed in reply, "I wasn't asleep." They saw each other for some time and still exchange letters, but she married someone else. "I guess that's why I've never married," Hetzel says. "I didn't want anyone to replace her."

It was not until 1947 that he started taking off his sweat jacket to shoot—"before, on account I was so slender, I was afraid there would be more people laughing at me, and the jacket made me feel a little fleshier. The greater freedom of movement helped him to keep up his distance shots; but he made his last 70-footer in '54, his last 30-footer four years ago. In the '50s he began to find it hard "to get my pep up," and sometimes when that happened he got "snotty" receptions and reviews. "Those few times when maybe I wasn't in form, no one asked for autographs," he says. "They looked on me as a fake or a cheat or a has-been. I get emotional when I think about the time, in Jeffersonville, Ind., some people were saying, 'He's not much,' and the coach there stood up and fairly exploded and said, 'I wish I could shoot half as good as that man.'"

In recent years he found that small, out-of-the-way black schools in the South were a fertile field, though once "they were envious— one of the boys came up and asked if I could spin the ball in my hands. I said if I could do those things, I'd have been a Globetrotter. But usually there's no resentment of me because I'm white. Without my saying it, the Negro kids come up to me and say, 'You're better than Alcindor.' Now that don't take no glory from him. He's still one of the greatest centers that ever lived. It's not the same competitive field."

In 1936 Hetzel heard Dr. James Naismith, the inventor of basketball, make a speech. "He said if you're doing something for humanity, don't think about getting a reward now, you'll get it later. I thought then, 'If I don't get a million dollars for it, I'll just enjoy it.' I do envy those football players. You know that commercial: 'Remember, Charley Conerly, such and such a day when you threw three TD passes,' and then they show the replay? I wish that on my best days they'd had TV cameras running. And I wish the people back in Minnesota that hated me and made fun of me and said, 'If there was money in it, somebody would be better at it'—I'd like to get all those people together in one gym and do all the greatest tricks I ever did."

But now, at Louisa County High School in Virginia, his audience is some 500 rural kids who have been charged twenty-five cents apiece by their student council for the benefit of a Korean orphan. And what Mr. Hetzel is saying now to the kids, in reference to all those doubters back in Minnesota, is "if they'd believed me back there in the beginning, when I tried to tell them I had made 98 out of 100, I might not be here now."

And he is advancing, in his gangly yet almost formal walk, to the foul line, where he begins to hit his underhanded shots, blim, blim, blim, coolly, crisply, now cross-legged, now on his toes, now on his heels, missing one occasionally but in command, running through his repertoire, down on his knees, up on one foot, and the kids are paying him mind. Mr. Hetzel's manner of shooting is memorable in many respects, but its most noteworthy feature is that when he releases the ball—even routinely in practice but especially when he knows he is going well—his face is lit by a proud and affectionate smile. The first time Wilfred Hetzel has ever tried a shot from behind a Louisa County backboard, over the crossed wires that raise and lower it, he scores. On his second try at that same shot backward, over his head, he scores. He scores on one more backspin bounce shot from his knees. And now, in closing: the dropkick. Short. Short. Off to the right. Short. Off to the right.

Short. Short. Off the rim. Off the rim. Off to the left. Off the rim. No, way short. A pause before the thirteenth try and then it is up, off the backboard, swish.

"Yaay! Aw-*right!* Sign him up!"

Stephen Dunn

Basketball: A Retrospective

My ethics were
    a good pair of hands,
        a good move
when things were difficult.

An exceptional man
    could change direction
        in the air,
could thread a needle.

Part Four

The Big Time

Jack Litewka

from *The View from Section III*

Far below the bottom of an orange bowl
are two baskets and a hardwood floor,
20,000 colored seats
and 20,000 people filing in.

We have all met before.
In Macy's.
In voting booths.
On opposite sides of tear gas in the streets.
Everyone forgets.
There is another war we are waiting for.

The athletes are warm.
The anthem is sung.
The play is about to begin.
I know
nothing else could have brought us together.

Nelson George

The First Three

Earl Lloyd, Chuck Cooper, and Sweetwater Clifton all have a valid claim as the first African-American in the National Basketball Association. At a Chicago hotel on April 25, 1950, Celtics owner Walter Brown selected Duquesne's Cooper in the second round of the college draft. According to *New York Times* columnist George Sullivan, this announcement silenced the room. Finally, another owner inquired, "Walter, don't you know he's a colored boy?" Brown responded, "I don't give a damn if he's striped, plaid, or polka-dot!" In the ninth round of that same draft the Washington Capitols picked Lloyd of West Virginia State. Within a few months the Knicks purchased Clifton's contract from the Trotters. So while Cooper was the first drafted, Clifton would be the first to sign an NBA contract. But it was the little-known Lloyd who, in an October 31, 1950, game in Rochester, New York, became the first of the trio to step on court as a player in uniform in the NBA.

When Brown picked Cooper he did more that break the color line: he challenged Abe Saperstein's stranglehold on Black talent. According to Wilt Chamberlain, when the Trotter honcho heard Brown selected Cooper, "Abe went crazy. He threatened to boycott the Boston Garden." During the NBA's early years Trotter appearances as an opening act guaranteed a large house, so Saperstein's threat carried weight. Other owners put pressure on Brown to back down on integration, but he held his position and that resolve decided the Trotter's future. Given the opportunity to play fewer games for more money with no clowning required, the best Black players started to

ignore Saperstein's blandishments against the NBA. It didn't happen
overnight—the Trotters were established, the NBA relative upstarts.
But an irreversible trend had begun.

Earl Lloyd is the least remembered of that pioneering trio, in large
part because of what happened to the Washington franchise. That
October 31st game in Rochester, in which Lloyd pulled down a game-
high ten rebounds, was supposed to be the first of sixty-eight. Unfortunately, on January 9, 1951, after compiling a 10–25 record, the Caps
disbanded, a victim of the same basketball apathy that killed the
Bears. Lloyd, a wiry, brown-skinned twenty-two-year-old, 6 foot 6,
220-pounder nicknamed Big Cat, had appeared in only seven games,
scoring forty-three points for a 6.1 average before being drafted into
the army. For the 1952—1953 season Lloyd signed with the Syracuse
Nationals, where he toiled as a hardworking rebounder or, in today's
jargon, power forward for six seasons and then two more in Detroit
before retiring in 1960. His best season was '54–'55, when he posted
career highs in minutes (2,212), field goals made (286), rebounds
(553), assists (283), points (731), and point average (10.2), this last
statistic his only season in double figures. It was a career year for
Lloyd that, not coincidentally, was the year Syracuse, perennial brides-
maids, won the NBA title against Fort Wayne in seven games.

Syracuse teammate Dolph Schayes recalled that Lloyd "got the
poor end of the stick as far as playing was concerned. He was always
doing the dirty work, fouling out of the game. Actually, he helped
me a great deal because with him in there I was free to rebound and
get a lot of glory, since his game was to guard the other team's offensive ace." Because Lloyd didn't play in a big city and wasn't a high
scorer or flashy on the court, his career is little noted today. Yet he
was unquestionably the first Black actually to suit up, and as such he
probably deserves the title of NBA African-American pioneer more
than Cooper or Clifton.

By some trick of fate, both Lloyd and Cooper wore number eleven.
They also both spent time at West Virginia State—Cooper for only
a year and a half before entering the navy for two years. But these
similarities aside, Lloyd and Cooper had very different careers. While
Lloyd developed into a valuable role player on championship-caliber
clubs, Cooper never fulfilled the promise he showed in college. The

barrel-chested, light-skinned, 6 feet 5, twenty-four-year-old guard-forward was a star at Duquesne, a Pittsburgh school with a history of Black athletes in football and basketball, though Cooper was its first Black roundball starter. His presence inspired racist reactions several times in college: the University of Tennessee, after traveling all the way up to Pittsburgh for a game, canceled just before tip-off when they found out Cooper didn't merely have a tan; Duquesne couldn't book any games against schools from Alabama and Mississippi; as players lined up for an inbounds play against the university of Cincinnati, a Cincy player shouted, "I got the nigger!" to which Cooper replied, "And I got your mother in a jockstrap!"

In four years in Boston, Cooper made a modest impact, mostly playing forward, though Red Auerbach used him a bit at guard. His rookie season was his best, as he recorded what would stand as career highs in rebounds (562), assists (174), and point average (9.3). In two years with the St. Louis Hawks Cooper posted decreasing numbers in all areas and in 1956 left the NBA for good. "The major thing I had to adjust to upon entering the pros," he told the *Amsterdam News* in 1978, "was the stationary pivot. In college, with my size and agility, I liked to go down low and utilize that space, but in the pros a big man in the middle would clog that area." Cooper also complained that his career was marred by coaching decisions that, similar to those made for Layne at CCNY and Lloyd at Syracuse, limited his offensive role. "There were things I had to adapt to throughout my career that I wouldn't have had to if I were white," he recalled. "I was expected to play good, sound intensified defense and really get under the boards for the heavy dirty work. Yet, I never received the frills or extra pay of white players."

Another problem that nagged Cooper, and dogs Blacks in pro ball to this day, was the perception that they exaggerated injuries due to a low threshold of pain or plain old laziness. "If I was hurt, they got suspicious," he remembered. "Auerbach, in fact, had me labeled a hypochondriac. In my four years in Boston, I never had an x-ray—lots of stitches, but never an x-ray. There were one or two white players on the Celtics that if they jammed a finger it was cause of great concern. But then you know how strong Black skin is. We don't hurt. Ha!"

After his exit from the NBA Cooper joined Marques Haynes's Harlem Magicians for a few years. His salary rivaled what he made in the NBA, but Cooper was getting tired of the road. An auto accident in the late fifties led to his retirement. In the years between the end of his career and death in 1984 Cooper made a comfortable life for himself as a Pittsburgh businessman. Still, even after his playing days were over, Cooper confronted other roadblocks. "I would have like to get into coaching," he said. "I felt I knew how to handle young men. But there were no opportunities for Black coaches then. I got one offer from a school in Piney Woods, Mississippi, but they were still killing Black people down there then. When my alma mater was looking for a coach, they approached me in a very roundabout way, but it was only for a position as an assistant coach."

The best and most colorful of the NBA's original brothers was Nat "Sweetwater" Clifton. Clifton, a soda-pop fanatic whose passion for the liquid led to his nickname, was a Chicago cabbie from his professional retirement in 1965 until his death in 1990. Of the NBA's original Blacks, Clifton was the one with the kind of leaping ability and flair we now associate with the contemporary game. The combination of Clifton's above-the-rim jumping and Trotter gamesmanship made him the NBA's first proponent of the Black athletic aesthetic.

His story began on the same Chicago streets he later cruised as a cabbie. After his family left Little Rock, Arkansas, in the 1930s, it settled on Chicago's South Side. By the time he entered DuSable High he was 6 feet 5, and in the 1940s that made him a dominating schoolboy center and the foundation for a rich postwar basketball tradition at the school. After fielding offers from several prominent Black colleges (Morris Brown, Clark, Tuskegee) Clifton chose Xavier in New Orleans because his DuSable teammates had already committed themselves to go there (just as the squad from Chicago's Wendell Phillips had in 1935). For three varsity years, led by Clifton, these Chicagoans terrorized the Southern Conference. In 1943 Xavier took the conference title and Sweetwater was the league's most valuable player. Upon graduation he served in Europe with the army's all-Black 369th Battalion from 1944 to 1947. Back home he joined the Dayton Metropolitans, an integrated bunch (three Blacks, nine whites) composed primarily of ex-Big Ten players. The Dayton experience led Clifton to a year as roundball gypsy: he moved from Dayton to the Harlem Rens for about six months before settling in Chicago with the Trotters in late '47. For the next three years Clifton was a member of the Trotters' best-ever lineup; playing beside Marques Haynes and Goose Tatum, Clifton's agility and good-natured personality meshed well with the team's style and comic reams.

A dispute over money ended his Trotter tenure. In the summer of 1950 Clifton found out that the white college all-stars the Trotters played in a very lucrative barnstorming series were making more per game than them. Clifton shared his knowledge with his teammates, which enraged Saperstein. So Saperstein, knowing how the Knicks were interested in having a Black player, sold his contract to New York. "He told me he had me sold for $5,000," Clifton remembered, "so he got $2,500 and gave me $2,500. . . . But later I came to find out that it was something like $20,000 he got, you understand what I mean?"

During his seven years in New York Clifton did well on court (averaging 10.3 for his career there, playing in the 1957 All-Star Game) and in salary negotiations (going from $7,500 in 1950 to $10,000). Still, Clifton felt his game was inhibited by Knick management: "When I first came to the Knicks I found I had to change over, you know. They didn't want me to do anything fancy or do anything like that. What I was supposed to do was rebound and play defense . . . I would have been happy playing with the Knicks, but the thing is all the time I played there they never did get another good Black ballplayer to play with me, somebody who knew what I was doing, you understand. And that kinda held me back 'cause you couldn't do something with the other guys because they played the straight way. I felt like I was sacrificing myself for some guy and I don't think other guys would have done that. I'll put it this way: at that time they weren't making any Black stars. You already had to be made."

Even mere flashes of Clifton's sweetness could cause trouble. Indeed, in an early fifties preseason game it even caused a fight. Boston's Bob Harris, a good old boy from Oklahoma, got upset when Clifton did "a little Globetrotter stuff to him and he said where he came from people didn't do him like that." After some cursing Clifton threw the fight's first and only blow, decking Harris with a right.

Referee Norm Drucker remembers, "Harris lost several front teeth. The Boston bench started to come toward Clifton, and when Sweetwater started to meet them, they all retreated." In 1958 Clifton, then wearing a Detroit Pistons uniform, got into a major melee in St. Louis backing up seven-foot Black teammate Walter Dukes. Dukes had stumbled into the crowd on a lay-up attempt. "Suddenly, Dukes is in a fight with some fans," says Drucker. "At this point Clifton runs towards the stands and with his humor yells, 'Walter, you take the first row, I've got the second row.'"

Clifton stayed with Detroit one season before reuniting with Haynes and Tatum for four years with the Harlem Magicians. Ironically, he ended his career back with the Trotters. He played for Saperstein until 1965, when his career was ended by a knee injury. Clifton wasn't a major star, but his occasional flourishes and refusal to be intimidated made a lasting impression on his peers. In terms of Black basketball history Clifton symbolizes the introduction of Black attitude into the NBA and, of equal long-term importance, the arrival of Blacks from Black colleges to the pros. As a Northern-bred African-American who attended a Southern Black college and moved on to the NBA, Clifton was a prototype for many African-American athletes of the next decade.

Clifton, and to some degree Cooper, were victims of a double standard based on race. While they were criticized for show-boating, the first celebrated white show-time player was revered. At this point in NBA history the prime exponent of what is now considered Black style was a skinny, white Catholic kid from Queens. Bob Cousy, a teammate of Cooper's, was a star precisely because of his use of the behind-the-back dribble and no-look pass. Cooper, a clear victim of this skewered perspective, had no beef with the Holy Cross College alum. "Cousy is about as free of the affliction of racism as any white person I've ever known," Cooper said. Unfortunately for this pioneering trio, the Celtic legend was in the minority.

Tom Meschery

Pro Basketball Players

pro basketball players
live in bat caves
upside down
hotel rooms
minds pointing
to darkness. . . .

Ted Vincent

Mo Udall's Denver Nuggets

Presidential candidate Morris K. Udall is said to be a pleasant fellow; but as a presidential hopeful it is said he appears to be too much the intellectual. Of late he has been trying to appear less erudite, more like one of the boys. He declares: "What this country needs is an athlete, a former professional basketball player"—meaning himself. Mo Udall is good at making wry comments, but the joke here, unfortunately, is lost on most of his listeners. They are unaware that the professional basketball team he played for was more representative of socialism than capitalism. It was the player-owned, player-controlled Denver Nuggets of the 1948–49 season.

Morris got into basketball following his brother Stewart, as Mo followed Stew, former Secretary of Interior, into national politics. Stew had led his Arizona University basketball team to a berth in the NIT in 1945. Morris's big moment in basketball came with the Nuggets. Mo says of his role, "I was a sub on an expansion team that went into a thirteen-game losing streak and then folded." Actually, Mo was the fifth best scorer on the Nuggets and a well respected rebounder. The team played all but the final two games of the season before folding, and despite the losing streak managed to end up second to last in the league, the National Basketball League. The following season a merger of the National Basketball League and the Basketball Association of America created the NBA.

The player-owned Nuggets were rather fortunate to survive financially until the last week of the season. The team was probably the most under-financed outfit in modern big-league sports history. Those who played for the Nuggets had to be committed to some kind of principle or ideal, since it was known from the start that the chance for profit was slim. By joint agreement the players would not be guaranteed a salary. They would try to live off the gate receipts. As described in a *Sporting News* article on this unusual team, players were recruited by manager Hal Davis who would explain, "We're just making a start this season. We're going to share whatever money we make, but probably it won't even be enough to keep us in groceries. We may break even next season. By the third year we ought to be well enough established to get a return on the time and money we've sunk in the first two years. And we'll be splitting the whole melon—there won't be any promoter getting the biggest slice." The Denver Nuggets were incorporated with stock distributed to the players; as Davis explained, "The value of this stock depends on the team's success. The harder we work at the game, the more we get out of it."

Manager Davis was granted authority to handle the club's day-to-day business affairs, but as pointed out in *Sporting News,* "important decisions were left to all the squad members. In one meeting the players voted to fine one of their number guilty of an outburst of temperament. He paid the fine and has behaved since."

In 1949, big-league basketball teams required an initial investment of from seventy-five to a hundred thousand dollars. Getting players to forgo a guaranteed salary saved much of this cost. And the Nuggets found other ways. Ralph Bishop doubled as player and coach. Forward Jack Cotton was an expert mechanic and kept the players' cars in running order. Guard Leonard Alterman was the team auditor; and forward Mo Udall, after passing his bar exam, became the team lawyer. An office secretary was the only paid staffer for the Denver Nuggets Incorporated.

To keep their families in groceries, the players held moonlighting jobs. Alterman's job made him miss games for business trips. In this informal atmosphere, guard Al Guokas got permission to go home to Philadelphia for Christmas, missing a game. Without salaries there had to be some side benefits.

Mo Udall was of course allowed to go to Arizona in January to take his bar exams. He sent the team a telegram on the eve of an important game he was missing. "Please fellas, win one for the old

Mormon," Udall being a Mormon. The next day the *Denver Post* sports page headline read, "Message from Mo Helps Nugs to Win."

The Nuggets became a pro expansion team under rather odd circumstances, at least by today's sports standards. The year prior to joining the National Basketball League, the Nuggets had been technically an amateur outfit, an AAU team, and had finished second to the Phillips 66 Oilers in the National AAU Tournament. The AAU had some tough teams, whose sponsors had scoured the country to win the services of good players by offering them paying jobs on the side. In those years, newspaper sports sections were filled during winter off-days with debate over who played the best basketball, the pros, or the AAU, or the collegians. The collegians usually whipped the pros in the annual All-Star game; and as for the bigtime AAU teams like the 66ers and the Nuggets, many people felt they were really just pros in disguise. A magazine article on the 66 Oilers was titled "The Amateur Professionals from Bartlesville Oklahoma." Some said the 66ers were pro because they played like pros, while others said it was because the Phillips petroleum company provided the players so many fringe benefits they might as well have been pros.

When the Denver Nuggets went professional for the '48–'49 season, they became the first major-league team in the West, an area where the pro game had been badmouthed as being a corrupt form of basketball, a commercial product rather than sport. In the years right after World War II, the so-called amateur AAU had an almost exclusive hold in the West, and openly professional teams in big-time ball in the East.

When Nuggets team manager Hal Davis, coach Ralph Bishop and a couple of players sat down to discuss the possibility of going pro, they were searching for a way to avoid some of the drawbacks of professionalism. They felt there was room for a new form of pro team. Genuine major-league pro basketball was still rather new, dating only from the end of World War II. New teams in the East, like the New York Knicks and Boston Celtics, were run with all the drawbacks, player reserve, player drafts, and much buying and trading around of players. The Knicks, in their first year, ran through twenty different players.

The Nuggets decided they would not hold their fellow athletes to a reserve if they wanted to leave, and they would try to avoid the temptation of trading. Rather unavoidably, coach Bishop had to be given the right to cut a player from the squad, but as manager Davis said, in the case of the Nuggets, "When a player slows up . . .he is likely to be the first to suggest that he be replaced. After all, the players themselves own the club and are looking after its best interests. Ordinarily, professional basketball is a pretty cold-blooded business with players bought and sold like so much livestock, but every Nugget is also a stockholder."

As a pro team in Denver the Nuggets were going to have a hard time getting established with the fans. Denver was the AAU capital of the world, the host city of the national AAU tournament, and a city that for years had fielded at least one, and often three, of the top dozen AAU teams in the nation. The Nuggets began their inaugural pro season in a rather second-fiddle position to the AAU Denver Chevoletts. The Cheves had radio coverage. The Nuggets didn't. The Cheves played in the Civic Auditorium, capacity 7000-plus. The Nuggets played in the Denver University fieldhouse, capacity 3,600.

So why would the Nuggets try to go pro, and at that with such slim financing that they hardly had the money for uniforms? The question is a generic one, a question of why America has professional sports at all. From the players' point of view, the AAU so-called amateur system must have appeared as a rip-off of their talents. Ticket prices for AAU games were comparable to those on most pro teams, and attendance was about the same. AAU teams took in a lot of money and all the players got was a moonlighting job on the side. As long as spectators are willing to pay to see a game there will be money interests trying to cash in on potential profits, and players will be concerned that they get something of a fair return for their performance. College players may be willing to perform at profitable games merely out of school spirit; but in the late 1940s even a good number of college players felt ripped off and took money from gamblers. College players in Madison Square Garden were particularly susceptible to overtures from gamblers. The Garden's college double-header programs packed in the fans, and in order to sell more high-priced seats, the college rooting sections were removed from center court to the second upper deck behind the backboard. The players found themselves performing before well-dressed socialites and, of course, the gamblers.

In going openly professional the Nuggets were cutting through the hypocrisy that was rampant then in so-called amateur basketball. Some of the Nuggets on the previous year's AAU team didn't like the pro idea, or didn't like the insecurity of no guaranteed salary, and they found positions on other AAU teams. There were plenty of replacements available, however; coach Bishop received letters from all over the country from players wishing a try-out on the player-owned Nuggets. Regrettably, only one experienced professional asked for a chance.

His case points out one of the problems faced by the Nuggets and facing any attempt today at player-owned, and under-financed sport. Bob Doll had been for two years one of the better guards in the Basketball Association of America, then the league of the Knicks, Celtics, Warriors, etc. Doll jumped to the Nuggets of the National League in order to play near home. He was a graduate of Colorado University. Like others on the Nuggets, Doll appears to have been a man of some principles. During World War II Doll had insisted on being sent overseas to fight the Nazis, rejecting an offer to remain in the states playing basketball for the military base team.

Now he was in a battle to test the possibility of player-controlled sport, and he failed the test. His two years of big league paychecks had given him the good things in life, and some debts. After a month with the Nuggets he asked permission to go back to the high-paying Basketball Association. Coach Bishop freely gave Doll his release. The Denver press, however, did not forgive him, running a number of stories on the allegedly money-hungry home town deserter.

Today it is highly doubtful that a player-owned team could get a franchise in any sports big league. Today's sports club owners are even reluctant to allow in a civic-funded team—of which there were two in the old National Basketball League. The National League allowed in all kinds of teams, including one sponsored by the Pittsburgh YMHA. The National League integrated big-league basketball when it granted the barnstorming New York Rens, an all-black outfit, a franchise in 1948.

Financially, the Nuggets failed. But as a test case for player ownership of pro basketball they appear to have made their point. No sooner had the season ended than the National League admitted a second, and better financed, player-owned team, the Indianapolis Olympians. The Olympians were composed of virtually the entire 1949 squad from Kentucky University, the NCAA champions. Six of these players had been on the 1948 Olympic team. The Olympians wanted to stick together as a team, as friends are wont to stick together. The Basketball Association of the New York Knicks and company would have selected them piecemeal through the typical college player draft. The National League gave them a chance to stay together. Having the Olympians in their league would prove a strong bargaining point in the negotiations that summer that resulted in the merger creating the NBA.

The Nuggets were reorganized under private ownership and entered the NBA. Mo Udall did not go along. He most likely would have made it as a player. He had been the "sixth man" on the Nuggets and a third of the time a starter. Probably his finest moment was in sinking the clutch basket in a game with the Syracuse Nats that had seen a street-fight-type brawl in which a ref had been twice punched and suffered a reported loss of a full inch of skin from his chin. Pro basketball was a rough sport in those days. *A Denver Post* headline after one game read, "Only One Fight as Nugs Lose."

The Nuggets might have lost less often had they been a more thoroughly professional outfit; had they been a team that didn't allow a player to take off for Christmas, a team that didn't have players showing up tired from working all day at a nine-to-five. When they did show up they could count on getting into the game; win or lose, coach Bishop almost always cleared the bench. Although the Nuggets ended up 18–44, the team did have a few glorious moments, as when Mo Udall put away the Syracuse Nats, the league champions and future NBA champions. When the Nuggets beat the Nats it was as if a bunch of working stiffs had gotten together, played a good game, and beaten the best, the champs. Things like that don't happen very much, anymore, in the world of sport.

Now an older Morris Udall stumps the country as a spokesman for a type of liberalism that isn't seen much anymore either.

William Matthews

Oscar Robertson: Peripheral Vision

They clear the left side for him.
An eye-fake, dip and ripple
of a shoulder, he runs his man
into a pick. He's done this so many times
it hurts him the right way.
The ball blooms away from his wrist.
The body is most vulnerable
when it claims space,
shadows in the moist
and painfully kept open
corners of his eyes.

Woody Allen

A Fan's Notes on Earl Monroe

Toward the end of the 1976–77 basketball season, the editors of this magazine, aware of my interest in the game, called me and asked how I'd feel about covering the NBA playoffs for them. At first the idea seemed provocative, but then the thought of traveling around, and the time required to do a good job, not to mention the disappointment of the Knicks not making the playoffs, rendered the whole notion unappealing. But I said I wouldn't mind writing something about Earl Monroe, who had given me a great deal of pleasure watching him play over the years. I didn't really know Monroe, although we had exchanged several sentences on the Madison Square Garden floor two years ago. I was filming a comic sequence for my movie, *Annie Hall,* in which certain actors, including myself, played basketball against the Knicks. The sequence was later cut from the film because it didn't come off funny enough, but I did get to meet Monroe, who said hello and mentioned that he had received a fan letter I once sent him. He said it had meant something to him and that he had carried it around and showed it to friends. I didn't believe him because, exposed as I am to gratuitous pleasantries all the time in my profession, I am not a trusting person.

That was two years ago and it was the first and last time I met or spoke with Earl Monroe for any reason. When I suggested writing about him, *Sport's* editors suggested I spend lots of time with him, at practice, in the Knick lockerroom, even travel with the team for an away game.

All these things seemed superfluous to me. My ideas on Monroe had nothing to do with getting the feel of the lockerroom, experiencing the smell of sweat, hearing the players curse, and all that rigamarole.

The truth was, I immediately saw myself cast in the role of the bespectacled, white, pseudo-intellectual trying to form a "heavy" thesis about a gift of grace and magical flair the black athlete possesses that can never be reduced to anything but poetry. I have always envied this gift and have often said that if I could live life over as someone else it would be wonderful to be Sugar Ray Robinson or Willie Mays. With my luck, however, I would undoubtedly wind up John Maynard Keynes.

Assured finally that Monroe was thrilled about the cover story and even invited by the great man to his house in eager anticipation of a long chat, I agreed to meet him for a few hours on the weekend. Of course, I knew there was also the outside chance that when I met the magician Earl Monroe he would be disappointing. This has happened to me before when I've met famous people whose work I've loved. Not every time. Not with Groucho Marx, for instance, but with certain other comedians and film directors who shall remain nameless. I did meet another magician who did not disappoint me. It was Stan Musial and he is indeed an amateur magician. For hours, in the bedroom at a party in Washington, D.C. he delighted me with astounding card tricks. It was quite thrilling to see the menacing lefthanded slugger who had made my Brooklyn childhood miserable by lining one shot after another off of and over the rightfield wall at Ebbets Field, produce from his wallet the restored ace of spades that I had moments before torn up.

I didn't follow basketball until 1967. Baseball, boxing and the theater provided most of my entertainment. The theater has since become boring and there are no plays approaching the pleasure given by a good sporting event. Even a game against a last-place team holds the possibility of thrills, whereas in the theater all seems relatively predictable. Baseball remains a joy for me, but basketball has emerged as the most beautiful of sports. In basketball, more than in virtually any other sport, personal style shines brightest. It allows for eccentric, individual play.

Give the basketball to such diverse talents as Julius Erving, Kareem

Abdul-Jabbar, Walt Frazier, Rick Barry, George McGinnis, Dave Bing or Bob McAdoo, to name a tiny fraction, and you get dramatically distinctive styles of dribbling, passing, shooting and defensive play. There is great room in basketball for demonstrable physical artistry that often can be compared to serious dance.

So there I was in 1967 leafing through the sports section of a newspaper one day (I still read that section first) when I came across the name Earl Monroe. I had never heard of Monroe, knew nothing of his daily rookie brilliance, nor ever heard of his astounding feats at Winston-Salem. I just liked the name, free-floating, three syllables and euphonious to me. Earl Monroe. The name worked. (Years later, when I did a film called *Sleeper,* I named myself Miles Monroe. On me it was kind of a funny name.) I came across Monroe's name again every few days as I glanced over the basketball boxscores in a casual, disinterested way and noticed that he invariably led the scoring column.

Monroe 34, Monroe 36, Monroe 24, Monroe 28, Monroe 40! I was impressed by the consistent high numbers and repeated his name every now and then like it was a mantra. It still sounded musical. Earl Monroe. I think I even recall seeing a picture of him on the cover of *Sports Illustrated* that year and thinking he was very interesting looking. I was, and I don't know why, aware of Monroe in some special way. Although I didn't follow his sport much then, if someone had awakened me in the middle of the night and said, "Quick, name your favorite basketball player," I'd have snapped back: "Earl Monroe." This was probably his first working of magic on me, though I had no real idea of what Baltimore Bullet fans were witnessing and feeling each night when they saw him play and referred to him as The Pearl or Black Jesus.

The first time I saw Monroe, an actor friend said, "Come with me to the Garden tonight. I want you to see this guy. You'll like his style. It's real herky-jerky." That was in 1968. By then I was more interested in basketball and had begun following the Knicks a little. They had made the playoffs and had captured the imagination of New York. I went and saw Monroe score thirty-two points against Walt Frazier. This is Walt Frazier, mind you, who played the guard position as perfectly as it has ever been played and who was to be voted on the all-defensive team seven years running. Thirty-two points and

Frazier said, "I had my hand in his face all night. He shoots without looking."

I went the next night too and while the Knicks double-teamed Monroe at every turn, he tore the place up with a buzzer beater that he flipped in as he ran across the midcourt line at halftime, and he kept running right into the lockerroom.

My impressions of Monroe then? I immediately ranked him with Willie Mays and Sugar Ray Robinson as athletes who went beyond the level of sports as sport to the realm of sports as art. Seemingly awkward and yet breathtakingly graceful, with an unimpressive physique, knobby knees, and the tiny ankles of a thoroughbred race-horse, Monroe, in seasons to come, would put on exhibition after exhibition of simply magical shot-making. One sportswriter wrote that his misses are more exciting than most guys' baskets. It's point-less to describe Monroe on the court. It's been done a thousand times by good writers who try vainly to communicate in print the excite-ment with which he plays. They refer to his head fakes, shoulder fakes, spins, double pumps, stutter steps, hip shots, arms and legs fly-ing in different directions at once, but these things in themselves do not sum up the ferocious rush he gives the audience. After all, there are players like Nate Archibald, Dave Bing, Walt Frazier, Julius Erv-ing, Connie Hawkins, who have unusual grace, beauty and excite-ment, and who also dip and twist and toss their bodies one way while their arms move another way as they hang in space.

What makes Monroe different is the indescribable heat of genius that burns deep inside him. Some kind of diabolical intensity comes across his face when he has the ball. One is suddenly transported to a more primitive place. It's roots time. The eyes are big and white, the teeth flash, the nostrils flare. He dribbles the ball too high, but with a controlled violence. The audience gets high with anticipation of some new type of thrill about to occur. Seconds later he is mov-ing in aggressively, one on one, against a defender and you sense the man is in trouble. Monroe is suddenly double-teamed and now there are two men hanging all over him. Then it happens. A quick twist, a sudden move and he's by both men. Either that or a series of flash-ing arm moves cease with a lightning pass to a teammate he has never even bothered to look at.

It's amazing, because the audience's "high" originates inside Monroe and seems to emerge over his exterior. He creates a sense of danger in the arena and yet has enough wit in his style to bring off funny ideas when he wants to. He has, as an athlete-performer, what few actors possess. Marlon Brando is one such actor. The audience never knows what will happen next and the potential for a sudden great thrill is always present. If we think of an actor like George C. Scott, for instance, we feel he is consistently first rate, but he cannot move a crowd the way Brando does. There is something indescribable in Brando that pins an audience on the edge of its seats at all times. Perhaps because we sense a possible peak experience at any given moment, and when it occurs, the performance transcends mere acting and soars into the sublime. On a basketball court, Monroe does this to spectators.

I began watching the Baltimore Bullets, and while still a Knicks fan, always rooted for Monroe when Baltimore played New York. "We had no set offense," one Bullet player once said. "We gave the ball to Earl. He *was* our offense." The Bullets did very well with Monroe (not to mention such other great stars as Wes Unseld and Gus Johnson) and I followed his career like any dedicated fan. I was sorry I had missed his rookie year and his college games and I tried to imagine what he must have been like at that age, before the problems with his arthritic knees set in. Monroe is not overly fast these days, though he once was, but like the magician he is, he creates the *illusion* of spend. When he takes off with the ball and races the length of the court, he resembles an animated cartoon character whose feet never touch the floor. I recall a newspaper interview with Monroe after he had scored clusters of points against the Knicks in a playoff game, and he confessed to the desire to be a comedian. I thought, *A comedian? But why? Why would anyone want to be a comedian when he can do what he does?*

Then in 1971 he got traded to the Knicks. Naturally, I was happy to be able to watch him more often, but there were two uneasy questions. Could he play alongside Walt Frazier? Frazier was then the premier all-around guard in basketball and had set standards so high that years later when he might be off his game a fraction and could no longer single-handedly win games, the fans could not deal with it and turned on him. I found this unforgivable and it certainly says something about the myth of the New York sports fan.

In those days, however, Walt Frazier played with a serene brilliance that made it seem that he could steal the ball *whenever he wanted to,* dribble it behind his back and score at will. He was wonderful to look at (great posture, perpetual "cool"), dressed flashy off the court, drove a Rolls and got an awful lot of rebounds for a guard.

Monroe, who when he joined the Knicks reportedly said, "Man, I got two Rolls," was also used to being the cynosure of his team. He had never had to be overly concerned with defense and never had to share the limelight with anyone approaching Frazier's greatness. This didn't worry me, because I felt the two guards would be simply breathtaking together, which they indeed were. They played brilliantly in tandem. Frazier was the steadier of the two. He did everything perfectly. Monroe was, as always, the more dramatic and explosive one. Consequently, when Frazier dribbled up the middle you could count on your two points because of his smooth-as-satin style. When Monroe drove, his lust for danger took him in directions where he might get the ball slapped away or might miss a shot because of spectacular gyrations. Again, like Brando, Monroe takes risks, and while some fail, enough come off to make him an artist.

The second and more irritating question to me was, can Monroe fit into the flow of team play? Can he become part of that superb combination of Bill Bradley, Walt Frazier, Willis Reed, Dave DeBusschere, etc., that hits the open man, retains poise, and sooner or later grinds up opponents like a well-oiled machine? Some said Monroe would not be able to adjust. Others felt Monroe could learn to give off the ball, to play defense, to sublimate his brilliant one-on-one skills and contribute to this championship club. But I asked, why would anyone want that of him? After all, here is the single most exciting player in basketball, a solo performer. Do we really want him to abandon his individuality and become a cog in a machine. Would we ask Heifitz to become a sublimated member of the string section? Great Knick fan that I was, I would rather have seen the team set up Monroe for his dazzling solo feats than the other way around. Is winning so important that we can afford to sacrifice Monroe's essential gift to the game of basketball?

Now there were those who argued with me and said they derived more aesthetic satisfaction out of watching a five-man unit execute with the precision of the Knicks at their height. Nothing was more beautiful, they said, than the ball going from Frazier to Bradley, to DeBusschere, back to Frazier, to Reed for a basket. Well, what can I say? I don't agree. Perhaps because I'm a performer. Artistry like Monroe's does not come along often and I for one feel sacrifices must be made for art. It's great if the team wins (Baltimore did quite well with a Monroe-oriented offense), but if the price included the conformity of Earl Monroe to a patterned offense, I didn't like it.

The outcome we now know. Monroe learned defense. He modified his style in favor of team play. He scored fewer points. At other times, his irrepressible genius on the court asserted itself. The Knicks won with him until Reed and DeBusschere retired. Then Frazier and Monroe carried the offense. The team acquired other stars in Spencer Haywood and Bob McAdoo, but the Knicks have yet to jell. Monroe at thirty-two years old has emerged as the toast of New York's basketball fans because with the team's demise as a power, more and more they turned to his older one-on-one skills to get them out of jams.

While Knickerbocker problems seem to run deep, Monroe again burns brightly and enjoyed a great season in 1976–77. He has grown in all his skills and has returned to much of his own style play. The difference now is, that if a given night demands it, he can play defense, hand off, steal, and quarterback the team. He is now the Knick captain. He is also still the magician. He might play a game as he did on January 1 and take ten shots and not miss one. Or he might win the game with a clutch basket in the last three seconds or, in the final ten minutes, score sixteen of the Knicks' last eighteen points. These are just a few feats he performed last year. When the fans see him pulling off his warmup jacket they get ready for the closest thing to a magical experience. They sense nature will be defied in some way.

At precisely two PM, the appointed hour, I ring the bell of a fine old townhouse on New York's upper West Side. The name on the bell reads: Monroe. I am buzzed in and stand at the bottom of a staircase like a supplicant before Dr. No or the head of SMERSH. Suddenly an unbelievably beautiful woman descends the staircase and says with

confidence unseen since the days of Mae West, "Hi—I'm Earl's lady."
I smile, cough, look at my shoe tops, and mutter something that
sounds like, "Aha-un-eh." As usual, I'm right on top of things. "Earl's
not back yet. Would you care to wait?"

"Wait? Yes. Sure." The music from the rock station on the radio
is flowing through the house at a level that would drown out the takeoff of an SST. I follow this utterly devastating woman up the stairs.
The juxtaposition of our bodies causes me to think, my God, she's
packed into those jeans with an ice cream scoop. We sit opposite one
another and I manage to achieve maximum awkwardness in thirty
seconds. To call "Earl's lady" beautiful is an understatement. I writhe,
shuffle. She tells me her name is Tina and assures me Earl had some
errands but was looking forward to our meeting. The house is simply furnished and here and there are mementoes of the great man's
career. Plaques, photos, a game ball under glass, certificates of athletic achievement that bear the name Vernon Earl Monroe. (Vernon?)
I learn through conversation with Tina that the photos of beautiful
kids on the wall are Monroe's children from previous love affairs in
other cities. "He's a good father," she tells me. "He loves his kids."

A half hour goes by as I chat with Tina. I learn how they met: at
a discodance. I am told that Earl adores watching television. "There's
a set in every room in the house and they're on all day and night."
Tina tells me Earl eats lightly. Fish mostly. She says Earl took up tennis as a hobby a year or so ago and swiftly achieved tournament level
ability. I learn that Knick players don't fraternize with one another
that much, although they are friendly. An hour is gone. Still no Earl.
Tina says that Earl has two cars and, unlike Clyde, no chauffeur
because, "He's such a fantastic driver he could never have anyone
else drive him." She says Dr. J has acknowledged Earl as an inspira-
tion and model. Now and then the two phones ring and since they
are identical but with different numbers, Tina must hold her hand on
each instrument and feel it in order to tell which one is ringing.

"Earl's not here," she would tell various callers in her Mae West
style, "he's been de-tained." I learn Earl and Tina stay in a lot, play
board games, now and then dine late, sometimes around midnight,
though then they might hit a dance hall and stay out late. They generally keep to themselves. I ask about a story on Earl wherein he

quoted Descartes and Tina tells me, "He likes reading sports magazines mostly."

Hours have now gone by and we are out of conversation. Finally I must leave for another appointment. "Earl will be so disappointed he missed you," Tina says.

I back out the door, fumbling and apologizing, for what, I don't know. Then, walking home this sunny, Saturday afternoon, I think to myself, how wonderful. This great athlete is so unconcerned about the usual nonsense of social protocol. Unimpressed by me, a cover interview and all the attendant fuss and adulation that so many people strive for, he simply fails to show up. Probably off playing tennis or fooling with his new Mercedes.

Whatever he was doing, I admired him for his total unconcern. Tina said he would be very upset that he had missed me, but I knew it was not the kind of thing Earl Monroe would dwell on with the anguish of a Raskolnikov.

That night Earl scored twenty-eight points and had eight misses against Washington; the next day he tossed in thirty-one points against the same team.

I thought about how *Sport's* editors had relayed Monroe's enthusiasm about the prospect of our interview. I thought, too, that if I had missed an interview I'd be consumed with guilt. But that's me and I'm not a guy who can ask for the ball with the team down by a point, two seconds left on the clock and, with two players hacking at my body and shielding my vision, score from the corner. If I miss that basket and lose the game for my team, I commit suicide. For Monroe, well, he's as nonchalant about that tension-strung situation as he is about keeping appointments. That's why I'd tense up and blow clutch shots, while Monroe's seem to drop through the hoop like magic.

Tom Meschery

To Bill Russell

I have never seen
an eagle with a beard
but if there is
in some strange
corner of the world
and the Hindu
belief is true,
you will return
and beat your wings
violently
over my grave.

Bill Bradley

from *Life on the Run*

The money and championships are reasons I play, but what I'm addicted to are nights like tonight when something special happens on the court. The experience is one of beautiful isolation. It cannot be deduced from the self-evident, like a philosophical proposition. It cannot be generally agreed upon, like an empirically verifiable fact, and it is far more than a passing emotion. It is as if a lightning bolt strikes, bringing insight into an uncharted area of human experience. It makes perfect sense, but at the same time seems new and undiscovered. The moment in basketball depends on the blending of human forces at the right time and in the right degree. It goes beyond the competition that brings goose pimples or the ecstasy of victory. With my team, before the crowd, against our opponents, no one else but me can feel what it all means. It's my private world. No one else can sense the inexorable rightness of the moment. A back-door play that comes with perfect execution at a critical time charges the crowd, but I sense an immediate transporting enthusiasm and a feeling that everything is in perfect balance.

These moments require a childlike imagination. "We can only know as adults what we can only feel as children," says Leslie Fiedler. In those moments on a basketball court I feel as a child and know as an adult. Experience rushes through my pores as if sucked by a strong vacuum. I feel the power of imagination that creates a sense of mystery and wonder I last accepted in childhood, before the mind hardened. When a friend tells me that his son cries when I miss a last-second shot, I know how he feels. I cry a little, too. That's why ultimately when I play for anyone outside the team, I play for children. With them the communication of joy or sorrow rings true, and through the playing that allowed me to continue feeling as a child, I sense a child's innocent yearning and love.

Mark Shechner

Elgin Baylor

you had to see it

the leap
        sudden
        selfgenerated
            the moment
bursting
        into golden petals
        arch
        of the neck

ex-
tension of the arm

you just had
to see
    the feint
            leading
    to a takeoff
    arms
    lifting
            the whole flower
glorious
and the great re-
              lease
                of energy

you had
        to see
Baylor
        before his knees went

            how
            he could
            dance

John Ross

In the Beginning

— to Kareem Abdul Jabbar
after the fourth game of the 1989 N.B.A. Finals

In a waking dream,
the movie flies backwards,
You get smaller,
You jump higher,
Your skyhook
swoops through the net
every single time
you launch it.
First you have more hair,
then you have a lot more hair,
then you are bald again,
your mama bounces you
on her trick knee,
you learn how
to dribble backwards,
Magic wasn't even born yet,
Allah only a glint in God's Eye,
the hoops hung golden
from the heavens back then
and the Lord played H O R S E
with Beelzebub
while Adam went one on one

with Eve.
The score was knotted zip to zip
when you threw up your first wish
and swish the universe dipped into
negative overtime.
You were named
The Most Valuable Plasma
in The Firmament.
It was a far better ending
than this one.

Eric Nadel

The Most Damaging Punch
in Basketball History

The most damaging punch in basketball history was thrown on December 9, 1977, in a game between the Lakers and the Houston Rockets at the Forum in Los Angeles. Early in the third quarter, seven-foot center Kevin Kunnert of the Rockets and 6 feet 8 Laker forward Kermit Washington collided under the boards. As the teams moved upcourt, the two men shoved each other and began fighting. Washington landed a punch that stunned Kunnert and left him holding the side of his face.

Meanwhile, 6 feet 8 forward Rudy Tomjanovich, the Rocket's captain and best player, raced back to help his teammate. As Rudy arrived on the scene, Washington whirled and landed a roundhouse to the face that flattened Tomjanovich. Rudy dropped to the court unconscious, bleeding from the nose, mouth, and ears.

Referee Bob Rakel later said it sounded like someone had hit a concrete wall with a baseball bat. And while Houston coach Tom Nissalke called the blow "a sucker punch," Washington contended that he acted in self-defense, believing that Tomjanovich was leading a second wave of Houston attackers.

While Washington has always maintained that the punch was an honest mistake, the damage was unmistakable. Tomjanovich suffered a broken nose, a double fracture of the jaw, and a concussion, requiring three operations to rebuild his face. One of the surgeons said, "His face had to be rebuilt like a jigsaw puzzle." Rudy spent two weeks in the hospital, covering the mirrors with towels for several days so he would not have to see his own face.

Tomjanovich, who had been an All-Star four times in his eight years in the league, was lost for the rest of the season. At the time of the injury, he was averaging twenty-two points a game and one of the league's premier power forwards. What happened to Kermit Washington?

Four days after throwing the tragic punch, Washington was fined $10,000 by N.B.A. commissioner Larry O'Brien, the largest fine in sports history at that time. He was also suspended without pay for sixty days, which cost him an additional $50,000.

Tomjanovich sued the Lakers for failing to control the actions of Washington, who was known around the league as an "enforcer." The Rockets sued the Lakers for the loss of their captain, who missed fifty-three games. When the case came to trial in the summer of 1979, a federal court jury in Houston awarded Tomjanovich $3.3 million, which was even more than he asked for. The jury concluded that the Lakers had failed to adequately train and supervise their employee, and that Washington had acted with reckless disregard for the safety of others.

The Lakers appealed the ruling and eventually settled with Tomjanovich for an undisclosed sum. They also settled the lawsuit filed against them by the Rockets.

Tomjanovich was able to return to action ten months after the incident and played well, helping the Rockets make the playoffs. He retired as a player in 1981, with a career average of 17.4 points a game.

Tomjanovich says he does not relive the incident, that there are no flashbacks, since he never saw the punch coming. In many ways, the aftermath was tougher on Washington than it was on Tomjanovich.

At 6 feet 8 and 230 pounds, Washington was one of the strongest men in the N.B.A. But despite his reputation as one of the league's "enforcers," the Tomjanovich incident was the only fight he was ever involved in. In his five years in pro ball, he had fouled out of only four games, hardly what you would expect from an overly aggressive player.

In fact, Washington was popular with players around the league. An honors graduate in psychology from American University, Washington was sensitive and gentle off the court, a peaceful, caring man. In the words of Lakers general manager Bill Sharman, "Kermit is just the opposite of mean. He's almost timid away from basketball."

Yet it was Washington who unloaded the punch that he claimed was thrown in self-defense, "an honest, unfortunate mistake." It cost Tomjanovich fifty-three games and untold anguish. It cost Washington almost as much.

Kermit's fine and sixty-day suspension came at a time when he was having his best pro season, averaging 10 points and 9 rebounds a game as a role player off the Laker's bench. Washington received hate mail from all over the country, including racial slurs and death threats. He was hounded by crank telephone calls. All this, despite the fact that he constantly expressed sorrow over the incident and made several attempts to contact Tomjanovich—calls that were never returned.

Three weeks into the suspension, Washington was traded by the Lakers to the Celtics, and when he returned to action, he was booed everywhere he played. Despite averaging eleven points and ten rebounds with Boston, they traded him that summer to San Diego.

Ironically, his first game with the Clippers was against Houston, the first game for Tomjanovich since the injury. The two men guarded each other for an entire quarter without a handshake or a word spoken. They did discuss the altercation before a game two years after the incident, following the trial in which the Lakers had been found negligent for retaining a player with "a tendency for violence while playing basketball."

Washington was unable to shake that reputation for years. But this supposedly malicious player later devised what may have been the most compassionate undertaking in N.B.A. history.

Late in his career, in 1983, Washington was attempting a comeback with the Portland Trail Blazers after injuries had limited him to just twenty games the previous year. In a stunning request, Washington asked the Trail Blazers for permission to give away his entire salary to fans who had fallen on hard times and needed the money to get back on their feet. Unfortunately, Washington's comeback attempt failed because of knee and back problems. But his program of assistance survived, with Trail Blazer players and management contributing.

Portland general manager Stu Inman said, "The world is going to be a better place because Kermit Washington walked through it." Unfortunately, one tragic moment kept most of America from ever knowing that.

Peter DeJonge

Talking Trash:
The Art of Conversation in the N.B.A.

John Starks and Reggie Miller had been in each other's face for two and a half games, shooting jump shots and their mouths with equal conviction. According to the prevailing customs of the National Basketball Association, outplaying an opponent is no longer sufficient—you have to rub his nose in it like an untrained puppy. As the third game in the first round of the Eastern Division playoffs wore on, Starks's teammate on the New York Knicks, Charles Oakley, began referring to Miller as "Cheryl," the name of his older and, until recently, more celebrated Olympic-basketball-playing sister. For his part, Miller, a guard with the Indiana Pacers, was punctuating his long-range jumpers with obscene references to a report that the Knicks, confident of ending the series that night, had checked out of their hotel before the game.

On this night, Cheryl's baby brother would get the last laugh. Eight minutes into the third period, Starks, who had just scored a basket to put the Knicks up 59—57, chased down Miller and fired a head butt into the Pacer's flapping chin. Starks was immediately ejected from the game and, with Miller leading the way, the Pacers were on the way to a rout.

With the playoffs driving to a climax, many of the most memorable matchups have been verbal rather than athletic, and 1993 seems destined to be remembered as the year of Trash Talk—the various gratuitous ways by which players distract, intimidate and infuriate their opponents. No longer limited to an occasional aside, inaudible to all but the players and invisible to the average fan, trash talking has become an inextricable part of the game, a permanent doubling of the stakes of humiliation.

In the current virulent strain, what is said is often secondary to the broad mime of self-congratulation and put-down, directed as much at television cameras as at beaten defenders. Media-conscious players, like the Charlotte Hornets' Dell Curry, sometimes suggest telecasts that embarrassed opponents might check for replays. "That's the Play of the Day," Curry told the Miami Heat's Bimbo Coles after his blocking his shot. "Tune in." The reference was to a nightly feature on CNN.

In the playoffs alone, we've seen and heard the Yugoslavian-born New Jersey Net, Drazen Petrovic, spewing his heavily accented trash all over Gerald Wilkins of the Cleveland Cavaliers, Phoenix's Cedric Ceballos jawing with Laker veteran James Worthy, Houston's Vernon Maxwell and Kenny Smith going back and forth with the Clipper's Ron Harper and Mark Jackson ("Don't you ever lay off on me," screamed Smith at Jackson while wagging an admonishing finger, after hitting an uncontested three-pointer).

Asked to name the most loquacious players in the league, Miami's Glen Rice doesn't know where to start. "It's not like there's one player who stands out like a sore thumb," he says. "Everybody, one way or another, says something."

Among those talking are rookies, veterans, big men, little men, superstars, guys on ten-day contracts, the chronically insecure and the profoundly self-confident. Last year, the Knicks had two trash-talking point guards, one of whom, Greg Anthony, is a registered Republican and another, Mark Jackson, who is a born-again Christian. The practice, like the N.B.A. itself, is an overwhelmingly black phenomenon, cultivated in inner-city neighborhoods and playgrounds, where it is called "signifying," "playing the dozens" and "selling woof tickets." Yet it is generally agreed that the most devastating practitioner was a shy, slow-footed low-jumping, fair-skinned man named Larry Bird who grew up in French Lick, Ind. (pop. 2,087).

As quickly as it's filtering down from the league's one-named superstars, it's flooding up even faster from below. "In the N.C.A.A. tournament, it looked like Dean Smith was one of the only coaches whose players weren't yammering," says the Bulls coach, Phil Jackson.

It's the youngest players in the league who are taking what had been a discreet form of gamesmanship and pushing it to the edge. A frontier of sorts may have been reached in a playoff game last month, when Seattle's Shawn Kemp performed an obscene dance while hanging from the rim after dunking off an alley-oop pass over Utah's Mike Brown. "Before, players did it for the win," says Doc Rivers of the Knicks. "Now, it's more of a show thing, to pump yourself, pump your own image. I hope it's not because they think they can get an endorsement deal."

The trash itself tends to be repetitive: "You tell people they can't check you," says Rice, "and on defense you tell them they don't even have a reason to have the ball in their hands." Only rarely are the exchanges as honed as the ones in the hit 1992 film "White Men Can't Jump," a celebration of playground basketball in which players say things like "Elevator's going to eleven, but I'm dropping you off at five" or "I'm going to take you to the hoop, and then I'm going to take your girl."

Nevertheless, trash talk can accommodate a range of purposes and shadings from good-natured competitive camaraderie to calculated campaigns of terror. After an N.B.A. All-Star Game, the Hornets' Larry Johnson, disgruntled over the scant playing time he received from the East (and Knicks) coach, Pat Riley, vowed to get eighty points in his next game against New York. "Maybe eighty stitches," responded the Knicks' Charles Oakley, who stayed in Johnson's face right through to the waning moments of the teams' playoff series, which the Knicks took in five games.

Trash can be a crude form of foreign relations. In last year's Olympics, as the Dream Team was warming up to play Angola, Charles Barkley spotted the players from several European teams in the stands. "Watch," he told them. "We're going to kick their butts. And when we're done, we're going to kick yours."

For Petrovic, who one night had to listen to Starks accuse him of complicity in the World Trade Center bombing, trash talking is a way of answering the xenophobic enmity his herky-jerky Eurostyle seems to provoke. "A guy start talking to you, you have to talk back," he says, "because they're going to take something away from your game."

In the increasingly stratified N.B.A., where a handful of super-stars get all the tout and everyone else plays for their two or three million a year, talking trash can be a way of maintaining a little dignity. "When you play a marquee player like Shaquille O'Neal, for instance, if you block his shot, you want to let him know," says Terry Mills, a 25-year-old Detroit Piston. "Don't come in here with that. Who do you think I am?"

For superstars, trash talk is a way of maintaining hegemony. When Dikembe Mutombo was blowing him smoke in Denver last year, Michael Jordan stepped to the foul line and asked, "Hey rook, can you do this?" and hit a foul shot with his eyes closed. And when Alonzo Mourning, following a Hornet victory over the Bulls in Chicago, started talking about how the Hornets were now at the same level as the two-time champions, Jordan came into Charlotte, dunked the ball in his face and then wouldn't even look at him. Jordan says that in his first few years, whenever he had to switch off and defend Larry Bird, the Celtics star would say, "I got a little one on me, give me the ball."

These days, initiating any kind of dialogue with Jordan is per-ceived as unseemly social climbing. "If it's people that I know, hope-fully Carolina guys or whoever that I have been around, I don't have a problem with it," he says. "But if it's people that I don't know, I won't say much and let my game do the talking." Early in the sea-son, after Seattle's point guard Gary Payton said something rash, Jor-dan stole the ball from him on three consecutive trips up court.

It's not always what's said, it's who says it. If Danny Ferry of the Cleveland Cavaliers were to say, "You can't stop me," it would be laughable in one sense. But when Manute Bol, a 7-foot-7 former Dinka tribesman says it, as he often does, it's hilarious. It was Bol who, after blocking shot after shot in Portland one night, turned to the home bench one night and asked, "Don't you get cable up here?"

Trash can be directed at opposing coaches—Payton recently told the new Timberwolves coach, Sidney Lowe, to "shut up you little Smurf"—and in the case of Jordan, Barkley and the Nets' Derrick Coleman, it has frequently been directed at teammates. In the heat of battle, Golden State's point guard, Tim Hardaway, drives to the hoop while emitting a paralyzing, full-throated "Oh, yeah."

But for the most part, trash talking is a way of hanging on to one of the world's most coveted jobs. "If you intimidate a guy, you've done your job," says Xavier McDaniel, a muscular small forward acquired by the Celtics from the Knicks before the season. "Sometimes you got to knock the heck out of someone. Sometimes you got to give hard fouls. Sometimes you got to talk."

"The biggest trash talker of all is gone," says a wistful M. L. Carr, who unabashedly hacked and talked his way though a ten-year career with the Pistons and Celtics. The preeminent woofer, says Carr, was Larry Bird, his former Celtics teammate and the man who by all accounts did more to unravel his opponents verbally than anyone who ever lived.

Not that Bird pioneered the form. In "Tall Tales" (an oral history of the early N.B.A.), Terry Pluto described how an earlier Celtic, Sam Jones, liked to torment Wilt Chamberlain by saying "too late baby" as he released a soft high jumper over the center's outstretched fingers. Just how annoying this got to be is revealed in a 1962 photograph in which Jones is fending off Chamberlain with a wooden stool. Even the cool, poised championship Knick teams of the late 60s and early 70s had a junk talker in Dick Barnett.

Bob McAdoo, an unstoppable shooter for seven different teams in the 70s and 80s, helped popularize "face"—the "in your" being understood—which he snapped off as the ball was spinning through the hoop. George Gervin, a scoring champion for the San Antonio Spurs, for whom he is now an assistant coach, would scold defenders: "You spanked me once, now I got to spank you twice."

But no one could get into your head like Bird. He would start softening up his man in the tunnel before the game, telling him: "I think I feel really good tonight. I think I might go for about 50." As the game wore on, he would lay out an escalating verbal assault that might start with his defender's lack of athletic ability and progress to unkind assessments of his masculinity and his girlfriend's attractiveness. "Bird was degrading," says Parish, grimacing. "He'd make it real personal."

What made Bird untouchable was the seamless connection between his dribbling and babbling, as if his tongue were one more incredibly coordinated limb. As he backed his defender down, Bird would matter-of-factly tell him where they were going and what was going to happen when they got there, going on to explain that his being able to do exactly what he wanted, and the defender being helpless to do anything but watch, was the reason for the huge discrepancy in their salaries. In the middle of this combination radio play-by-play and TV color commentary, without any telltale grunt, the ball would be flying toward the basket with the concluding remarks: "Don't even turn around. It's all net." Another Bird ploy was to shoot and score while yelling at a teammate for setting such a horrible pick.

There was nothing good-natured about Bird's trash. Matched against Julius Erving when Erving was at the end of his career and Bird in his prime, Bird twice provoked the gentlemanly Erving into fights. On one occasion, he repeated their respective totals for the game—"36–5, Doc, 36–5"—until Erving's fingers had to be pried from Bird's throat.

For Bird, trash talking was a remarkably graceful way both of acknowledging he was playing a black man's game and announcing that he had come to take his place in it. In an interview after his retirement, Bird described a pickup game twenty years earlier at his college, Indiana State: "I always went to the gym and practiced on my own game, and in the middle court—I always called them brothers— all the brothers would play and the only way you could get in the game was if you picked a team and you was up or whatever. So I never played with them, I just worked on my game by myself. One day they didn't have enough players, so somebody asked me to play. So I went over and all of a sudden everybody's eyes were popping and the next day I got to the gym, they all turned and said, 'There's that guy I was talking about, watch him play.' That's the first time I ever knew that I got respect from the black player. In the pro league, I had to do the same thing, over and over. I knew that and I did it, in a way that I thought was best.

Whether all the talking has made the league more violent has been debated all year, particularly after a late-season brawl between its two winningest teams, the Phoenix Suns and the Knicks, and separate incidents that resulted in one-game suspensions for Michael Jordan and Shaquille O'Neal. "It's something the league is looking at very closely," says Rod Thorn, the N.B.A.'s vice president of operations and chief disciplinarian. "We're starting to call some technicals. Maybe we should call some more." Although Thorn suspects that talking does lead to more altercations, he says trash talk was a factor in only one of seven serious fights all year, supporting the players' contentions that hard fouls are more incendiary than words.

Former players and coaches seem to take trash talking the most personally. Like older people everywhere confronted with a youth movement they don't understand, they shake their heads and wonder whatever happened to common courtesy and decency. "The people who have been around the league a long time, I think are unanimous that they are sick and tired of this trash talking," says Hubie Brown, who as a coach would challenge suspected drug abusers on his team to fistfights and is wound so tight he seems perpetually on the threshold of apoplexy.

"There were things you just didn't do," says Paul Silas, who in his lengthy N.B.A. career doubled as a rebounder and a "cop," one of the players on each team responsible for enforcing an unwritten code of conduct that barred things like embarrassing a player or undercutting him as he went to the basket. "I don't see that anymore."

Brown concurs. "The days of the cops are gone, and it's a shame, because they kept everything under control."

And while no one has proved that trash talking leads to more fighting, it's obvious to veterans that the league's severe crackdown on fighting has encouraged more talking. "It's like nah-nah nah-nah, you can't punch me or you'll get fined $100,000," says Carr, who recalls a stretch in his second year when the Pistons got into five fights in six games. One night, Carr says, he took a swing at Tom Boerwinkle, the enormous and plodding center for the Chicago Bulls, and missed. "He didn't see it, or he would have killed me. So I slapped him on the butt, and said, 'Come on big guy, let's go break it up.'"

It's hard to find any coach who likes trash talk. "It works against everything you're trying to do," says the Knicks' Riley. "What players have to understand is that the game is about control more than anything. You got to want to win more than you want to talk. You got to want to win more than you want to fight."

Yet when trash talking fits a team's style of play as well as it does the Knicks, one wonders how vociferously Riley really opposes it.

True, he benched Starks for two games and Greg Anthony and Anthony Mason for one, after a trash talking blowup with their ex-teammate Mark Jackson in Los Angeles early in the season. But he wasn't trying to rein in Xavier McDaniel when he was battering and taunting Scottie Pippen into submission in last year's vicious playoff series with the Bulls.

The league itself has been largely mum on the matter. In the last decade, the N.B.A., long considered too black to attract a mainstream audience, has prospered by giving middle-class whites, desperate for some semblance of a connection to black America, a series of un-threatening yet bigger-than-life superheroes called Magic, Michael, Charles and Shaquille. In many ways, trash talking, a genuine form of black culture, fits right into this scheme. It's colorful. It's over the top. It plays great in snippets on the nightly news.

Among the other major sports, trash talk is a factor only in the National Football League, which once outlawed excessive celebrations after touchdowns and big plays. Stung by articles calling it the "No Fun League," football dropped the ban last year. Now, the league penalizes only "flagrant acts or remarks that deride, mock or embarrass an opponent."

The sneaker manufacturers, whose fortunes are so closely linked to the N.B.A.'s, have embraced trash talking. "The shoe companies say, 'Let's make our shoe the street-est, blackest shoe out there,' because the kids want to be like the city kids," says Doc Rivers. "They want to dress like them, talk like them, everything except live in the same neighborhood."

Virtually every basketball sneaker spot has a trash element. "Come Strong or Don't Come at All" screams one ad. Another features the Charlotte Hornets' Larry Johnson as a 250-pound, moustached, gold-toothed, trash-talking grandma. "I throw elbows," says Johnson in drag. "A lot. I step on your feet. I will hold you. Basically, I will work you till you die."

"In my opinion, all it is a bunch of immature guys showing off," says the point guard of the Orlando Magic, Scott Skiles, furiously working on a wad of gum as he sits in one of the chartreuse seats beside the court in Charlotte before a crucial late-season game against the Hornets. "It's rookies who think they're bigger than their game and bigger than the team they're on. So many of the guys now are built up beyond belief in high school. Then they get to college and their coaches don't have the nerve to say anything to them, and then they come into our league. I'm from the old school. I think you should go out, play hard, and keep your mouth shut."

With his receding hairline, combative jaw and pale squat body packed into unfashionably tight shorts, Skiles looks more like a frustrated gym rat, not an N.B.A. starter making three million dollars a year. In fact, Skiles was the model for the unprepossessing white ringer in "White Men Can't Jump."

"It's a nightly thing," continues Skiles. "How long is it going to be before every single play needs some kind of trash talking or celebration?"

Stretching in a corner of the court fifteen feet away stands Skiles' backcourt teammate Nick Anderson, a fourth-year player and the team's second-leading scorer after O'Neal. Anderson, whose relaxed regal bearing makes him look taller than his listed 6 feet 6 height, has a diamond stud in his right ear, the thinnest wisp of a mustache and slightly hooded eyes.

Trash talk, says Anderson, who grew up in one of the most dangerous neighborhoods in Chicago, is part of the game: "It's all in the play. You got these talented young guys like Shaq and Alonzo coming in the league, guys with a lot of skill, doing well, and they want to set a tone for themselves, let the other guys know, 'Hey, I'm here.' I think it's good. I'm all for it."

Doesn't it make the atmosphere on the court a lot nastier? "I think it makes it a lot more fun," he replies. Well, how does he like it when some guy dunks on him and starts screaming in his face? "Don't get dunked on and it won't happen."

Anderson's sentiments were echoed by almost every other player, from rookies like Mourning to 17-year-veteran Robert Parish of the Celtics. Far from poisoning the atmosphere on the court, they say, trash talking lightens things up and makes everybody play harder.

"I think it's motivating," says the thirty-nine-year-old Parish. "It gets the guy who is talking motivated, and hopefully it ticks off the other guy and gets him motivated. I know if someone talked trash to me, I'd want to kick his butt."

And just as Skiles is nostalgic for the game he remembers growing up in Plymouth, Indiana, where basketball is a kind of joyless religion, black players feel the pull of the game as they recall it on ghetto playgrounds. Says Anderson: "The areas we come from, the inner-city areas, a guy gets on the playground court, it's 'You can't check me, you never have, you never will.' You know we've been listening to that for years."

As fans started to file into the enormous new arena, and as chubby dancers, tiny acrobats, and two Hornet mascots entertained them, it wasn't hard to see why black players feel such a proprietary allegiance to the playground culture of their game. Although the league is three to one black, the fans are almost all white and the games are played in arenas—like this one—located as far as possible from the dangerous neighborhoods that produce the players.

Ten minutes into the game, the nearly seven-foot Mourning receives a perfect pass from Muggsy Bogues and throws it down so hard on the late-arriving Anderson that Anderson is sent sprawling on his back while Mourning dangles from the rim. Mourning then drops into a crouch over the still-prostrate Anderson, pretends his hands are pistols and furiously pumps them back and forth like Yosemite Sam, as the crowd goes bonkers.

Jeff Coplon

The Right Call

Last April 6, Earl Strom, a stocky, silver-haired man of sixty-two, stepped onto the court at Madison Square Garden to officiate at a game between the New York Knicks and the Philadelphia 76ers—a group of ambitious young men who were generally half his age and almost half again his size. For Strom, the dean of National Basketball Association referees, this would be the last of more than two hundred nights on the job at the Garden. Over the past thirty-three years, he had seen basketball evolve from a waltz-paced and virtually all-white game played by two-hand set shooters into the gliding, anti-gravitational, inner-city-inspired version of the sport, which made pro basketball one of the growth industries of the 1980s. Strom had presided over the game's greatest teams and most incandescent players, and had also made a little basketball history himself. Had he been a player of equivalent stature, or even a coach, the evening might have lent itself to sentiment: a heartfelt introduction to spur the fans into a standing ovation; a ceremony at half-time with gifts from the Retirees' Catalogue (a rocking chair, a Lincoln Town Car); a chorus of long goodbyes from the guys who knew him when. But a referee remains isolated even in his valedictory, and not a word about Strom's leave-taking would pass the PA announcer's lips. They would have to miss him after he was gone.

It was a bad time for nostalgia, in any case. The six-month regular season had come down to its last few weeks, and the all-important playoffs—"money time," in Magic Johnson's phrase—loomed. Both the Knicks and the 76ers were playoff-bound, but there all likeness ended. After struggling since February, New York craved what had been depressingly rare of late—a win over a good opponent—to help it regroup for the postseason. The Sixers, meanwhile, had won eight straight games and flown to the top of the Atlantic Division. They were eager to kick a Knick or two while the New Yorkers were down—a desire strengthened, no doubt, by the memory of the 1989 playoffs, when the Knicks had celebrated a three-game sweep against Philadelphia by sweeping the court with a push broom.

From the moment Strom tossed up the ball at center court for the opening tap, it was evident that this game had "playoff intensity" as the sportscasters say. The pace was fast, the errors few, and the physical contact unbridled. Most of this contact was, if not strictly legal, at least within the NBA's usual limits: a crash against an opponent's hip and thigh to carve some turf closer to the basket; a tug at his jersey or waistband, the better to keep him earthbound; even the occasional push (applied discreetly, at the small of the back) to force a man out of the play. But midway through the first quarter, with the Knicks owning a six-point lead and the ball, New York's Patrick Ewing sidled over to cut off the Sixers' Charles Barkley and thereby free a Knick forward on offense. This was a moving pick—technically a foul but often overlooked by the officials. Unhappy with the obstruction, Barkley threw Ewing to the floor.

Ewing is listed at seven feet and 240 pounds, and isn't shy about throwing that weight around. Barkley, six-five and 250, is famous for his raw power, startling speed, and manic flair. Neither man is much good at retreating, and it was no surprise when Ewing jumped up to challenge Barkley. The two shoved each other once, then again, and Ewing went sprawling to the floor a second time. Other players stepped in to intercede, and, just as the incident seemed to be over, into the fray jumped a third large man: Charles Oakley, the Knicks' resident enforcer, who'd been shelved with a broken hand, and was watching from the bench in his street clothes. Glowering, he moved toward Barkley and appeared, as the league office noted when it later fined Oakley $1,500, to be "serving as other than a peacemaker." (Barkley was fined the same amount, for "instigating the altercation," and Ewing was dunned $500 for "adding to the fight.")

Earl Strom had enough. He had already whistled Barkley for a technical foul, or "T'd him up." Now he did the same for Oakley, and summarily threw him out of the arena; Strom pointed dramatically toward the locker room several times to make sure that Oakley and everyone else got the point. Then he called the players from both teams into a huddle and launched into a profanity-laced scolding, loud enough for their coaches to hear. "I told them that people had paid money to see the greatest players in the world, not to see a bunch of hoodlums out on the floor, punching and shoving," Strom recounted to me after the game. "I told them that I was going to toss the next guy who as much as raised his hand to scratch his head."

It was a classic Strom solution. A less experienced or less confident referee might have overreacted and bounced Barkley from the game as well, thereby compromising the 76ers' chances and damaging the show. But Strom had managed to restore order while keeping the teams' stars in action. His masterstroke was the ejection of Oakley—a strong statement with no effect on the game's outcome. And by issuing *two* technicals Strom canceled the free throws that such fouls ordinarily call for, and dodged another potential distortion of the final score. The play resumed with no loss of fervor and no further incidents. The Knicks won, as they deserved to. And Strom packed his black leather uniform bag and moved on to his next assignment, in Charlotte—another stop on a mostly unacknowledged farewell tour.

"I like Barkley," Strom told me a few days later. "He has a lot of enthusiasm, and he does a lot of things out of his anxiousness to perform so well—he's not a vicious individual." Many NBA referees privately admire some of their more wayward charges. But in Strom these feelings seemed to run deeper—toward affection, even protectiveness.

Though Strom is old enough to be a rookie's grandfather, he has kept a young man's looks, save for a few mild furrows in his forehead and some faint crow's-feet around his eyes: his hair is still thick and bristly; his eyebrows are bushy and black. Strom's complexion reddens when he is provoked or exerting himself, and he has deep-set hazel eyes, which flash in a moment's heat. In civilian life, he frequently wears aviator glasses, which soften his face, but on the court he wore contacts, and his features came at you in waves: fleshy nose, full mouth, large teeth, and, not least, magnificent lantern jaw. When he confronted an obstreperous coach or player, that jaw was a jutting edifice—a target that could never be touched. (He was punched just once in the line of duty: it happened more than twenty years ago, when Richie Guerin, then with New York, swung at an opponent and struck the referee instead.) Strom is spreading slightly about the middle, but his body remains firm and compact, down twenty pounds since he began following a low-cholesterol diet six years ago. He has thick forearms and wrists, large hands, and blunt, untapered fingers— the better to punctuate an unpopular call, something he did more flamboyantly than anyone else.

Strom is not a stylish runner (there is a slight shuffle to his gait, and his elbows flap out from his sides), but his legs, toned by years of off-duty jogging and by the five miles he covered during each game, are lean and sinewy. Over the past several years, those legs charted new ground every time he stepped on the court: no one else had refereed major league basketball for as long as Strom had—more than three thousand games, in five different decades, before he finally retired last June—and no one else had stayed active beyond his sixtieth birthday.

Strom has been called the Kareem Abdul-Jabbar of referees, but the analogy is inexact. While Abdul-Jabbar faded noticeably in the last year or so of his unparalleled career, Strom performed agelessly to the end. This past season, when he might have drawn Social Security, he worked as brilliantly as he had in the past—undaunted by nightly races with some of the fastest young athletes in the world, or by the mental strain of making a hundred instant judgment calls a game, or by an itinerary that exceeded seventy thousand miles of air travel annually. If he lost a step over the years—something that Strom denies ("I was *always* slow," he says)—he compensated with anticipation and positioning, and with an iron will to excel.

Strom's stamina is famous even by NBA standards. In June of 1985, during the fifth game of the Celtic-Laker championship finals, the temperature in Boston Garden reached ninety-seven degrees. Abdul-Jabbar took oxygen from a portable tank and still played miserably. Strom's partner, Hugh Evans, had to be replaced in the second half. Strom, then fifty-seven years old, just chugged on, never missing a beat, his face only slightly pinker than usual. Throughout his long career, Strom missed two games, and one of those came when a granddaughter had meningitis. In 1974, after an off-season knee operation, he came back at full tilt two months earlier than his doctor had projected; in 1977, he worked through the protracted NBA playoffs with a stress fracture in his foot. To this day, his sole concession to age remains a two-hour afternoon nap.

Strom was a star official in the early sixties, the era of Sid Borgia and Mendy Rudolph, celebrity referees who ruled the fledgling NBA with arrogance, theatrics, and impeccable judgment. He was *the* star official of the 1980s, despite the recent vogue for low-profile, by-the-book types—"robots" and "clones" in the eyes of scornful old-timers. Like one of those rare silent-film actors who thrived in the talkies, Strom lasted through six supervisors, five commissioners, three professional leagues, and two generations of players: he reffed Dolph Schayes, a star forward with Syracuse in the 1950s, and Dolph's son, Danny, now with Milwaukee. In 1988, when *USA Today* polled the NBA's players and coaches to choose the league's best referee, Strom won in a landslide, with 83 votes out of 193 cast. (His supporters mostly cited his consistency and his fairness, particularly toward road teams, but one player said he voted for Strom because Strom reminded him of his grandfather.) Finishing second, with 43 votes, was Jake O'Donnell, who had risen to prominence only after Strom jumped from the NBA to the American Basketball Association in 1969. Darell Garretson, Strom's supervisor, placed a distant third.

The results surprised no one. According to a prominent team official, Strom had been perennially rated first by the NBA's coaches and general managers in their reports to the league office. For twenty-five of his last twenty-six years in the league, he worked the NBA finals—the only mark of excellence that mattered to Strom, because it not only translated into national network exposure, not to mention more money (Strom is a free spender and an extravagant tipper, and a bulldog for every check), but reflected his unique and unconditional acceptance among coaches and players—the single overriding criterion for any official's success.

"He was the only ref who was relaxed enough or confident enough or crazy enough to come over a minute before tipoff and tell you his latest dirty joke, or ask you what you were doing after the game," Ted Green, a writer for the sports daily *The National,* said recently. "Most referees approach the business with some kind of fear—a fear of losing control, a fear of not being respected, of showing you're too human, of having anyone perceive you as being biased. Earl seemed to have got beyond all those fears."

In the last phase of Strom's career, his acceptance allowed him unparalleled flexibility in handling the occasional player challenge. Two years ago, in Milwaukee, the hometown Bucks coasted into the fourth quarter with a thirteen-point lead over the Phoenix Suns. But Paul Mokeski, then the Bucks' reserve center, was aggrieved. While boxing out his man and getting ready to rebound a Phoenix shot, Mokeski had been diverted by a forearm to the head. Even though the shot went in, and there wasn't any rebound, Mokeski wanted a call for such presumption, and he didn't get one. As he lurched upcourt toward his own basket, he complained to Strom, loudly enough to be heard at the courtside press table, "You're going to have trouble down there if you don't call that."

A typical NBA referee counters such threats in one of two ways. The first is simply to ignore the protest from behind a wall of authority—to say, in effect, "Don't bother me." The second, used if a player or coach carries on too long or abusively (a standard defined by the official's threshold at that moment), is to sting him with a technical, which brings with it a $100 fine. (In extreme' cases, when a player or a coach reacts to a technical with yet more verbal rage or with some other display—throwing a sports jacket on the court, for example— a second technical is called, grounds for automatic ejection and an additional, $150 fine.) There is a third course, a middle road, but it is expressly prohibited by the *National Basketball Association Official's Manual:* "No game is to be stopped while the ball is in play to warn a player or coach regarding his conduct. If any interruption is necessary then call a technical foul. Do not stop the action for a warning!"

That, however, is what Strom proceeded to do. He threw up a hand to freeze the clock, then met Mokeski at a spot near the Milwaukee foul line. "I'll start calling it, but I didn't see that one," he said.

"But it was very obvious," Mokeski insisted.

"It was obvious to you, but not obvious to me, O.K.?" Strom said, his nose nearly scraping the player's collarbone, and with a hint of menace in his voice.

The interruption of play had now stretched to fifteen seconds— an eternity in basketball—and Mokeski squirmed, and said, "Are you done?"

"No, I'm not," Strom replied. "The next time you open your mouth, I'm going to throw your ass out of here." He marched the ball out of bounds and blew his whistle to resume play. Officially, nothing had happened.

"Other guys would probably just call a technical," Mokeski said afterward. "They wouldn't talk to you or try to explain, but we get frustrated, just like the refs. At least, Earl gave me that much respect."

Quincy Troupe

A Poem for Magic

take it to the hoop, "magic" johnson
take the ball dazzling down the open lane
herk & jerk & raise your six feet nine inch
frame into air sweating screams of your neon name
"magic" johnson, nicknamed "windex" way back
    in high school
cause you wiped glass backboards so clean
where you first juked & shook
wiled your way to glory
a new style fusion of shake & bake energy
using everything possible, you created your own space
to fly through—any moment now, we expect your wings
to spread feathers for that spooky take off of yours—
then shake & glide, till you hammer home
a clotheslining deuce off glass
now, come back down with a reverse hoodoo gem
off the spin, & stick it in sweet, popping nets, clean
from twenty feet, right-side

put the ball on the floor, "magic"
slide the dribble behind your back, ease it deftly
between your bony, stork legs, head bobbing everwhichaway
up & down, you see everything on the court
off the high, yoyo patter, stop & go dribble, you shoot
a threading needle rope pass, sweet home to kareem

cutting through the lane, his skyhook pops cords
now lead the fastbreak, hit worthy on the fly
now, blindside a behind the back pinpointpass for two more
off the fake, looking the other way
you raise off balance into space
sweating chants of your name, turn, 180 degrees
off the move, your legs scissoring space, like a swimmer's
yoyoing motion, in deep water, stretching out now toward free
flight, you double pump through human trees, hand in place
slip the ball into your left hand
then deal it like a las vegas card dealer
off squared glass, into nets, living up to your singular nickname
so "bad," you cartwheel the crowd towards frenzy
wearing now your electric smile, neon as your name

in victory, we suddenly sense your glorious uplift
your urgent need to be champion
& so we cheer, rejoicing with you, for this quicksilver,
quicksilver
    quicksilver
moment of fame, so put the ball on the floor again, "magic"
juke & dazzle, shake & bake down the lane
take the sucker to the hoop, "magic" johnson,
recreate reverse hoodoo gems off the spin,
deal alley-oop-dunk-a-thon-magician passes
now, double-pump, scissor, vamp through space
hang in place & put it all up in the sucker's face, "magic"
johnson, & deal the roundball, like the juju man that you am
like the sho-nuff shaman man that you am
"magic," like the sho-nuff spaceman, you am

Bob Greene

from *Hang Time:*
Days and Dreams with Michael Jordan

"I do dream," he said one night.

We had been talking about that word—the word "dream"—and how often people seemed to use it when referring to him. The word came up so frequently in conversations when people were discussing him, it was almost as if the usage was involuntary. People would use it when trying to explain how he inspired young boys and girls: "Michael Jordan teaches children to dream." People would use it when endeavoring to make the point that no goal should be considered unreachable: "Michael Jordan shows that you should never give up your dreams." It had become a part of his job, really—he stood constant visible sentry as living, public proof that dreams can come true.

Not that he was entirely comfortable with it; who would be? And anyway, the dreams that were always talked about when his name was mentioned—dreams as inspirations, dreams as goals—were not literal dreams. A dream is something that happens when you aren't in control; a dream is what takes over when you have finally fallen asleep for the night, and you have had to temporarily give up the task of attempting to direct your life. A dream is not yours to determine.

"Most of the time I'll sleep right through the night," Jordan said. "But on the nights when I do have dreams, I wake up remembering them."

Most of the people who speak about Jordan and dreams are people who don't know him; that's another aspect of being who he is.

We'd been talking about this, and I had brought up the subject of real dreams. Dreams like the rest of us have, two-o'clock-in-the-morning dreams that sneak into our heads when we're lost to the world and can't help it.

"I have very few sports dreams," he said. "It's not very often in my dreams that I'll be playing sports. Usually when I dream it will be about problems."

He stopped, but I knew not to interrupt. With Jordan, so often people will not allow even a few moments of silence to form during a conversation. It's as if they fear he will walk away—as if they assume he is so busy and so constantly behind schedule that if a bubble of emptiness is permitted to build, he'll be gone. That's not how you would behave with anyone else. Think about it—think about talking to a friend and not permitting the conversation ever to take a breath. It's something else Jordan had reluctantly become accustomed to: knowing that he had given up the luxury of pausing in wordless contemplation.

I waited for him to continue.

"What would happen if I had a bad problem," he said. "What I would do about it. In the dreams there will be negative things. I've had dreams in which I am an alcoholic. What would I do? I'm an alcoholic in the dream, and because of it all the things I've worked so hard for will be taken away. I wake up numb after those dreams. Those are the kind of dreams when you want to make yourself wake up, because they trouble you so badly. In the dreams I'm making bad mistakes, and I'm not perfect, but I don't know what to do about it because I might lose everything."

What about good dreams? The kind of dreams that make you wake up with a smile on your face?

"Not really," he said. "Oh, sometimes I'll have a baseball dream."

Baseball?

"I'll dream I'm a baseball pitcher," he said. "In the dream, I'm all alone on the pitcher's mound. I'm a pitcher, but I also want to hit the ball. I'm not a pitcher who has to bat ninth. I'm a pitcher who bats third. And in the dream I will hear the crowd cheering for me, but the cheers are different than the cheers I hear every night on the basketball court.

"In the baseball dream, everyone has been saying that I can't do it—that I'm not good enough to be a good pitcher. And the cheers I hear are from people in the stands who are feeling: 'I hope he'll do well.'"

So in the dream he can actually discern a sound that's different from the sound he has grown accustomed to hearing in basketball arenas around the globe?

"In the baseball dream, they're more cheers of hope than cheers of expecting me to be good. They're cheering for me even though they don't know that I'll be good. No one knows if I'll do well, but they hope that I might. In the baseball dream, when I'm at the plate I don't hit home runs, but I don't strike out, either. I'm just a baseball player who always connects with the ball. Or when I'm pitching in the dream, I won't be pitching a no-hitter, but I will always protect my team's lead. And the crowd is on my side because they don't know too much about me, but they hope I'll do okay."

Is that the only sports dream he has? Is there any dream in which he's a basketball player?

"I don't dream about basketball anymore," he said.

Part Five

Warriors

John Ross

Al Attles: Flashes from the Past

"I went to Weequachic High School—now, if you're familiar with Philip Roth's *Portnoy's Complaint,* that was the high school. I grew up around Avon playground—it became the kind of playground where the great players hung out. You remember Sherman White? He was big around there, one of the best who ever played. Because of him, a lot of players came around—Oscar Robertson was one. . . ."

Sherman white, an All-American, was one of three Long Island University players banished from basketball after the infamous point-shaving scandals of 1950–51.

Al Attles, fifty-seven, once known as "The Destroyer" when he rampaged through N.B.A. backcourts, folds into an Oakland Coliseum seat and reminisces about his earlier years on the playgrounds of Newark, New Jersey.

"Even if you had a home playground, you played at a lot of others. One was in East Orange, a place called Elmwood. Guys like Maurice Stokes would come down and Tommy Heinsohn, he was from Union City, he played at the Colombia playground. Growing up back there you could always find a game and being right across from New York, you went over and played in Brooklyn or up at Rucker playground. You always found good players.

"There were a number of guys on the playground that never got an opportunity. There were some that were just as good as those who became stars. There were guys who were the best that ever played but they never got a chance to attend certain schools.

"I could have gotten a scholarship to St. John's, Manhattan, and

N.Y.U., but I wasn't as academically oriented as I should have been. My folks got on me, but still . . . that's why I went to a black school.

"I came out in '55, when all these big schools were de-emphasizing sports—it was right after the scandals of the fixes and you had to be academically inclined. So I went to North Carolina A&T in Greensboro.

"I grew up in New Jersey. You would hear all these things about what would happen to you if you crossed the Mason-Dixon line. This was the time of Emmet Till.

"In the South, the white schools didn't do much recruiting at black high schools. If Michael Jordan had been around then and wanted to stay in North Carolina, he couldn't have gone to the University of North Carolina because of the color bar. He would have had to go to a black school like A&T. That's why so many good ballplayers never got the attention. Sam Jones grew up in Laurenberg, North Carolina, but couldn't go to the University so he went to North Carolina College and he didn't get drafted. Finally, he got drafted out of the Army. Tennessee State was another school like A&T—that was Dick Barnett and that group.

"For every black player that got to make it, there were hundreds just as good who got away. You hear about Earl Manigault, Helicopter Knowles, Rabbit Walthough. Rabbit went to the Celtic camp just when Cousy got started—blacks weren't in the league yet, so he didn't make it. He just came at the wrong time."

Attles is asked about the lunch counter sit-ins conducted by the Student Non-Violent Coordinating Committee at the Greensboro Woolworth's in the winter and spring of 1960, his senior year at A&T. SNCC's historic Greensboro sit-ins became the model for similar direct action desegregation efforts throughout the South.

"It started with these four freshmen sitting around the dormitory playing cards. They couldn't understand why they couldn't go to Woolworth's, they could buy things but they couldn't sit down and eat there. That was the genesis and it hit the campus like wildfire, everyone was in the same frame of mind. We had these meetings on campus and anyone who felt they couldn't go out and deal with this in a non-violent way, they were asked to stay on campus. I mean, the last thing they needed was a confrontation. So the athletes had to stay on campus. You know how we are—if anyone spits on me or throws anything, I'm going to retaliate.

"It was a positive time, but it had a lot of nervous moments. The sit-ins had inflamed the surrounding area—if you wanted to walk uptown to go shopping, you had to go there in groups. They didn't want you to go by yourself. They warned you to look both ways before you stepped off the curb, because of the violence."

In 1960, Al Attles was drafted out of North Carolina A&T by the old Philadelphia Warriors. Thirty-four years later, he is a still a vital part of the franchise—its vice president and general manager, in fact. On a recent autumn afternoon, Attles sat in a darkened arena and talked about his rookie year with the franchise.

"There were only eight teams in the league when I came in. The teams were sort of a continuation of college. The Warriors had Paul Arizin from Villanova, Tom Gola from Lasalle, Guy Rogers from Temple, even Wilt Chamberlain—he was from Overbrook high school and they worked him in. He was considered territorial. They were all from Philadelphia and that way people came to see them continue the college thing.

"They didn't know me from Adam in Philadelphia so I knew it was going to be hard to make the team. I never thought I would—I mean, I'm not a name guy. My main competition is Pickles Kennedy, who had played at Temple and who was from Philly. This guy played with Guy Rogers—now this is a marquee name and he's got a bigger name around Philly. But when I got on the floor—I'm not going to say who was better—but I knew I could play with those guys.

"You know what kind of money you made? Remember, the A.A.U. was big then. You got a job in the off season if you played for the Peoria Caterpillars or the Phillips Oilers. In the N.B.A., it was different. You didn't have a starting salary. My first salary was $5,000 for seventy-nine games. My class was Jerry West, Oscar, Lenny Wilkins, Darrel Imhof. Jerry was the second player picked and he's getting $15,000.

"Now, I had passed the national teacher's exam and I was offered a job teaching school in Newark starting at $4,500. The difference was this: teaching was nine months and basketball was six—that thousand and three months made up my mind.

"But I would have played for nothing, you know. I mean, I never thought about playing in the N.B.A., but when I finally made the team, what came to mind immediately was that now I'm going to play in Madison Square Garden. That was all I thought about. If they had said, we'll pay your ticket to Penn Station and give you a meal every day and I could have played at the Garden, I would have done it . . . back then, money was not so much the issue. You might be making more than the average joe, but not that much more. Hey, I felt like I was one of eighty-eight people in the world selected to play in the league.

"A lot of players never got that opportunity. Look at the way it worked: in order for any player to come to camp now, he has to have a signed contract. We didn't. If I was running on the floor and blew out my knee, I'd get a ticket home if I was lucky. When I went to camp, I found out that I was the only player without a contract.

"We played twenty pre-season games—now it's only eight. We had two months of practice. Now they can only practice twenty-eight days. The final exhibition game [in 1960] was at the auditorium in St. Louis—it was more like a theatre. We had little rooms to dress in. Guy and I were dressing when Eddie Gottlieb, the owner, came up and said, 'I want to talk to you outside.

"Eddie says, 'We're going to keep you.' Remember, this was my first time I negotiated. think of the difference between 'We're going to keep you' and 'You made the team'—if they say you made the team, that means you got a leg up. But if they say they're going to keep you, it seems like you're not very good, but we're going to let you hang around.

"No one talks about it, but there was an unwritten rule on the number of blacks that could be on a team. The Warriors already had four—Andy Johnson, Guy, Wilt, and Woody Sauldsberry and they were all coming back. Woody had been rookie of the year. So Woody knows I'm coming and he hears I'm pretty good. Now, one of us is going to be traded and, lo and behold, Woody got traded to St. Louis right at the deadline. If you go back and look at the rosters of the teams back then, no team had more than four blacks on it. People will say there were no quotas, but you can have a quota without writing it down.

"See, when you try out for a team, you hope all the competition is across the board. It's one against twelve. But with this kind of quota system, the blacks are competing against each other for those four spots. This is how the league was controlled. First, it was the marquee value. And then how you looked. Sometimes, it had nothing at all to do with the way that you played.

"We came out here in '62. No one believed it was going to happen. All the players we had were Philadelphia born and bred. There was no way we were moving out of Philly. We didn't think about it when we went home for the summer and the radio and TV didn't report much on it. And then, all of a sudden, there it was on the sports page, the Warriors were going—and you didn't have anything to do with it. Our big thing was now we were going to make all this money. My second year, I'm making $7,000. Now I'm going to San Francisco and they're going to double, triple our salaries. But it didn't quite work out that way all of a sudden. But eventually it did raise the ceiling because it spread the country. It opened the coast as a new market. The move laid down a base for the whole network of teams on the West Coast.

"This building right here—we sell it out every night now. That was Franklin Mieuli's vision when he bought the team, but it took him from 1962 till '86–'87 to turn the corner. I mean, we used to play here with 8,000 people in the house—now you can't buy a ticket. Where's it going to stop? It's a paradox. You look at the economy— these are bad times. But whenever there are bad times what is able to sustain is entertainment and sports. People complain, but they still get to the game. People want to be a part of it, no matter what it costs.

"Hey, look at professional football. Thirty years ago, Franklin Mieuli had a piece of the '49ers and you could go to Kezar five minutes before game time and buy a ticket. Go sit any place you wanted. It's not that way now.

"You guys got me talking now. Today, people will pay what it takes. That's how Chris Webber's going to get paid. Look at the marketing. In '74–'75 we win the championship and late that summer, someone had a great idea: we needed to sell something. So what we did was take a picture of the trophy and put it on a shirt. On the back, they put all the players' names, from Butch Beard on down, and they sold them at the game—this was the only thing you could buy as a souvenir of the championship. I can go downstairs right now and get our catalogue. We have golf club heads, pencils, even baby booties. They all say 'Golden State Warriors' on them. It's a gold mine.

"Before we came over to Oakland, we played at the Richmond Auditorium, the San Francisco Civic Center, the Cow Palace, down in San Jose. When we first came out here, we had home games in Omaha, in San Diego, San Jose, the Civic. It was small, but you were glad to be there.

"Gottlieb first and then Mieuli used to make their payroll for the season on the exhibition games. Particularly with the Dipper as the attraction. We'd go on a midwest tour with the St. Louis Hawks every year. You'd draw so well during the pre-season, you'd make your payroll by the time the season came around.

"One time in Missouri, they hadn't given Franklin the guarantee yet, so we get a phone call: stay in your rooms until we get the cash. They had to wake up the mayor and judge before we suited up.

"Eddie Gottlieb used to have games up there in Pennsylvania Dutch Country. They'd give us shoo fly pie, whatever. It was a dollar to see Wilt Chamberlain—here's your only opportunity to see a legend play even if it was just a practice. We'd make like it was a real game.

"We came over to Oakland in '69. Up until then, we played about thirteen games in the East Bay. The fact is that until you have a place where you play all your games, you're not really a professional team. See, even in Philly, we played games all over the state—the game in which Wilt scored a hundred was in Hershey, Pennsylvania.

"I became a player-coach in '69–'70. It is a concept that has only worked for Bill Russell. Why? Because Russell the coach had Russell the player to coach.

"The reason player-coaches came about was to save money. You saved a coach's salary. One guy did two jobs. You had to have someone who knew the players, played with them. I agreed to do it for one season. But I never tried to make it work. I told them from the first day, I was either a player or a coach. The only time I would put myself in was to take the extra foul—there used to be a rule, it was a terrible rule, that you had a foul to give so you'd send someone in to foul.

That's what I would do—it wouldn't hurt me and it wouldn't embarrass the players. It was a joke.

"I turned down the job a lot of times. Finally, I took it under the stipulation that there were thirty games left in the season and I said I'd take it for those games. Then, I'd go back to playing. That was the agreement I had with Franklin. We did just like we'd been doing after I became coach. We kept losing. We were eight and twenty-two. It was the end of the season, way past trade deadline. I was stuck with the players I had. I told Franklin I'd come back only because those guys had worked so hard for me. They never quit. And the next year, we made the playoffs and that started it.

"I coached for a long time. I enjoyed it while I was doing it, but when you walk away from it, you have no desire to go back. John Madden asked me once, did I miss it. He had walked away from the Raiders right around the same time I got out. Nobody knows when you've had enough but you."

Did you win the championship too early? Attles is asked.

"Probably. I never said it that way but I won it in four years. I had been on the team fourteen years by then."

Al remembers his championship team: "Phil Smith, Jamal Wilkes, Frank Kendrick. They were in their first year. Jeff Mullen, he had maybe fifteen years in the league. The rookies didn't understand that you don't win championships every year. Jamal was out of U.C.L.A., he won every year. For him, it was a carryover to win the championship.

"Winning the championship, that was fun. Those guys were committed. We had fourteen people, twelve players, two coaches. We played a lot of people each game. But, most importantly, we were all on the same page. They liked each other. That's not necessarily a prerequisite for winning. But they banded together because everyone kept saying these guys weren't very good. They never believed it. They pulled together and they got better and better.

"Were we a better team than the Bullets? No. They beat us, they won sixty games, we won only forty-eight. But if you win a series, then you are the best if that series is the finals. I remember we won game three of the finals against them at the Cow Palace. Mike Riordan took a shot that went in and out. I remember flying back East right after. I never once said we'd win the championship. I just told them if they won one more game, they would achieve something no one ever thought we were capable of.

"Regardless of how they looked at us, it's in the record books now. The winners of the 1974–75 championship will always be the Golden State Warriors. No, I don't think we got our proper due. We were supposed to be on the cover of *Sports Illustrated,* but the skier Jean-Claude Killy did something spectacular that week and we got knocked off. But that wasn't important. We had proved something. Did Franklin Mieuli believe we could win it? To a point—but Franklin didn't score one basket. No one scored a basket but the guys on the floor.

"A lot of people got caught up in it. I remember media people here after we beat Chicago telling me, we had done enough, you don't have to do anymore. But, you know, in sports there's no continuity from one year to the next. We had to get it right then. Not wait for next year.

"Sure, the next year, '75–'76, we came out and won fifty games. Then right here at that basket down there, we had a bad twelve minutes and the franchise just went down. Guys started leaving because of free agency. We had some personality problems.

"The two best Warrior teams didn't win championships. Two years back, we won fifty-five games and the guys were having fun. You never know what's going to happen—it has a lot to do with expectations. See, the year we won it, we were picked to finish last. Now we win it, and the expectations go way up.

"That fifty-nine win team was the best that ever played around here. We won one game in Milwaukee on Thanksgiving night 1975—we're thirty-one points down at half-time and we come back and take it. We were so confident. We had a lot of young players—Jamal Wilkes was rookie of the year, Phil Smith is a comer, he makes all-pro in his second year. You got Rick Barry, an old pro, an all-star. You got Gus Williams, a rookie, all Pac-10. But free agency gets into it. Bob Feerick was the GM around here then. He taught me some things: you have x amount of money, your best player gets the largest percentage. Then you go down the line—but under free agency, you got some guy coming in making more than your best player. So that started to creep in. Your guys are getting nervous about the money.

Philadelphia Warriors (169)

Player	Pos.	Min.	FGA	FGM	FTA	FTM	Reb.	Ast.	PF	Pts.
Paul Arizin	F	31	18	7	2	2	5	4	0	16
Ed Conlin		14	4	0	0	0	4	1	1	0
Joe Ruklick		8	1	0	2	0	2	1	2	0
Tom Meschery	F	40	12	7	2	2	7	3	4	16
Ted Luckinbill		3	0	0	0	0	1	0	2	0
Wilt Chamberlin	C	48	53	36	32	28	25	2	2	100
Guy Rodgers	G	48	4	1	12	9	7	20	9	11
Al Attles	**G**	**34**	**8**	**8**	**1**	**1**	**5**	**6**	**4**	**17**
York Larese		14	5	4	1	1	1	2	5	9
Totals		**240**	**115**	**63**	**52**	**43**	**60**	**39**	**25**	**169**

New York Knicks (147)

Player	Pos.	Min.	FGA	FGM	FTA	FTM	Reb.	Ast.	PF	Pts.
Willie Naulls	F	43	22	9	15	13	7	2	5	31
Johnny Green	F	21	7	3	0	0	7	1	5	6
Cleveland Buckner		33	26	16	1	1	8	0	4	33
Darrall Imhoff	C	20	7	3	1	1	6	0	6	7
Dave Budd		27	8	6	1	1	10	1	1	13
Richie Guerin	G	46	29	13	17	13	8	6	5	39
Al Butler	G	32	13	4	0	0	7	3	1	8
Dannie Butcher		18	6	3	6	4	3	4	5	10
Totals		**240**	**118**	**57**	**41**	**33**	**60**	**17**	**32**	**147**

"That team wouldn't have come apart if we hadn't lost in Phoenix here by four points. That final twelve minutes and all the other pressures that followed. Now the team is falling apart. Jamal, he played one more year, but he wanted to go to L.A. and play with Kareem. Let's be honest: to get Jamal on the floor, he's got to play Elvin Hayes, 6 feet 10 to 6 feet 5. Now Jamal's thinking, my career won't last very long if I have to play these monsters every night. With Rick on the floor, we got two small forwards but I don't know how else to play

these guys. Now I got Gus—he sees how good he is, but he's playing behind some guys. And the Warriors couldn't afford to pay him
what the guys in front of him are getting.

"Then Phil Smith gets hurt right over there in that corner. It was
an Achilles' tendon. He had just had a fifty-one point game against
the Suns was on his way to another one. He had like twenty something in the first quarter when he gets hurt. He was never the same
after that.

"The '91–'92 team was just as enjoyable. They were all such bud-
dies. Chris, Roony, Tim, they played together and hung out together.
That's an advantage. You know, you can't practice every day and
bump and knock each other without getting into a fight, but not these
guys. There was such a togetherness."

Al Attles is questioned about the franchise he has worked for for
the past thirty-three years.

"Thirty-four . . . Well, Franklin Mieuli has never received his due
for having the vision. it wasn't just a business to him. Franklin didn't
create free agency, but he had to live with it. A number of his players were stripped from him because he couldn't afford to keep them.

"This used to be a real mom-and-pop operation when Gottlieb
had it. Mieuli gets it because he's an advertising executive for Burg-
ermeister Beer and his client was the '49ers so they sold him a part
of the team. So then he gets some partners and goes after Gottlieb.
He brings the franchise out here.

"We didn't do well out here at first. We won a division, but we
were bucking college ball. U.S.F. had been so popular. People didn't
want pro ball.

"It started to look like it would click in '67 when we played Philly
in the finals. But Rick went to the A.B.A. and that was the dynasty
for us. Then, we got socked with free agency and that finished Franklin.
So he started looking to sell the team.

"Now I was in a meeting with a potential buyer—that guy was
taking the team out of here. Franklin wouldn't do it. He held on for
a few more years. He kept taking hits but he waited until he could
find someone like him to sell the team to. I think the present owners
are just like him—maybe, they don't wear the same hats . . . Franklin
found someone who cared about the fans, the Bay Area, the integrity

of the game. These are traits Franklin had—he just didn't have the financing. If he hadn't held on and had sold the team to Jim Fitzgerald and Dan Finane, we wouldn't be sitting here talking about the Warriors. They would have been long gone."

Do you still play the game, Al?

"Nope. The last time was here on this floor—the year after Phil Smith tore his Achilles. We had a lot of injuries. We had played a Sunday night in Portland. On Tuesday, we had practice but only nine players showed up. I came that morning and filled in. I was mad because the team was doing badly. Then I felt a little knot in my leg. First thing, I look up here. I thought someone had thrown a ball at me. John Lucas came running over. He was crying and carrying on. Phil Smith started feeling my leg. He said it was the same thing that happened to him. Are you a doctor or something I said to him—but he was right, it was torn. So that was it.

"Sure, every once in a while I throw one up, but I don't play. My son and I used to play some. I used to shut him out when he was smaller but then he got big. So here we are, going for a rebound and he goes up and his elbow comes out. Oh, I said. Just give me the ball. I put it down on the court. Nope, I said, that's it. I'm not playing with you again. What am I supposed to do? Have a fight with my own son?"

Interviewed by John Ross and Fred Gardner at the Oakland Coliseum Arena, October 21, 1993, three hours after Tim Hardaway injured his knee and finished his season.

Youth Radio, Berkeley, California

Interview with Tim Hardaway, December 4, 1993

When did you start playing basketball?

I started playing basketball when I was, in third or fourth grade, not throwing up all the way to the hoop, ten feet up, but probably had my own basketball hoop at my house that my dad and my mom bought me for Christmas and stuff like that. I carried on till when I was really ... really when I got into it was when I was in sixth grade, that's when I played on the eighth grade basketball team, made the basketball team and was successful from there.

I was just wondering, your wife just had a 7 lb. 12 oz. baby?

7 lb. 10 oz.

How has that affected you, being away from your kids?

Well, this year, since I'm hurt, it's not affecting me at all. I'm loving it right now, being with my son, my family, my wife, and my daughter. So, this is going to be a year which I get to spend with them. Just gotta take an off-year and just have fun with my family. You know, like, during the season I wouldn't be able to, so now I can.

Are you going to introduce your son to basketball?

No, I'm going to introduce my son to whatever he wants to play. Whatever he wants to play, I'll be supportive and be right behind him.

I want him to play basketball—football is kind of harsh, baseball is kind of boring, and that's it. You know, if he plays basketball, that's fine, but if he doesn't, that's fine, too.

Did you have any heroes or mentors when you were growing up? Basketball or non-basketball related?

Well, there was one, well, two heroes, that I had, that I idolized. One was . . . really, three. One was Isaiah Thomas because I liked the way he played on the basketball court—smiled, had fun while he was playing, tricking people—doing all the things I like to do on a basketball court. The second one was my high school coach who passed away after senior year at high school, during my freshman year at college. He just carried himself off court very well, very outspoken, very intelligent, and I admired him for that. He taught me a lot of things beside basketball. And, my dad. My dad taught me a lot of things about basketball, about life. You gotta have your parents, you gotta always listen to your parents, because they're not going to steer you wrong, they're always going to steer you right, so my dad was a big part in that, too.

What are the best parts about being a Warrior?

Just being in the Bay Area, being around fans, you sell out every night. You are playing with some great players. Chris Mullen, we have Mitch Richmond here, now we got Chris Webber, Billy Owens. You know, the whole team is just playing very well. The organization is nice. What can I say? San Francisco. . . . It's just fun, being in the NBA, period. That was one of my goals, and I feel it.

Can you talk a little about your emergence as a team leader?

Everywhere I played, I was always a team leader. I never thought, or wanted to be a team leader—I'm just very outspoken, very aggressive, just told people where to go, told 'em to have confidence in yourself, play hard. So, they just put me as team leader. Now, if I go out there and lollygag in practice, they're going to lollygag in practice. If I lollygag in a game, they're going to lollygag in the game. So, all the coaches that I had, they said every time you come out on the basketball court, just play hard, just try to play well for your team, and your team will follow you. That's what I tried doing, and they said, you're the team leader. I'm still trying to figure out how I got this "team leader," y'know?

What were some of the high points of your career?

One of my high points in my career was going to college and getting an education. Making the NBA, that's a high point in my career. Providing for my mom and my dad and my brother and my family. All the things I do out on the basketball court are just fun to do, fun to play, but you know, off the court is where it's at—my family.

Is your knee injury the worst thing that's happened up to now in your career?

The worst. The extreme worst. I never had an injury that was going to keep me out for the whole season, where I'm not going to be able to do anything but rehab the whole season. But, I look at it on the bright side. I just had a new baby, and got a son that's twenty months, so what can I say? I'm happy. Right now, I've just gotta go ahead and rehab and get ready for next year.

Do you worry that too many kids think "Well, you know, I wanna be an NBA star, forget about school, I wanna play basketball."

No, you can't think like that. Education is where it's at. I was listening to Charles Barkley on a tv show last night. He said, "People always say that basketball or sports can make you a better person, can make a better life for yourself, which it can. But you know, we as role models, as they say, don't tell kids about being a doctor, being a lawyer, being president, but setting goals to those standards first. School is very important. If you go to school you get an education." Charles Barkley also made the point, he said, "There are three important jobs in this life—being a doctor, being a fireman, and being a teacher. Doctors save lives, firemen save lives, and teachers go out there and they try to save lives, too, now." But teachers do a great job, and why not give them more money, because they almost have to baby-sit you when you leave the house. I think they're doing a great job, teachers are.

Do you think that star players have an obligation to provide a positive image for kids?

You know, we, being basketball players, we can't act ourselves. We can't walk around and act ourselves. If we act ourselves—you know, most basketball players are crazy. It's as simple as that. We're crazy—we like to have fun, we enjoy what we're doing, and.... But we can't act the way we want to act, normally. Every day when we walk out of the house, we gotta act in a way so that people can see us in a positive way. We can't walk out in a negative way, like you can't walk out and go into bad neighborhoods, and just hang out with your friends in bad neighborhoods. That'll get back [to you], you know, "you're hanging out with whoever," and that's supposed to be bad. So, we always gotta hangout somewhere nice or do something nice to please somebody else. It's always bad when we are seen in that sense, as role models to keep the kids in the right perspective. I think that's the parent's jobs and the parents need to get on that job, too.

How has the style of African-American players changed the game?

You know, Afro-Americans have changed the game a lot. We jump a lot higher, run a lot faster, it's just . . . I'm never racist, you know, I like Hispanics, Mexicans, or whatever, you know, Puerto Ricans, whatever. I'm never, never, what's the word I'm looking for? Racist. People perceive this in the wrong way, and it's not a subject that you can take too lightly, but if you take it too lightly, then a lot of people will be saying that you're not . . . that you don't involve yourself in it, something like that, you know. It's always something. So, I really don't like to talk about it, 'cause it gets a lot of people riled up about. So, I just leave it as is. If I have to face it, I face it. But if I don't, I won't.

Do you feel bad for the team because of the injuries that took place early in the season?

I feel bad for the team about the injuries, for all the injuries that we have sustained, last year and this year. You know, like I told the team before, "You don't need me to go on. Go out there and play your hardest, you'll win basketball games. Just go . . . Don't think about,

'Well, you know, if we had Tim Hardaway or Sarunas Marciulionis or if we had Chris Mullen,' y'all are out there now, y'all are playing basketball. Y'all need to go out there and play basketball the way y'all are taught, in a confident way. Go out there and play hard and don't worry about me, Marciulionis, or Chris. We'll be back. Unfortunately, it just takes me and Marciulionis a lot longer than Chris Mullen. But, you all gotta go ahead and make the playoffs, and do what you can and win. Make this a successful season." So, that's what I tell them.

Do you feel you'll be the same player after your knee heals?

Oh, most definitely. I'm going to come back and tear it up; I'm looking to come back and just tear it up.

What's it like for you, Mullen, and Cherones to sit and watch the team, especially the way Billy Owens and Chris Webber are playing this season?

Well, I feel that—and I can't speak for Chris Mullen and Marciulionis—but I can't come to the games. It's just—I can't come to the games because I'm just so worked up and ready to play. I'd be over there sweatin' and . . . . So I just look at the games on tv, so I got a rim and me and my son, we play on this little court that I got him and we go over there and we dunk the ball and we shoot the ball and I take all my frustrations out on him! [*laughter*]

After basketball . . . what are your plans?

Well, right now I'm not going to say that I'm glad I'm hurt, but I'm using this being hurt in a positive way, to start making business ventures for myself, so when I get out of this game, I can be set for life and my kids can be set, and when I go pass away, they'll still be set and won't have to worry about anything, except going to school, getting an education, and becoming a doctor or a lawyer. It doesn't have to be a doctor or lawyer, it can be anything, as long as they succeed in life.

Well, my dad wanted me to ask you this one, you know, we both watch you. He said that he read somewhere that you are one of the best point guards and also one of the best "trash talkers." He asked who else were the best "trash talkers."

Well, Michael Jordan talks trash, Charles Barkley, Larry Byrd, Magic, you know, a lot of people talk trash, but you have to talk it in a way where if you dish it out, you gotta be able to take it. A lot of people are not able to take trash talk. John Starks—he showed that in the playoffs last year. He's not able to take trash talking when he is losing. So, when you're losing, you know, you just got to take it. There are no ifs, ands, or buts about it. If you're winnin', the other guy has to be able to take it, if he's going to trash talk. So, that's the way I feel. In this game, right now, a lot of people have taken trash talkin' to another level, "If you're gonna trash talk me, well, we're just gonna have to fight." That's the wrong way. .... If I trash talk to you, and you're not playing well, or you're trying to trash talk to me and you're losing, and your game is not up to my game, you need to go home and practice on your game. That's the way I was taught and that's the way I've learned. All right, so a lot of people don't understand that, and they want to fight and they want to do this and they want to do that, well, don't fight *me,* fight yourself. Go home and practice on your game so maybe the next time when you come and meet me, maybe you'll get a "W" [win], but I doubt it.

So, probably it doesn't spill over till after the game with you, but does it spill over with any of your other teammates?

Oh, no, no. After the game is over with, the game is over with. If you want to take it to another level, after the game is over with, you go ahead and I'll see you later. There are a lot of guys in the NBA that I don't associate with because once you're out there trash talking, they take it off the court and want to be all upset and do other things to you. That's uncalled for.

I also understand you give a lot money to literacy programs—what is your reason for doing that?

Well, to give back. You know, I wasn't a great student when I was coming up. I had to work hard, very hard to try to get my grades, get my books, stuff like that. It was hard for the teachers or for the programs I was going to, to raise money. It was just hard. I think that if I give back to education programs, I am contributing to what somebody else contributed to help me get to where I am at today—to get to college and improve my study habits. So, that's what I do it for.

The Warriors have a lot of All-Star caliber players, like yourself or Mullen. Can you give me some comments on Sprewell's performance this season? I mean, I think he's emerging and that he should be on the All-Star team.

Yeah, he should be on the All-Star team, no doubt about it. This year, as one of the guards, he's one of the reasons why we're winning. Making those big shots. You know, Billy Owens is going to be an All-Star, Chris Webber is going to be an All-Star. Sprewell is definitely All-Star in my eyes. Hopefully, he'll make it this year.

Our radio show, Youth Radio, plays different types of music. On my show it's hiphop and rap. What type of music do you enjoy? Do you have a favorite?

I like hiphop, rap, slow songs, jazz. All that stuff.

What do you think of Shaq's new singing group?

It's terrible, it's terrible. He can't rap! He can't rap. He thinks he can, but he can't rap. You know more power to him, I hope he accomplishes all he wants to, but I don't . . . the song is terrible to me.

I just wanted to ask something on a lighter note. Do you think they have your game down pretty well on NBA Jams?

[*Laughs*] They do. They got it to a tee. They should, they've been putting me on there, haven't they? So, they should. But I'm going to come out with something new next year. They're going to have to put something new on screen next year.

Thirty points, thirty steals.

[*Laughs*] I could do thirty points, I don't know about thirty steals a game.

When I play NBA Jams, I always use you, and I always get thirty points, thirty steals.

Oh, okay, that's good, that's good. But not in the real world. [*Laughs*] Can't get thirty steals.

Who's this little guy?

That's my son, you've been hearing him hollering? We're trying to get him to talk. His name is Tim Hardaway, Jr. This is Junior right here. Say something, man. . . . Say hi! Oh no.

Could you do a couple of little promos for the show — "I'm Hardaway," etc.

Okay. This is Tim Hardaway from the Golden State Warriors, and, yeah, I got skills. But so do my friends at Youth Radio. You're listening to Youth in Control, 89.3 KPFB.

John Boe

Religion and Basketball

On any given Sabbath day people gather to watch ball games. In many ways these games are pagan substitutes for the collective religious experience of church. I've often seen newspaper photos of basketball games—the eyes of all the players and all the fans are fixed upon the ball frozen above the rim. When the game is on T.V. there are millions of eyes focused upon that same ball. This is a *collective* spiritual experience; the group consciousness is united by a single thing, the ball. The ball acts like the mandala in Tibetan systems of concentration and meditation, focusing the psyche of the individual, uniting the consciousness of the group.

Shortly before his death, Black Elk, a priest of the Oglala Sioux, gave an account of the seven rites of his people. These were recorded and edited by Joseph Brown in *The Sacred Pipe*. The seventh and last rite is a game that was revealed in a vision, "The Throwing of the Ball." A ball is painted red (the color of the world) and, with blue (the color of the heavens), dots are made at the four quarters. Then, by making two blue circles around the ball, Heaven and Earth are united into one sacred sphere. (This ball makes me wish our culture had a more symbolic ball, perhaps a whole earth ball, a rubber, bouncing globe). In the Sioux rite, a little girl takes the ball, which is both the world and the great spirit, *Wakan-Tanka,* and throws it to the west, where someone catches it, embraces it, offers it to the six directions (East, West, North, South, Up and Down), and gives it back to the girl. She then throws it to the north and the other directions. Black Elk explains this rite:

Just as the ball is thrown from the center to the quarters, so *Wakan-Tanka* is at every direction and is everywhere in the world; and as the ball descends upon the people so does His power, which is only received by a very few people, especially in these last days.

In the man's vision, which gave birth to this game, the little girl who threw the ball turned into a buffalo calf, nudged the ball towards the man, and said: "This universe really belongs to the two-leggeds, for we four-legged people cannot play with a ball."

Black Elk says that "it is the two-legged men alone who, if they purify and humiliate themselves, may become one with—or may know—*Wakan-Tanka*." The unique spiritual capacity of us two-legged ones is symbolically related to our ability to play ball; we are the creature who plays with a ball (the symbolic union of heaven and earth), and so the universe belongs to us. *The Sacred Pipe* ends with Black Elk's moving words:

> At this sad time today among our own people, we are scrambling for the ball, and some are not even trying to catch it, which makes me cry when I think of it. But soon I know it will be caught, for the end is rapidly approaching, and then it will be returned to the center, and our people will be with it. It is my prayer that this be so, and it is in order to aid in this recovery of the ball, that I have wished to make this book.

I sometimes feel, when I play basketball, that I am in some large sense trying to recover *the ball*. To play well is to unite body and mind; to play badly is to be out of Tao. What a fine feeling it is to go up for a jump shot and as you release the ball, to know it is going in; to be able to say in your mind or out loud, "Swish." Sometimes you don't even need to see the basket; you can go up for a shot with a defender or the sun in your eyes and still know the ball is going in. It almost feels as if there is telekinesis involved—you think the ball into the basket. I play basketball in order to experience those moments when I feel rhythm, and it is more a matter of the rhythm having me than of my having the rhythm. I find myself moving to the open spot at the right time and putting the ball surely in the empty circle that the rim defines. It is like the skill defined in *Zen and the Art of Archery*— it moves me on the court, it shoots the ball.

Usually you don't have time to think out what you are going to do—you move and react instinctively, unconsciously. At magic moments you and your teammates can seem to read each other's minds; you can throw a blind pass knowing that a teammate will have moved to that spot. You feel a part of a greater whole, a group mind, a Team. But while It may shoot the ball, and It may move you on the court, this does not mean that consciousness is eliminated. What is demanded is a sort of union of consciousness and unconsciousness; you can perceive and analyze, discuss and plan, but the analyses and plans have to blend with unconscious knowledge in a flow and rhythm. In the flow of a five-man team, you sink to the level of group mind while at the same time intensifying your own individual concentration, heightening your own consciousness by focusing it on the narrow field of a basketball game. It is popular to talk about rhythm and flow in basketball, and when playing basketball you do indeed feel the rhythm, flow with the group mind in a way that is much like improvising music in a small group; you are all improvising together, paying attention to each other and to the structure of the game (or the music), trying to let the It within you, the individual, direct your flow, all the while maintaining awareness of what the group is actually doing. And the problem in both music and basketball is often playing *together.* It can be relatively easy to "synch in" with someone you have played a lot with before. If you two can play together as a unit, then that dual unity can reach out to include a third, and eventually, all five will be playing together.

The ball is the focus of the group consciousness; it is *Wakan-Tanka,* the great mandala relating to the basic rule of defense—to see the ball; even when watching your own man, you must be conscious of the ball. On offense, to have the ball is to be the center of attention. It is easy to understand how difficult it can be for gifted offensive players to learn the selfless art of giving up the ball.

My favorite way of passing involves jumping into the air, hanging in mid-air as if preparing to shoot, and as the defense freezes awaiting the shot, pass off. The sensation of hanging in the air before shooting or passing is one of the most pleasurable in basketball. When you are hanging in the air, time can seem to stretch out as the moment fills with the perception of a variety of alternatives. Oscar Robertson, a truly great, if not flashy ballplayer, urged players never to go up into the air unless they knew what they were going to do with the ball. More and more contemporary players choose the pleasure and uncertainty of going up in the air in order to create a situation, deciding what to do when in full flight. As a player, I have an ambivalent attitude towards flying; it is such a pleasure that I leave my feet too often, get hung up in the air with nothing to do with the ball. The problem of when to fly and when to stay grounded is a symbolic one for me; I have had to learn, in my non-athletic life as well, when to keep my feet on the ground.

Julius Erving, "Dr. J.," says, "My game is in the air." Dr. J. was probably the first player to fly, to really defy the laws of gravity. Scientists used to say a baseball couldn't curve, just as they would now say a person couldn't fly; but certain basketball players do sometimes fly, or so it seems. Dr. J. inspired me to write a little poem in which I envisioned a great basketball player of the far future: "Wondrous bird-man, enlightened athlete-monk,/Flying through the air and then, slam-dunk!" I love the vision of some future shaman-athlete. Flying has always been a symbol of spiritual power—in many cultures the shaman was the bird-man, the man who could fly. I only wish that the symbolic flying power of current players was matched by flights of consciousness, of spiritual soaring.

Like many men, I root for my team today as I did as a child, with an almost religious fervor. Since I live in the San Francisco Bay Area, I root for the Golden State Warriors. The Warriors are not so much my team as my totem. It is interesting to consider sports teams, so often named after animals, as totems of specific areas, magic representatives of a certain group of people. I know my friends and I felt uplifted, blessed with luck (a gift of the gods) when, a few years ago, the Warriors won the championship.

To go to a ball game is to participate in a "primitive" rite, a Dionysian revel. The Oakland Coliseum, where my totem-team plays, takes on a ceremonial character. Between the parking lot and the arena there is a long winding row of small stone penis-shaped pillars. In

India they would be recognized immediately as *lingams,* ceremonial stone phalluses. Ascending along the line of *lingams,* you approach the great round colossus, the Coliseum, looking like the Great Mother at the end of a row of her sons.

After giving your ticket to the gatekeeper, you pass into the other, ceremonial realm. The attendants help the confused find their way through the maze of seats and sections to their spot. Down below, at the bottom of the great circle that is the Coliseum, stands the rectangular court. As a magic space within its own center circle, the rectangular court within the circular building suggests the proverbial perfection of the squared circle. At a prearranged time, the players symmetrically distribute themselves around the middle of the symmetrical court. The referee throws the ball above the exact center of the court and the game begins. Anyone profane enough to step onto the sacred space during the game will of course be subject to ejection and arrest. The players move in waves, from north to south and south to north, as all attention focuses upon the special space, with its special rules and own time frame. As the game progresses the crowd becomes less inhibited; an exciting playoff game can almost *possess* a crowd. Conscious control slips away, mass mind takes over. A wonderful relief or purge occurs in this sinking into unconsciousness, as a mass of people focus on a simple game; it can also be rather frightening, as base emotions surge to the surface.

Basketball was invented by James Naismith in 1891, in Springfield, Massachusetts. While Dr. Naismith deserves credit for his invention and ingenuity, the roots of basketball also reach into Native American culture. It is important to realize that before the discovery of the "New World" there was no rubber in Europe. Rubber was called "India Rubber" because it was first brought to Europe from the West Indies, the land Columbus mistakenly thought was India. Archeological evidence suggests that rubber was used by the Mayans perhaps as early as the eleventh century. A Native American invention, the hoop game with a rubber ball was popular throughout Native American culture.

There were a number of different rubber ball games, but I am interested in those which used a stone ring, through which the rubber ball was to be propelled. There was no real parallel to the use of a ring in

European games. The game played throughout Mexico was like a combination of basketball and volleyball. The object was to score points by sending the ball into the opposing team's court so it could not be returned. Generally, the ball was to be struck with the hips, buttocks, or knee; to use the hands or another part of the body was to forfeit a point. There was a stone ring in each team's court, and if a player sent the ball through the ring (a very difficult feat) he won the game outright. Such a lucky player had the right to claim gifts from the losing team (who would abuse him as bewitched and run away), and would be honored by his teammates. He would also make sacrifices to the game's patron deity and to the stone ring itself.

The magical-religious elements in the ancient rubber ball games was obvious. Every court had images of the patron deity (or deities) of the game. Players might magically prepare the game balls the night before a game, and ask for supernatural help during the game. The referees were likely to be priests.

But if the magical-religious element in the ancient games is obvious, so is the aggressive component. The players understood the game to symbolize warfare, and sometimes it would even be used as a substitute for battle. The duality implicit in this and similar competitive games was made conscious by making the god of twins a deity of the game. The game itself was quite violent, in that the ball (often made of solid rubber) was heavy enough to cause serious injury (and even death) to the player struck in the wrong place. And like the rubber ball games played today, the Native American rubber ball games were inextricably linked to gambling. Players and spectators inevitably wagered upon the outcome, and used all their aggressive energy and magical power to achieve victory.

A modern American rubber ball game, basketball is like the ancient American rubber ball games. It involves competitive as well as religious energy, aggression, and ritual. I love the intensity with which I play and watch basketball, but I must admit that my attempts to see basketball as a religion are inadequate. Basketball is a very *primitive* spiritual event. The Native American rubber games were religious and secular events, but the players were at least conscious of the spiritual symbolism of their game and court. I have written this essay in an attempt to make conscious some of the spiritual implications in my game, basketball. Basketball does play an important part in my spiritual life; but I am sad to admit how limited and unconscious that spiritual life really is. The problem comes, I think, from the way in which the spiritual has been cut off from the secular. In our modern world it is unnaturally difficult to see the spiritual dimension in anything so secular as a ball game (or a dance, a carnival, a party). In Europe, as late as the sixteenth century there were ceremonial ball-dances held in churches. Priests danced to the rhythm of the chant, and a ball was thrown or handed around. This game was finally banned as too secular, and not "spiritual" enough for priests and churches. We have forgotten that the Olympics are celebrated in honor of the Great God; we have separated the secular from the spiritual. I envy those so-called "primitive" cultures in which this division was not so clear cut. I can only wish, with Black Elk, that we might begin to try to recover the ball.

Selected Bibliography

Phlegon, *History of Olympia,* c.AD 138.

Black Elk, *The Sacred Pipe,* ed. Joseph Brown, Penguin, 1971.

Theodore Stern, *The Rubber-Ball Games of the Americas,* University of Washington Press, 1966.

Part Six

Downhill Slide

John Valenti with Ron Naclerio

from *Swee'pea and Other Playground Legends: Tales of Drugs, Violence, and Basketball*

He walked with a comfortable gait. Not an attitude walk, the kind of strut owned by new jack punks and assorted common street hoods, but rather a step like that of a man who had once been a king but who had never quite found it to be his role in life. It was humble, dignified. It was a walk that cut the fine line between self-assurance and self-doubt.

He was wearing a pair of old black-and-white Chuck Taylor Cons. In one hand he held an unlit cigarette and, in the other, a brown paper bag, the business end of an aluminum can stuck through its opening, tab popped. He seemed quite in control of his faculties, and he was. But as he approached, a sense of alcohol seemed to overwhelm the fresh morning air, air as fresh and upstanding as it could be at ten o'clock on a humid mid-summer morning on the asphalt of Harlem.

"Hi," he said, eyes cast downward in sudden, sheepish fashion, yet with a voice possessing a certain strange resonance, low and with a gravel edge that undercut its mellifluous tones with betrayal. "I'm Earl."

The man was an intriguing contradiction. There he stood, skin dark, rich and deeply textured, body surprisingly lean after all these years, legs still strong. But missing were two lower front teeth that seemed to make his face, when you looked close, appear hardened and worn. Endless railroads ventured across his arms, their lines darker than that of his darkest days, their maze of scar tissue an eerie sort of avant-garde reminder of the bad habit that had nearly killed him. His weary, weathered eyes remained fast to notice interest. Almost instantly he offered up his arms, the tracks.

"Curious?" he asked. There came a nod.

"It's from 'The White Lady,'" he said with what sounded to be a hint of self-contempt. "*Her-ron.* The old days.

"You know, on the streets I still hear people say, 'There goes "The Goat." He used to be the baddest dude in the world. But drugs brought him down.' People tried to show me the way, but I didn't want to listen. At the time, I really enjoyed doing it. Later, I found out it wasn't shit."

"It lost me my whole career."

Twenty-five years ago, it seemed Earl Manigault soared over every park in New York City. He could entertain the crowd, picking quarters off the top of the backboard during warmups. He could spin and shake defenders almost at will. He commanded a repertoire of moves unmatched and unparalleled. Though just a thinly built six-foot-two forward, he often challenged the likes of Wilt Chamberlain, Connie Hawkins and Lew Alcindor. He would even throw it down on them. Just because of what it said.

On the uneven asphalt courts blended into the fabric of a neighborhood bordered by a world of burned-out buildings and burned-out dreams, he dominated the playground game with a flair and panache that earned him a street reputation as a player with few equals.

So moved by his ability, Alcindor, later Kareem Abdul-Jabbar, once called him "the best basketball player his size in the history of New York City." To those who could not pronounce his last name, he became known simply as The Goat. On the streets, the name alone commanded respect.

"No question, but that from fifteen feet in you weren't going to stop this man," Sonny Johnson said. "From the foul line to the basket, if he put a move on you, he had you. Period. You had to get it in your mind that you had to face the embarrassment. He might put it down backward on you. Or anything he wanted. The other nine players, two referees and everyone watching knew he was the center of attention."

"I still remember the first time I saw him," Bob McCullough, Sr., recalled. "I walked into this gym and there was this kid playing with weights on his ankles. I said, 'Why don't you take them off, so you can move?' He told me, 'Oh, it's all right.' Then, like he was runnin' up a wall, he came in and dunked something fierce. The man could defy the laws of gravity."

But for some, there is also a wicked gravity to be found on the streets of New York, its lure so illicit, its power so overwhelming that only the most strong-minded can overcome it. Earl Manigault couldn't.

As a result, he never made it out of the playgrounds and into the National Basketball Association, even though he briefly played in the Eastern League. Instead, he became a heroin addict by his late teens, a convict by his early twenties and a symbol, as predecessor to the likes of Lloyd, Joe Hammond, Fly Williams, Red Bruin, Richie Adams and a host of others, of everything both good and bad about the inner-city, its playgrounds and its players.

"Sometimes," Johnson said, "no matter how good a person you are, you can't help but fall prey to the sidewalks of New York."

Some men are afraid of success, some merely too impatient to wait for it to come, and so they fail. And some, like Earl Manigault, simply wake one morning and realize the reality that, sometimes, talent isn't nearly enough; that due to no particular fate, their chance for success has passed and, with it, their hopes and dreams. "The city," Manigault said, "can take it all away. For every Michael Jordan, there's an Earl Manigault. We all can't make it. Somebody has to fail. I was the one."

Gino Sky

from *Appaloosa Rising*

Ranger pulled a ball out of the sky and started to dribble. Easy at first, but as soon as he rediscovered his touch he went through all of his old moves: behind the back and the floater; between his legs and chasing the caboose; half-moon spins and the high-pocket drift; and a doublecross lay-over with a reverse spin called the dancing arrow polka. With the exercise over Ranger settled down and broke into the game with jump shots, set shots, fakes, steals, picks, fadeaways, lay-aways, pumps and double pumps, reverse spins, floating lay-ups, stuffs, dunks, and then the Grand Dunk: leaving the ground from fifteen feet out, going into a full twist as he moved the ball behind his back the opposite direction and then slamming it into the hoop. POW! By the time Ranger stopped, the game was over because the bad guys had thrown in the towel when the score became triple-infinity to ZeeRow-zip. Ranger walked out into the middle of the meadow and bowed to all of his fans as he accepted the trophy which was the Granddaddy of all trophies: the Cowboy Buddha dribbling twelve planets while tap dancing and tai-chiing at the same time. He lifted it in the air for everyone to see as he turned in a circle. He held up one finger to show everyone how he felt about his earthquake renaissance. The middle finger, presented to all of he demons, dragons, and wart-nosed, back-shootin' gargoyles, who had been riding inside his body, rentfree, for so long. To them . . . and all of their kids and children's kids . . . Old Numero Fucko!

"Fuckum all!" he shouted to all of the invisible dwellers of the sky, plus one eagle who was trying to decide whether to have rainbow trout at Jenny lake, or just hang around and see if any ham sand-wiches were left in the picnic grounds. "Fuckum all! Especially the ugly ones. They thought they had won, but I fooled them. Bastards! I fooled them. I was only red-shirting. Now, I'm back. And they'd better have their moves a lot smoother and quicker because I'm rollin' and I've got all of mine back plus a few more. So watch out! My pickup has been smashed flatter than an English saddle. My clothes, wallet, and my all-time favorite ... old Numero Five-X ratinfested Beaver Stetson are all floating in the middle of the lake and I ain't down. Virginia is gone and I ain't down. She thinks she's gonna have my kid and I ain't down. My kid. Ha! She thinks it's God's. Damn! Do you hear that, God? I've fooled you this time. I beat you. You know? Beat you at your own game. I didn't have to pull off a plus-eight on the Richter Scale quake to get laid. That was a mean trick, God. Real bad! Look at all the people you killed just so you could sneak into Virginia's pants. Was it worth it? Huh? Was it? Well ... I'll tell you something and I want you to listen. I'm cutting out of here. Understand? Leaving. Going home, and you ain't gonna stop me. Not this time. I've finally got you figured out. Yeh ... figured out. And you're nothing but a con, a dirty old man, a fly-by-nighter, and a flimflam man. I can't believe it. You! Well ... I'm finished. Through. So leave me alone. Just back off and let me be. Fuck off! Get lost ... adios and sooooo long." Ranger started walking through the meadow. Ten steps beyond his farewell he spun around to check his tracks. Nothing. He raised one fist and shook it out into space. "*Adios,* moth-erfuckers .... Aaaa-deee-ooossss!"

With his trophy in one hand and the magic ball in the other, he walked through the town, spinning with this newly discovered feel-ing of ecstasy and tranquillity. His walk was about ten feet all and just about that much off the ground. "It's all perfect," he kept on chanting to himself. "It's all perfect. I can feel it now. Everything. And it's all perfect." On the beginning side of town he slipped into the corral where he had delivered the four horses. He picked out a strong-looking mare with soft, dark eyes, and a long, flowing mane and tail. In the barn he found a bridle, blankets, saddle, saddlebags, and an old plaid coat that had been used for a dog's bed. He filled the bags with grain and took an old sleeping cowboy hat that was hanging on the barn's center support post. He walked the horse through the trees until they were a mile from the barn, and then he mounted the Appaloosa. He was going back home. He was going to find his mother, the moon woman of the alfalfa fields, and he as going to find his older brother ... Jus' One More Cowboy, Jonquil Rose. He was going back to that great long valley that touches the White Clouds and reaches out into the Sawtooth Mountains. Home. A little west and to the south. All downhill. Before the sun could pull down its shades and declare itself a magnificent sunset, Ranger Rose was long gone.

David Hilton

The Poet Tries to Turn in His Jock

> *The way I see it, is that when*
> *I step out on that court and feel*
> *inside that I can't make the plays,*
> *it'll be time to call it quits.*
> —Elgin Baylor

Going up for the jump shot,
Giving the kid the head-fakes and all
'Til he's jocked right out the door of the gym
And I'm free at the top with the ball and my touch,
Lofting the arc off my fingertips,
I feel my left calf turn to stone
And my ankle warp inward to form when I land
A neat right angle with my leg,
And I'm on the floor,
A pile of sweat and sick muscles,
Saying,
Hilton,
You're 29, getting fat,
Can't drive to your right anymore,
You can think of better things to do
On Saturday afternoons than be a chump
For a bunch of sophomore third-stringers;
Join the Y, steam and martinis and muscletone.
But, shit,
The shot goes in.

Peter Najarian

For We Would Be That Boy Again

We still play. And pray that our legs will last.

For we would be that boy again, alone in the schoolyard, his heart filled with the sky and the vision of the hoop. The winter clouds explode with his longing, his feet numb on the frozen pavement, his hands red and swollen.

Step light, sweet child, weave through the cold air and glide for your layup. Make it.

He practices, he practices.

Driven by his legs and the dream of flying, he prays: Please let me make it.

Not for fame, not for fortune, not even for a girl, but himself deep in the vision of his own magnificence. There is no end to his desire. He must be perfect. Nothing is more important. The clouds wait for him to reach their thunder, and he pivots, leaps, twirls until the twilight.

He dribbles dark streets and shoots to himself through the market town. *Whiff, Whiff,* he never misses.

And comes home exhausted, ball at his side, hungry for a huge dinner to grow immense. Pores over the sports page and tapes his heroes on the bedroom wall. Adventures into the night to watch them close. They are gods in their luminous uniforms and he's in love with them. He too will one day carry a duffle and wear a letter on his coat. Read his name in the paper and take his place in eternity.

Then comes the night on the court and the flash of the bright gym. Earth odor of the lockerroom and his genitals snug in the jockstrap.

Touch of the magic floor and the drum of balls in warm-up. His heart leaps.

And now his arms will shine, his face become flushed and throbbing. He bobs. He shakes his hands.

Will he make it? Will he float beatific through the wild chanting? Please, he prays, please let me make it.

And become beautiful like the deer and the wolf and even the eagle, the glorious animal he would worship in himself, eternally hunting and hunted, body to body in the sacred dance.

Please.

But neither struggle nor desire nor the clouds themselves can help him, and no boy escapes the inevitable wound.

For he's not as good as he wants to be, and someone else is always better.

He learns to hate in order to win. He can't stand to lose.

He turns and punches his best friend.

The crowd is merciless and he lets go of his vision.

He falls.

He becomes a man.

And years pass on the long journey of retreat.

Yet always beneath the scar in his eyes lives the image of that angel who once ran to get chosen in every saturday morning, the longing to be great and the joy of pretzels and soda while he waited.

And now we are forty.

And come to the court from a troubled marriage, from money problems, career worries and a painful failure in the mirror when we shave.

Now there is no crowd as we walk into the gym and undress. The butcher, the baker, the lawyer, the teacher, the writer, the painter, the cabinet-maker, the builder, the salesman, and the therapist. Cigarette smokers. Beer drinkers. Dreamers of beautiful women and a perfect work. Praising athletes half our age.

We want him back, the boy now bald and grey who puffs and grunts up court, gluttonous for another shot.

Our knees won't last forever but we know again we want to love ourselves and feel good.

Now we need each other to make sides.

269

Apologize for bursts of rage.

And recognize each other's wound.

Dear life, we are humble in your grace and praise our breath.

Send us out to other men in other cities as the boy who roams a strange neighborhood in his search of the hoop.

Stephen Dunn

Losing Steps

It's probably a Sunday morning
and it's clear
you've begun to leave
fewer people behind. Perhaps

your fakes are as good as ever,
but when you move
you are like the Southern Pacific
the first time a car kept up with it,

your opponent at your hip,
with you all the way
to the rim. Five years earlier
he would have been part of the air

that trickled behind you
in your ascendance.
On the sidelines they are saying
he has lost a step,

it is something you've said
about others, harsh as clerk's talk
about the early dotage
of a superior.

Stephen Dunn

Then it's Wednesday evening,
adult's night in some gymnasium
streaked with the abrupt scuff marks
of highschoolers, and another step

leaves you like some wire you never
thought about, leading to another wire.
This time you're playing defense,
someone gives you an old hesitation

and you're not fooled,
and he's past you anyway,
something more than dust
in your eyes, and points against you.

It's a Friday afternoon,
if you know anything about steps
you're playing chess
with an old, easy friend.

But you're probably walking
to a schoolyard where kids
are playing half court,
telling yourself the value of experience,

sneakers under your arm,
your legs hanging from your waist
like sloths from a branch
and so many leopards nearby.

alta

no handicaps

when i was in high school, at the age of 17, mind you (exactly half of what i am now!), i was one of the hot shots of the girl's basketball team. there was no thought of integrated basketball. forget it. boys were big, & strong, & nuts made them physically much more capable of carrying something nut shaped. none of us thought—at least i didn't—of not going to the boy's games to protest this separate but equal bullshit, nor did we think it odd that parents, little siblings, & assorted students came out en masse to sit in bleachers & yell for the boys to run & bounce their nut shaped thing while their nuts bounced. when we played, the gym was empty, except for the two teams & a couple of referees, whom we were all sure were dykes. i never heard the male coaches called fags, but the female coaches were all called dykes. at any rate, i loved basketball, & while no great shakes running from one spot to another, i could make a basket from almost anywhere on the court. all i had to do was stand somewhere & wait for the ball. when i got it, i would (usually) make points.

my boyfriend during the winter of 1959–60 was one of the varsity basketball team. letter sweater. gave me a bottle of MY SIN perfume for christmas (at my request). actually, we had broken up by christmas, but who the hell else could he give it to? one only has so many sins. but hudson had some endearing aspects: one being that he never pushed sexually, on the theory that it was oppressive to the girl, who might get preggies; & the other that he was the only one in the whole world who was proud that i was a star on the girl's basketball team. it is true that the gym was empty for our games, but in my

last year of school, when i was going with hudson, & wearing the
sweater he won for doing the same thing i did every wednesday, hudson would show up, wearing the sweater, carring two pom-poms, &
whenever i got the ball—which i did often, my teammates being anxious to have us get points—he would yell, "GO ALTA!" i didnt realize how important that was to me, that he showed up. but i've told
that story for years. it is one of the reasons high school was a great
place for me. in college, basketball was frowned on by the girls in my
dorm, & none of the boys gave a shit what my talents were—having
two tits was all the talent they demanded—so i ended up in figure
control, swimming, & ballet. & after college, i had this husband who
was built like muhammad ali, & but he didnt get that way from
sports—he got that way from being a farm boy, & he had no inten-
tions of embarrassing himself publicly by playing ball where anybody could see him. i had no women friends.

in my second marriage, simon & i were much more sports & games
minded, & we trucked over to the park to play a lil basketball. two
tall type men were having a bit of a game. simon asked if we could
join. they laughed, "sure. & you can have a handicap." "why the
handicap?" he naively asked. "cause you got *her!*" one said, aston-
ished that simon would need to ask. "i dont think you wanta do that,"
simon smiled. "no, it's ok." they insisted. "i dont take it." i said. "no
handicap." they shrugged, "ok, but dont say we didnt offer!"

simon has what i dont have—speed—& he ran all over the court,
retrieving the ball from those guys who were so high up they couldnt
touch their dribble until it was past their 3 foot tall knees, by which
time simon would have it & be spiriting it to me, waiting unguarded,
(what big man would be mean enuf to guard the little lady?) and i'd
sink it in. we beat the pants off those motherfuckers. the second game,
they said, "well, we underestimated the little lady. give us a chance
to save face." they played their best; sweat was pouring down so heavy
they could hardly see. we won, 21 to 19. i smiled at them & thanked
them for the game. simon shook their hands & said, "see you." they
didnt answer. i like that story almost as much as the story about hudson.

for a half a dozen years, i have had no one to play with, nor nowhere to play. a month ago, a guy at the med told me when i yelled

at him that i was sick of hearing about his goddamn basketball practice all the damn time, that he would play with me whenever i wanted.
& he invited me to wednesday practice. & from there, i learned about
the women's game at the y. so i was gonna go with jane, but she hurt
her ankle (playing basketball; sports, they say, are good for your health.
compared to what. i broke my elbow skateboarding, jane sprained
her ankle basketballing, joe namath's knees are the pits . . .sports are
for FUN, & that's it—for health, you go walking with a mastedon
to eat muggers, you dont play football or go skiing.) i decided without jane to introduce me, i wouldnt go. then i thought about that. art
doesnt wait for some man to introduce him to the guys at the park:
he just shows up, & stands around, & pretty soon, he's playing. (i
tried that at live oak park, but the men resisted me ferociously. when
they finally did let me in, they spent the whole game grabbing tit.) so
i thot, if i werent a woman, i'd go, jane or no jane. so i went.

it didn't last very long; 20 minutes total. full court, but stamina
wasnt my gig even in high school; & it's the first time i've played full
court in 17 years! & they were patient with me at first, then that wore
off & we just played, & i loved it. & one woman said, "come back."
& when i got out, i was still a woman going thru yet another divorce,
with notices from both the highway patrol & the bank on my desk
about how i'm such a lousy, irresponsible person; but for one glorious hour, there was just me & the basket, & a round, tan ball that did
what i wanted just enough of the time, & people yelling, "Here!" &
i was able to forget the entire rest of my life, for one whole, wonderful hour.

John Updike

Ex-Basketball Player

Pearl Avenue runs past the high-school lot,
Bends with the trolley tracks, and stops, cut off
Before it has a chance to go two blocks,
At Colonel McComsky Plaza. Berth's Garage
Is on the corner facing west, and there,
Most days, you'll find Flick Webb, who helps Berth out.

Flick stands tall among the idiot pumps—
Five on a side, the old bubble-head style,
Their rubber elbows hanging loose and low.
One's nostrils are two S's, and his eyes
An E and O. And one is squat, without
A head at all—more of a football type.

Once Flick played for the high-school team, the Wizards.
He was good: in fact, the best. In '46,
He bucketed three hundred ninety points,
A county record still. The ball loved Flick.
I saw him rack up thirty-eight of forty
In one home game. His hands were like wild birds.

He never learned a trade, he just sells gas,
Checks oil, and changes flats. Once in a while,
As a gag, he dribbled an inner tube,
But most of us remember anyway.

His hands are fine and nervous on the lug wrench.
It makes no difference to the lug wrench, though.

Off work, he hangs around Mae's Luncheonette.
Grease-grey and kind of coiled, he plays pinball,
Sips lemon cokes, and smokes those thin cigars;
Flick seldom speaks to Mae, just sits and nods
Beyond her face towards bright applauding tiers
Of Necco Wafers, Nibs, and Juju Beads.

Charles Entrekin

At Codornices Park

for Bruce Hawkins,
poet and Sunday morning guard

And when pores open, legs pumping,
I see that his court awareness still survives,
a forty-year-old four eyes who understands
this language of fast breaks and finger-tip
finesse, the backdoor pass and give and go,
and easy lay-ups.
    Because here is control
and that fun of full extension,
the face and flush of perfect
pick and roll. Because his hands
are filled with suggestions.
Because always his inscrutable sentences
begin in the arc of a hook shot.
    And the ball falls, spinning backwards
a prescribed imagistic route,
a will creating its own reasons
for grinning: sunlight, trees,
this irrevocable letting go
of what is already falling,
that sense of sweetest swish
thru unbroken string.

Thomas Rogers

Pete Maravich, a Hall of Famer Who Set Basketball Marks, Dies

January 8, 1988

Pete Maravich, the leading career and single-season scorer in major college basketball history, died yesterday in Pasadena, California, after suffering an apparent heart attack while playing in a pickup game. He was forty years old.

Mr. Maravich collapsed during a half-court game with friends, and died about half an hour later. Gary Lydick, a member of the group playing, said that just before he collapsed, Mr. Maravich had told him he had played only once in a year but felt "really good."

Last May, Mr. Maravich was inducted into the Basketball Hall of Fame in Springfield, Massachusetts, a tribute to his efforts as a pro that included a 24.2 scoring average and one league scoring championship. But it was as a player at Louisiana State University that he truly sparkled.

For three straight seasons, between 1967 and 1970, he led the nation in scoring while performing under the coaching of his father, Press Maravich, who died last April. In acquiring the nickname Pistol for his penchant for shooting the ball, he amassed 3,667 points in college for an average of 44.2 over eighty-three games, a National Collegiate Athletic Association record. In his senior year, the 1969–70 season, he scored 1,381 points for a 44.5 average.

He scored more than fifty points in a game twenty-eight times and hit sixty-nine points against Alabama in 1970, his collegiate high point. As a loose-limbed, floppy-haired six-foot-five-inch guard with sagging gray socks as his trademark, he was an enormous drawing card.

He averaged about thirty-eight shots a game, of which about seventeen hit the mark, but he also had a knack for brilliant ball-handling, dribbling and passing.

"Shooting is nothing," he once said. "Anybody can shoot. The big charge is putting on a show for the crowd."

Peter Press Maravich was born on June 22, 1947, at Aliquippa, Pennsylvania, while his father was playing professional basketball for the Pittsburgh Ironmen. He grew up in the Carolinas while his father coached at Clemson and at North Carolina State before moving on to Louisiana State.

After his college career, Mr. Maravich took advantage of a bidding war between the Atlanta Hawks of the National Basketball Association and the Carolina Cougars of the American Basketball Association to get a five-year contract with Atlanta worth a reported $1.6 million, the richest contract for a rookie to that time.

As in college, he never played for a championship team in the pros, and his ten pro seasons never surpassed the ones at L.S.U. Still, he won the N.B.A. scoring championship in 1977 when he averaged 31.1 points a game for the New Orleans Jazz. The next season he suffered a knee injury that dogged him until his retirement in the fall of 1980 after he was released by the Boston Celtics.

After leaving basketball, Mr. Maravich was involved in work within the religious community and recently as a basketball broadcaster for the USA cable network. He also ran basketball camps in Clearwater, Florida, and near his home in Covington, Louisiana.

"Most of my career was negative," he said a few years ago. "I accomplished what I set out to do, but I lost my discipline and my career. I got involved in going out. I got by on talent. That was my fatal mistake."

He is survived by his wife, Jackie, and his sons, Jaeson, eight, and Joshua, five.

John Ross

Play Off

When Music,
the other side of Air,
played itself
for the Champeenship
of the Kingdom of Sound,
the stars did not miss a hoop,
the power forwards slamdunked
like they'd found God
at the bottom of a bucket,
the point guards
pulled strings
with fingers
taut as arrows
and hit the rimshots
like rainbows on the run,
The Center held.
Who won?
All won.
All One.